The Ganges
in Myth and History

The Ganges
in Myth and History

STEVEN G. DARIAN

THE UNIVERSITY PRESS OF HAWAII
HONOLULU

Library of Congress Cataloging in Publication Data

Darian, Steven G
  The Ganges in myth and history.

  Bibliography: p.
  Includes index.
  1. Ganges River.   I.   Title.
DS485.G25D37   954'.1   77–21374
ISBN 0–8248–0509–7

To Geez,
>   Whose greatness slipped
>   through my fingers.

To Geez,
>   Who taught me a passion
>   for the Word.

To Geez,
>   Who found the dawn
>   too soon.

Contents

Illustrations

FIGURES

MAPS

Foreword

A SOUND AND COMPREHENSIVE STUDY of the Gaṅgā in all its
aspects has long been a desideratum, for no river in the world's
history has achieved such fame as the sacred river of India—the Nile
is its only possible rival. From its origins in the cold Himalayan
peaks to its merging with the ocean in the Bay of Bengal, in all its
majestic length, it forms the main artery carrying the lifeblood of
northern India. Surely there is not a river anywhere in the world
which has not something of beauty and mystery, something of poetry about it. And no river is endowed with these qualities in such
full measure as the Gaṅgā. It is not in the least surprising that ancient Indians thought of the Gaṅgā as sacred, a goddess in her own
right, descending from the head of the great god Śiva himself.

Dr. Darian is, at least figuratively speaking, a convinced devotee
of that goddess. He has traveled her banks for their full length and
has lived among those who dwell by her side. He evidently loves her
with an intensity which few modern Indians can match. This book
offers a wealth of information about the geography, history, and religious significance of the Gaṅgā. It is important both as a scholarly
study and as a work of interpretation that explores the hidden rela-
tionships between Indian art and religion. But thanks to his deep
love for his subject and his excellent literary gifts, Dr. Darian has

also conveyed something of the grandeur and poetry of the Gaṅgā to his readers. And, indirectly, nearly all aspects of India's history and culture are touched on in these pages, reflected in the clear sunlit waters of the sacred river.

A verse in one of the many sacred books of Hinduism reads as follows:

> What need of expensive sacrifices,
>   or of difficult penances?
> Worship Gaṅgā, asking for happiness
>   and good fortune,
>   and she will bring you heaven
>   and salvation.

Padma Purāṇa V. 60.39

To the reader who has not seen the Gaṅgā, this verse may seem to express a mere ancient superstition. Those who know something of the great river, though they may not take the verse literally, will see the point. Readers of this fine book will not only learn many interesting facts about the Gaṅgā, past and present, but also understand why this mighty river has been for three thousand years considered holy, and why, at least in a poetic sense, she *is* holy, and why those who truly love her are, again in a poetic sense, *mukta—* set free.

A. L. BASHAM
Professor of Asian Civilizations
Australian National University
Canberra

Preface

IN THE BEGINNING, there was no mythology; there was no art. There was only experience. To the early Aryan settlers of the Ganges Valley, the river loomed massive and omnipresent. Its waters nourished, its current allowed communication with other settlements, old and new, its route pointed ever east toward some unknown fulfillment. As civilization grew on its banks and cities rose, Ganga became more and more a part of the Indian ethos. With the flourishing of commerce and agriculture, its water was called upon for a thousand functions. Just as in love few men can resist an utterly devoted woman, so people came to worship the river that offered them so much. From the time of the *Vishnu Dharma Shastra* in the third century A.D., Ganga has played a vital role in Hindu ceremony: in rituals of birth and initiation, of marriage and death. As a goddess, she has moved among the great celestials of Hinduism: at times the child of Brahma, the wife of Shiva, the metaphysical product of Vishnu, or mother to the Vasus and to Karttikeya, god of war. But ever and always, she confers a benediction. She shares none of the chthonian affinities associated with Kali or Durga or the sepulchral goddesses of Greece. Even in the underworld, the river has pointed the way to paradise.

In time the fame and sanctity of Ganga reached the western

world. She became the goal of Alexander the Great, who regarded the river as the farthest limits of the earth. Alexander hoped to reach the Ganges and then, continuing east, return to Europe by sailing through the Pillars of Hercules. Virgil, Ovid, and Dante all mention Ganga. The river also played a unique role in medieval thought. With a curious blend of Scripture and classical geography, the Church Fathers came to regard Ganga as the Phison, first river of Eden. The belief prevailed throughout the Middle Ages, accepted by such great figures as St. Augustine, Ambrose, and Jerome. It remained until the end of the fifteenth century, when Columbus, on his fourth voyage to the New World, touched the coast of Panama and thought he heard the natives speak of the great river Ganges, which lay ten days' journey from the coast.

Ganga's power is felt more in Bengal than elsewhere along its course. Here its shifting current has created and destroyed great cities; its changing distribution of silt has left entire regions desolate. It is no wonder, then, that Ganga plays a prominent part in the literature and folk religion of the delta.

With the general reader in mind, I have omitted the diacritics normally used for transliterating Sanskrit words into English; I have retained them, however, in the notes and the index.

In this book I have tried to present the image of Ganga in her totality. The *Rig Veda* reminds us that god is one; we call him by many names. In the same way, the river is one. It is not history or art, geography or literature, but all these and always something more. If this study has led me beyond my poor powers, I have followed for a single reason: to preserve that oneness.

Acknowledgments

TO RECALL IS TO FORGET. For those I have mentioned here with appreciation, there remain others whose words have strengthened me in ways that only I will know. Let me mention here Renell Lazar and Royal Weiler. My thanks as well to Floyd and Baba, who made the journey so much more worthwhile.

Among Indian colleagues, I owe a special debt of gratitude to Dr. Dhanesh Jain of Nehru University. Likewise to Professor Asutosh Bhattacharyya of the University of Calcutta, and to Jayashree Bhattacharyya, for their help with the Bengali translations in chapter 11. My thanks as well to Dr. U. N. Roy of Allahabad for information on ancient Prayag.

My work in India and America has been supported by the American Philosophical Society, by the Rutgers University Research Council, and by Mr. A. B. Griswold and the Breezewood Foundation. To all of them, my deepest appreciation.

I am further indebted to Don Yoder, our copy editor, to Janyce Blair and the rest of The University Press of Hawaii, and to Professor James Bier for his cartographic work.

My wife Jean has offered important editorial comments and has sustained me in a thousand ways. This book was to be dedicated to her, except that another obligation intervened.

For his Foreword and encouragement, a special word is due Professor A. L. Basham, whose true greatness lies in his knowledge of the human heart.

1
The Source

BEYOND THE HIGH HIMALAYAS, in the vast reaches of the Tibetan plateau, lies Mount Kailasa. In the Indian tradition, it holds the same meaning as Jerusalem to the medieval Christians and Mecca to the followers of Islam. As such it seems less a place than a state of mind, constellated with the dreams and aspirations of a thousand pilgrims who shall never make the journey except in their hearts. But Kailasa *is* a place, a shimmering mountain of twenty thousand feet. In some of the ancient writings—Hindu, Buddhist, even Chinese and Tibetan—Kailasa is also the home of Ganga, which flows from its slopes, dividing into four streams, to grace the world of men. (See Map 1.)

Near the foot of Kailasa lies Manasarovar, the Lake of the Mind (*sarovar,* in Sanskrit, signifying lake; *manas,* mind or thought), another supposed source of Ganga. Like the great mountain, it has been a center of pilgrimage since the early centuries of the Christian era, famous among Hindus and among Buddhists of all the northern countries: Tibet, China, Japan. At fifteen thousand feet, the ice-blue water covers an area of two hundred square miles, its regularly indented shore set in a cluster of mountains that rise abruptly from the endless expanse of plains.

In the figurative geography of the Puranas, Indian religious texts

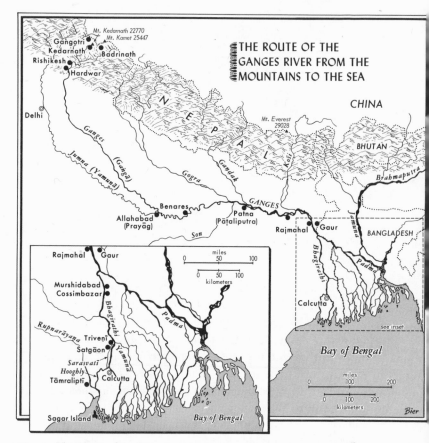

Map 1. The Route of the Ganges.

from the first eight centuries of our era, we confront the image of Asia as a four-sided lotus, each petal containing one of the great regions: China to the east, Persia to the west, India to the south, and, to the north, the obscure realms of Turkestan.[1] And out of Manasarovar, the Lake of the Mind, went a river in each direction to water the land. Within India itself, the four great rivers of the north—Ganga, Yamuna, the Indus, and the Brahmaputra—all take rise in the Himalayas and were thought of as flowing from Manasarovar, which in reality lies slightly to their north. But this was not known until the early nineteenth century.

The Ganges itself is born several hundred miles south of Kailasa in the Gangotri glacier, a mountain of ice nearly twenty miles long and three miles wide, surrounded by peaks twenty-one thousand to twenty-four thousand feet high. From here its two main sources— the Alakananda and the Bhagirathi—flow past the sacred villages of Badrinath and Gangotri, long since regarded as the most revered centers of pilgrimage. The journey from Rishikesh, nearly two hundred miles south, once lay across dirt tracks and over precarious bridges that swayed violently in the wind. These bridges, called jhulas, which still exist in remote places, are made from two pieces of twisted rope strung between the cliffs. Smaller ropes hang down, supporting short pieces of wood at right angles to the railings. Across these strips are placed lengths of split bamboo that provide the actual walkway.[2] The track is seldom more than ten inches wide. Since the 1940s, the Indian government has developed long stretches of the road, but the last few miles to Gangotri are still done on foot.

Badrinath is ancient and first appears in the *Mahabharata,* the great Indian epic often compared with the *Iliad.* Though composed between 400 B.C. and A.D. 400, it describes real and mythological events that return to the beginnings of Indian civilization. It is said that Manu—the first man—built an ark at the time of the deluge. Eventually it settled on a peak at Badrinath, where Manu recreated the human race. By his eponymous role as well as certain linguistic affinities, Manu is related to Adam and to Minos, the legendary king of Crete. India's greatest poet, Kalidasa, who lived in the fifth century A.D., describes the mythical Himalayan city of Alaka, perhaps a shortened form of Alakananda:

> Where maidens who the gods would gladly wed
> are fanned by breezes cool with Ganga's foam
> in the shadows that the trees of heaven spread.

The town of Badrinath lies on the western bank of the Alakananda in a mile-wide valley set between the ridges of Nar and Narayana, the somber rock cathedrals of Vishnu that rise to 19,500 feet, "higher than the flight of eagles," and behind them Nilakantha Peak, a dazzling pyramid of snow touching 21,600 (Figure 1).

The source of the river descends from Vasudhara Falls, seven or

Figure 1. The Town of Badrinath beneath Nilakantha Peak. Courtesy of R. R. Bharadvaj.

eight miles beyond the town, and can be reached by following a route long used by merchants and pilgrims traveling to and from Tibet. Starting from Badrinath, the road runs north along the Alakananda, then across a broad rocky plain to the tiny village of Mana, where it branches, one track leading to the Mana Pass at eighteen thousand feet and on to Manasarovar, 238 miles away, the other following the river to Vasudhara. Pilgrims follow the 2½-

mile track from Mana to immerse themselves for a moment in the icy waters of the falls where Ganga is born. It is a place of beginnings; for in Indian tradition, water—as a substance without shape—reminds us of the potential *(pralaya)* that all things have before they assume name and form, before they become unalterable. At Vasudhara the stream is sometimes cut off by the fierce winds that blow through the gorge. The natives regard this as a sign that someone of evil temperament has come to absolve himself by touching the source (Figure 2).

The village of Mana is like a hundred other Himalayan settlements: tiny stone houses cling to the mountainside; along the terraces and in unlikely places grow stands of wheat, corn, and other vegetables. Its inhabitants are Bhotiyas, a Tibetan people found along the mountains as far as Sikkim and Darjeeling. Their name itself means the people of Bhot, an Indian word for Tibet. Its men are short and powerful, the women full-bodied, with rich Mongolian faces and an openness that comes from working the fields and tending sheep. The few archaeological remains from the village include several carved figures of lamas and an early Brahmi script that date to the sixth century A.D.

Through hidden tracks among the mountains, the people of Mana carry on a considerable trade with the little-known kingdom of Bhutan. Toward the end of July, when the snows have melted and the passes are clear, they set off in groups of a hundred or so with merchandise, chiefly grain, carried by sheep or goats. The entire affair takes about a month; ten days each way plus time for rest and provisioning—and the endless subtleties of buying and selling, sitting in the marketplace sipping tea and talking of clouds and weather, flocks and grain, and intimations of the world beyond that drift down through the mountains like a wayward snowflake in September.

As for Badrinath, its heart is the temple, a small stone building covered with a copper-plated roof and surmounted by a gilded ball (Figure 3). According to tradition, it was first established in the eighth century by the famous philosopher Shankara, though it has been destroyed a hundred times by icefalls rushing down from Narayana Parvat. The statute may be older yet. For though it is wor-

Figure 2. Vasudhara Falls, Source of the Alakananda near Badrinath. Courtesy of R. R. Bharadvaj.

shipped as an image of Vishnu, there is every reason to believe it was originally meant to portray the Buddha,[3] at a time when the Himalayas were subject to strong Buddhist influence, especially under the Tibetan king Srong-tsang-Gampo (A.D. 629–647). Half concealed in the violet shadows of the sanctum, the black stone figure sits with legs crossed. One hand is raised, the palm facing outward in a gesture of benediction, the other resting in its lap, a pose typical of the Buddha. Another indication of its Buddhist affinities

Figure 3. The Temple at Badrinath. Courtesy of R. R. Bharadvaj.

is the regular gifts sent to the temple by the Tholing lamasery in Tibet, from an unknown time in the past up until the border closing in the 1950s.

The chief priest is a Numbudiri Brahman from Kerala, on the southwest coast of India, the original home of Shankara, and the contact has been maintained for over a thousand years. Near the temple is Tapta Kund, a hot spring that serves the appurtenances of pilgrimage. Throughout the year, even with snow covering the ground, it discharges boiling water that may be channeled to huts and private homes, providing a semblance of warmth. But except for the summer months—from May to November—the temple is closed, and most residents descend to villages at lower altitudes. Besides a handful of sadhus and sannyasins (holy men), there are few indications of life. Swami Tapovan, a saint of the Himalayas, describes the scene at the height of winter: "No bird stirs; no animal moves about. . . . Even as the face is seen reflected in a mirror, the Soul perceives itself in the stillness of Nature."[4] The temple service itself is austere: the chanting of a short litany and then bathing in the spring. For widows and orphans, there is shaving of the head, a custom practiced during the great Mela (bathing fair) at Allahabad, where three rivers meet and the true devotee steps beyond time.

Further south the Alakananda River is joined by the Mandakini, a lesser source that rises near Kedarnath, another center of pilgrimage. The shrine at Kedar is set on a broad treeless plain studded with glacial lakes. Certain architectural features as well as several of the sculptural panels devoted to Shiva all date from the tenth or eleventh century, while other characteristics seem as late as the sixteenth. The river itself flows from Kedar Peak, which looms above the temple at a height of twenty-one thousand feet. During the months of travel—in May and September—the entire route is thick with pilgrims, who come by foot and by bus, young and old, men and women, the rich and the penniless, the aged and the infirm, driven at times by something less than faith but more than curiosity. For, despite the occasional inns offering simple meals and shelter, it is not an easy journey.

At Deoprayag, the Alakananda joins the Bhagirathi, the other main source of Ganga, which rises beyond the pilgrimage center of Gangotri. The route to Gangotri follows steep mountainsides along the Bhagirathi Valley, passing among dense forests of cedar and pine and through little towns all with a curious sameness about them. The approach is through a rocky defile that booms with the sound of the river. Considering its age, the town seems almost makeshift. Apart from pilgrims, the only inhabitants are priests, yogis, and a few shopkeepers. In the surrounding caves, sannyasins often spend their last days in meditation before embracing the mystery. From November to May, everything is closed. Only a few ascetics stay on, sustaining themselves one way or another. Besides the temple, most structures are built from wood and tin, though the cedar, if properly cured, can last for centuries. The temple itself is made of stone and dedicated to Bhagiratha, whose name is intimately connected with the birth of Ganga. Inside there is a small statue of the river goddess with her companions the rivers Yamuna and Sarasvati.

But the true source of Ganga is at Gomukh (13,500 feet), the giant ice cave fourteen miles beyond the town (Figure 4). The journey is difficult; but the site, strange and compelling, says all that can be said about beginnings. No fixed road leads from Gangotri; only modest stone cairns guide the traveler. Clay pillars three hundred feet high cling precariously to the enclosing walls of the valley. Gradually the land levels to a boulder-covered plain nearly a mile long, sloping always upward toward the thick pine forest of Chirbasa. Here, at 11,800 feet, lies the only habitation along the way, a large pilgrim shelter *(dharmashala)* that accommodates forty or fifty people. The pines of Chirbasa have achieved a sanctity all their own. Even the poet Kalidasa speaks of Ganga flowing toward the pines along the high peaks of Himalaya. From Chirbasa it is another six miles, and most pilgrims set off at dawn, completing the full circle by nightfall. The last few miles run through stands of birch trees that recede near the perpetual snow line,[5] and the only things remaining are wizened shrubs and the yellow Brahma lotus that smells with the sweetness of the sun.

The ice cave—facing onto a tiny pool—rises over two hundred feet beneath its granite shell, and standing just above it is the peak of Shivalinga (19,630 feet), golden gray, the color of sea relics. For this is Gomukh, source of all begotten things, where shadows struggle into form "against the white unending canvass of eternity," where all that has ever been exists unuttered. Besides the occasional pilgrim, there are only shepherds pasturing their sheep along the small upland valleys. Men of incredible endurance, they often

Figure 4. The Ice Cave at Gomukh, Source of the Bhagirathi. Courtesy of R. R. Bharadvaj.

camp out on the plains—at thirteen thousand feet—without tents or firewood.

The shape of the cave forms a natural amphitheater that catches distant sounds: the shifting of ice, frost shattering on high peaks. At night the wind runs stronger; the entire atmosphere hums with the susurrous discourse of yakshas and gandharvas, divine beings believed to inhabit remote places that humans never see. Ordinarily such a scene might be terrifying, except that one can never think of death at Gomukh.

From here and Badrinath, the great sources descend to the *sangam* (the confluence) at Deoprayag, where they become the Ganges, the River of India. Flowing south, it passes through Rishikesh, the last point in the Himalayas before Ganga enters the plains. Unlike many other religious centers, Rishikesh is not mentioned in early literature and the town itself speaks nothing of antiquity. Here the sacred and profane are formally divided by the river. On one side: the endless rows of simple houses, workmen's sheds, and piles of dismembered auto parts. On the other: the ashrams, the centers of learning, and in the nearby hills the caves of holy men. Aside from a footbridge at the far end and a power launch that runs every half hour from dawn to sunset, nothing connects the two worlds but the agreement that the town is a holy place.

At the point where Ganga enters the plains, breaking out between the hills, lies Hardwar, the Gate of Vishnu (*Hari,* a name of Vishnu; *dvara,* the Sanskrit word for door or gate). The pilgrims gather here—in May and September—provisioning for the long journey north. At all times, the shops are filled with emollients for the spiritual traveler: tins of food, coarse coal-brown handwoven blankets, modest camp stoves, pots and cooking utensils, no two exactly the same, and brass-tipped walking sticks stained black. Everywhere too are earthen pots, often in pairs and joined with a bamboo pole. For here and at Rishikesh, Ganga water is considered its holiest. People come from all over the country—servants, pilgrims—to fill the pots and take them home for special occasions such as marriage or death or other times when Ganga is called upon to remind them of the dreams that have faded from their hearts. It is an old custom. Abul Fazl, a sixteenth-century chronicler, records the habits of the great Moghul king Akbar: "His majesty calls this source of life the water of immortality. . . . Both at home and on his travels he drinks Ganges water. Trustworthy persons stationed on the banks of the river dispatch the water in sealed jars. . . . Now that his majesty is in the Punjab, water is brought from Hardwar."[6]

As a wedding drink at Hindu marriages, Ganges water was accorded the highest honor. We glimpse the custom from the diary of Jean Tavernier, a French jeweler who visited India several times in the seventeenth century. Ganges water, he explains, "must be brought from a great distance by the Brahmins, in earthen vessels glazed inside, which the Grand Brahmin has placed his seal upon. This water is not given except at the end of the repast . . . for each of the guests three or four cupfuls are poured out and the more of it the bridegroom gives . . . so is he esteemed the more generous and magnificent. As this water comes from so far and the Chief Brahmin charges a certain tax on each pot . . . there is sometimes 2,000 or 3,000 Rupees worth of it consumed at a wedding."[7]

The life of Hardwar revolves around the ghats, the stone steps and causeways leading to the water. One may spend a day watching the endless coming and going of things: little troops of men from Delhi, Rajasthan, or towns without names, gathering pots of water for the journey of a thousand miles, this perhaps their only chance to visit Hardwar, the holy place, before they die. Then there are the bathers, some of whom rent small thatched one-room shelters at the water's edge, alternately immersing themselves and withdrawing into the huts, for hours on end. At sunset bells toll from the temples near the shore, and those with hopes or prayers launch tiny boats of leaves, filled with rose petals and a lighted candle. The shells gather slowly, forming a long line of tiny flames that moves tentatively but ineluctably along the current, out into the great river that widens here to a mile. At times the line wobbles and disappears, but always somewhere, further off, appears a tip of flame, a prayer that, one way or another, finds the sea.

Hardwar is an ancient town. Its name appears in different forms since the time of *Mahabharata* over two thousand years ago. It has been known as Mokshadvara (the Door of Freedom), Mayapura (the City of Illusion), and Gangadvara (the Gate of Ganga), its most common name. Sculpture fragments, coins, and numerous foundations allude to its antiquity, but nothing visual remains. We glimpse it but briefly in the early literature. The seers sang hymns at Gangadvara, and several heroes of the *Mahabharata*—Bhishma and Arjuna—do penance here at the point where Ganga meets the plains.

Unlike many other ancient cities, Hardwar has escaped the anonymous embrace of time, perhaps because it never was a kingdom or a capital or a place where armies fought. It never threw up palaces or monuments, and so it remains what it has always been: a kingdom of the mind, frequented by pilgrims and travelers who gather wherever highways meet, where roads begin and end. In the seventh century A.D. the Buddhist pilgrim Hiuen Tsiang reached Hardwar after an incredible overland journey from China. He describes the town as roughly "twenty *li* [3½ miles] in circuit. The inhabitants are very numerous, and the pure streams of the river flow round on every side; it produces native copper . . . pure crystal, and precious vases. There are always hundreds and thousands of people gathered together here from distant quarters to bathe and wash in its waters."[8] In Moghul times, Hardwar remained an unimportant though not forgotten outpost. Under Akbar it was one of the twenty-eight towns where copper coins were produced; silver and gold were minted elsewhere, at more important centers.[9]

As we will see later, the image of Ganga is intimately connected with Himalaya. She is "the child of the mountain" in a very real sense. For it is during the summer months of March and April— when the plains grow hot and dry and dusty—that the snows melt on the high peaks and the river, fed by a thousand icy streams, carries its life-giving water to the parched earth and its inhabitants.

2

The Waters of Creation

AMONG THE MANY SYMBOLS of India endowed with spirituality, water is the most sacred, at once the purifier and the origin of the mystery. It is the real and imagined source of life. "He who was born of old," speculates the *Katha Upanishad,* "was born of water. Right from the Waters, the Soul drew forth and shaped a person."[1] What was this thing culled from the waters? "Golden in form is he," rhapsodizes the *Rig Veda,* "like gold to look upon, the Son of the Waters."[2]

The sanctity of water has been part of the Indian tradition from its beginnings in the Indus Valley over four thousand years ago and has remained so ever since. Water in general and Ganges water in particular is used today for rituals of birth and death. It is still served at weddings, as it was three centuries ago when Tavernier described the ceremony. Water from Ganga may be offered to god at morning or evening worship. In Bengal, during the initiation or sacred thread ceremony *(upanayana),* a young man takes nothing but bread and Ganges water. At the end of life, it is the wish of every pious Hindu to die at Banaras and have his or her ashes scattered on the sacred river.

How shall we understand this primacy of the Ganges as a living tradition for over two thousand years? Just as all great traditions emerge from the interplay of many forces, so Ganga's fame has grown through time, enhanced by different people and cultures as they came in contact with the river, adding to it their vision of reality. These forces are numerous and varied; we will examine them throughout the book. But beneath the art and the ritual and the dazzling myths lies the physical reality of the Ganges Valley; the red heat of summer, the life-restoring monsoon, and, of course, the river itself.

The Plains

In March the grain ripens; it is harvest time. It is also the beginning of summer, which lasts until the rains in mid-June. By late April, the heat grows intense and a dry wind begins to wither the trees and grass. By May it reaches 110° in the shade and by June as much as 120°. Dust storms gather, sometimes advancing in a solid wall up to three hundred feet high. It is in these months, before the monsoon, that shortages occur and the periodic famines reach their climax. India has known scarcity since ancient times. The process is a complex one involving a confluence of misfortunes. If the monsoon fails in June and July, rice planting is delayed, and even a September rain seldom restores the withered crop. In October and early November, the farmer sows his wheat, which depends on the winter rain of December and January. If it is too light, he may lose this crop as well, facing a bleak summer and possibly starvation. The worst famines have seldom resulted from one bad year but rather from two or three in succession. Not only are there droughts: the farmer has sometimes found his rice planting swept away by sudden floods. Even toward the end of a good year, a promising harvest can be ruined in March by hail and thunderstorms that smash the wheat and the fruit trees.[3]

A shortage occurs roughly every five years in limited areas. Every ten years, famine breaks out over a wider region. Every fifty or a hundred years witnesses a major disaster extending over several states. One of the first recorded famines occured in 1291 under the reign of Firoz Shah Khalji, a Muslim king of Delhi. People streamed into the capital and "in the extremity of their hunger," says the chronicler, "drowned themselves in the Jumna. The Sultan did all he could to help them." Travelers' journals, the works of Muslim

court historians, and the records of the East India Company are filled with such reports.[4]

In the famine year of 1769, so many cattle died that tigers, unable to find their normal prey, attacked the town of Bhavapar, kill-
ing over four hundred people.[5] Famine struck the province again in
1873, and we read accounts of women, stripped naked, plowing the
fields at night as an invocation to the god of rain.[6] Even today offerings are made to the power behind the monsoon. When the rains
are delayed, the village potter may be told to turn his wheel in the
opposite direction. Thus Indra the rain god will reverse the order of
events.

If the rains have been poor since the previous monsoon, the
water level drops and the wells may run dry. Under such conditions, Ganga provides the only source of water in these sere summer
months. Even in the best of times, people depend on the river to
see them through until the rainy season.

With the coming of the rains in mid-June, the brittle earth is
healed and life rises up from the waters. Rain clouds, drifting in
from the Bay of Bengal, strike the summits of the mountains and,
rebuffed, move slowly up the Ganges Valley. In his poem "The
Seasons" Kalidasa heralds the monsoon:

> Slowly clouds appear,
> bent down by the weight of water.
>
> Strings of rain fall like arrows.
> Peacocks start to dance once more,
> and seek their mates
> with heightened sensuality.
>
> The new fallen water,
> heavy with insects, dust, and brittle grass,
> rushes onward,
> observed by a troop of startled frogs.
>
> The heat within the forest
> cools beneath the sprinkled rain.
> Kadamba flowers blossom.

More than 70 percent of the yearly rainfall gathers in the months
from June through September. The Arabic word *mausim* means

simply "a season," but in India it is *par excellence* the season of growth and of increase. Grass spreads across the dry earth. Vast stretches of the Ganges Valley turn to swamp. In a thousand mud villages, farmers yoke their oxen to a plow, preparing the ground for rice and millet.

The onset of the monsoon is celebrated as Ganga-dussera. It is a time for cleansing one's sins, a time for beginnings. Those with special reverence for Ganga rise early and fill their bath with water brought entirely from the river. If this is not possible, they add a small amount of Ganges water to their normal source, for as an old Gujarati proverb says: "Where the heart is true, there will Ganga be." While the monsoon provides the occasion, Ganga-dussera itself commemorates the descent of Ganga from heaven. The correspondence at once reveals the primal role of Ganga as both source and symbol of plenitude. Since Vedic times, from 1000 B.C., Indian thought has provided the elements with a human counterpart. This personification, in the form of myth, allows humans some recourse from the otherwise malevolent forces of nature. People pray not to water but to the life within the water.

The Descent of Ganga

Accordingly, the descent of Ganga has evolved through the centuries in the form of an elaborate myth. It is a lengthy tale, but central to any understanding of Ganga in her entirety. It begins with King Sagara, a just and mighty ruler whose name in Sanskrit signifies the ocean *(sagara)*. After years of childlessness, the king retired to Mount Kailasa with his two wives, Keshini and Sumati, where he lived, practicing austerity and praying for a son. Finally his wish was granted by Bhrigu, a great sage dwelling on the mountain. But the sage's pronouncement was strangely reminiscent of the kings of Greece and their misfortunes: "You will beget many sons," he predicted, "and your fame will be immeasurable. From one of your queens will come one son, and from the other 60,000."[7] Sagara returned to his kingdom, and in time a son was born to Keshini. Sumati, in turn, brought forth a gourd containing sixty thousand male seeds, which the nurses hurriedly placed in jars filled with butter, tending them daily. After a while, they attained to a state of adolescence, radiantly beautiful, and thereafter grew to manhood.

Sagara was jubilant and enjoyed the blessings of his kingdom during the long years of peace. Eventually he aspired to the title of Chakravartin, or world conqueror, a term referring to both spiritual and temporal ascendance. To realize this purpose, he undertook an *ashvamedha* (horse sacrifice), a ceremony followed by many historical Indian rulers. A horse was turned loose for a year, and the country where it wandered would become the land of the king. The outcome could be contested, but only by war. At year's end, the king was proclaimed Chakravartin and the horse was sacrificed as an offering and a notice that the ruler had attained to spiritual authority.

And so the horse was freed to wander, roaming through valleys, across mountains, over rivers; and all who saw him understood and accepted Sagara, for he was wise and treated all men according to their due. As the prescribed period drew to a close, the gods were troubled by Sagara's empire, which touched the oceans. Fearful he would reach heaven itself, they stole the horse and sequestered it by the hermitage of Rishi Kapila.

When the horse was taken, Sagara spoke to his sons: "You must find the animal and bring it to me. I cannot rest until you do; you must catch the thief and punish him, for he has kept your father from the doors of heaven." As a result, they hunted everywhere, in jungles and on mountaintops, rooting up the earth; in their frenzy they even descended to the underworld, where they saw the giant elephant Virupaksha, guardian of the Eastern Quarter. Finally, in an ashram by the sea, they came upon Rishi Kapila, deep in meditation, and near him the sacrificial horse. Whereupon they rushed toward the sage accusingly, hurling imprecations. In this way, the ascetic's fury was roused, and with the fire of his glance the sons of Sagara were reduced to ashes. The misfortune was revealed to the king by his grandson Anshuman, who had been sent to find the princes. Instead he returned with the news and the Rishi's promise that they would attain heaven when the waters of the Ganges were brought from heaven to purify their ashes.

Sagara grew old and died unable to bring Ganga from heaven.

Anshuman and his descendants came and went their way, but none possessed the singleness of mind to stir the celestial river. At length a son of the royal family—Bhagiratha—became king. An earnest seeker of truth, he entrusted his kingdom to his counselors and retired to Himalaya, where he spent years in penance and ascetic practice. The gods were pleased; his wish was granted; even Lord Shiva agreed to catch the river as it fell from heaven. Otherwise its tumultuous descent would sunder the earth with its force. Shiva, standing on the high peak of Himalaya, commanded the river. And Ganga, in her hubris, thought: "Who is this god that calls me down? I will sweep him away." And with her current circling the moon, she rushed upon him.

Shiva, understanding all thoughts, angered, caught the river in his matted hair dense as the forest of time, and held her there. "And Ganga wandered round and round amidst his locks and could find no egress." But out of kindness to Bhagiratha, he released the river, which entered Lake Manasarovar, dividing into seven streams that flowed to the far corners of the earth. And the seventh, the Alakananda (the river's name as it flows past Badrinath), followed Bhagiratha on his long journey down the mountains, a thousand miles across the plains, through the jungles of the delta, to Kapila's ashram, and there, at the end of the world, graced the ashes of the sons of Sagara, lifting them to paradise.

Of the many tales and legends associated with Ganga, the river's descent from heaven (Gangavatarana) provided the greatest challenge to the Indian artist. The theme has been rendered in diverse and imaginative ways. The most dramatic representation is found thirty-two miles south of Madras at the deserted seaport town of Mamallapuram. Now totally abandoned, it served as the harbor for Conjeeveram, capital of the great South Indian Pallava Empire, in the seventh century A.D. Near the shore, rising a hundred feet from the sand, is a granite rock half a mile long that contains the amazing collection of secular and religious architecture known as Mamallapuram.

The Descent of Ganga, a colossal sculpture cut from the east face of the rock, depicts the river rushing from its source in the distant Himalayas. In its day, water stored in a receptacle above tumbled down a natural fissure at the center of the great carved relief. Now the water is still, but at one time the city boasted an extensive irrigation system drawn from the Palar River and distributed throughout the port by a network of canals and tanks. Besides its public function, the water served for religious purposes, possibly combining with the naga or serpent cult as an object of worship:[8]

> It is difficult to reconcile this deserted area consisting of a bare rocky hill, and desolate sand dunes, with what was once a populous maritime center. The drifting sands have covered up and obliterated most of its landmarks, while the warring elements of wind and tide have altered the contours of the coastline, so that its ancient appearance can only be imagined. . . . But there is little doubt that from Mamallapuram, in the middle of the first millennium, many deep-laden argosies set forth, first with merchandise and then with emigrants, eventually to carry the light of Indian culture over the . . . ocean into the . . . countries of Hither Asia.[9]

The entire stone pulses with life: gods, mortals, animals, all hurrying to witness the event—the celestial river tumbling down from heaven to nourish humanity and restore the sons of Sagara. The river forms a natural cleavage halfway across the face of the rock and provides a center for the myriad converging forms on either side (Figure 5). We will never know, of course, but the scene seems directly inspired by the description of Gangavatarana found in the second great Indian epic, the *Ramayana:*

> Devas, Rishis, Yakshas, and all the Celestial Beings . . . hastened there to witness the marvelous and auspicious descent of the Ganges to the world. And the Gods, as they alighted from the sky, irradiated that cloudless canopy of heaven with the splendor of their divine ornaments, so that it seemed a thousand suns had risen there.[10]

From a deep slash in the rock rises a serpent king (naga) paying homage, his hands folded before him (Figure 6). Under the cobra hood one sees a face lost in reverie, lips half-parted in a mystical dream of paradise. Below his serpent body, winding between the cleft shores of the river, we find the naga queen, her hands similarly raised before her (Figure 7). She too is absorbed in some inner ecstasy, though less intensely than her lord, and beneath her, its

Figure 5. Descent of the Ganges. Mamallapuram. Seventh Century. Cliché: Victor Goloubew, Musée Guimet, Paris.

coil buried in the sand, rises a huge hooded cobra, its quivering body held firm in the stone that utters it. To the far left, facing the naga king, the yogi Bhagiratha balances on one leg (Figure 8). According to legend, he stood for a thousand years before obtaining his request. Slightly above and to the left, a smiling Shiva points with pride to the yogi, reminding us of the powers within, if only the will is strong and the heart is pure. One of the most striking

Figure 6. Naga King. Mamallapuram. Cliché: Victor Goloubew, Musée Guimet, Paris.

features at Mamallapuram is the singularity of forms, especially those nearest the center. The couples beside the river represent more than ideas of Pallava beauty: they reveal distinctly human, individualized expressions. To the left and slightly lower than the serpent queen, a naga prince stands awed and serene before the mystery while his lady waits respectfully (Figure 10).

In contrast to the enormous rock face, the images seem to float in

Figure 7. Naga Queen. Mamallapuram. Cliché: Victor Goloubew, Musée Guimet, Paris.

air. There is nothing massive here. All blends in a perfect expression, half mystical, half visual, part of the effect created by the figures on the upper half of the relief. With bodies swaying gently forward and legs beneath them, they move not as human beings but as gods (Figure 9).

Along with the Gangavatarana theme, the artist—by the placement of figures—stresses the triple nature of the river: Ganga as

Figure 8. Shiva and the Sage Bhagiratha. Mamallapuram. Cliché: Victor Goloubew, Musée Guimet, Paris.

Figure 9. Men and Celestials. Mamallapuram. Cliché: Victor Goloubew, Musée Guimet, Paris.

Figure 10. Couple Observing the Descent of the Ganges. Mamallapuram. Cliché: Victor Goloubew, Musée Guimet, Paris.

flowing in the three worlds. From their manner of movement, the figures at the top are clearly celestials, while the elephants, animals of the underworld, are found at the base together with the serpents rising from the earth. We will examine this threefold nature of Ganga more fully in the chapter on Ganga and Artemis.

Underlying the entire piece is the Maya quality of Indian art: the realization that all embodied shapes are but a moment's inflection

of Brahman, the formless essence of matter. In religion, the mode
of Brahman is water; in art it is stone. Here the sculptor, confronted
by the great face of Mamallapuram, has rendered the figures with
varying degrees of manifestation: some figures remain half within
the stone *(ardha-citra)* while others are fully rounded *(citra)*. In this
way, the artist has struck a vivid balance between the Brahman nature of the stone and the Maya manifestation of its fleeting images.
The scene may end at any moment. Bhagiratha, his penance over,
will step down from the pedestal and lead Ganga away to Kapila's
hermitage and to the ashes of the dead warriors, the gods will in-
cline their bodies and ascend into the heavens, the elephants and
serpents will seek the earth once more, and the rock will return to
its silent unbecoming *(pralaya)* and its discourse with the wind and
the sea.

Another sculpture depicting the descent of Ganga is found in the
temple of Nirmal Jahara—the ''Clear Springs''—near the village of
Kallikote in the jungles of Orissa. The site is virtually unknown; the
age of the temple can only be guessed.[11] It lies near the base of a
long sloping hill and receives a small but nearly constant stream of
water, which is channeled into a large tank through the mouth of a
stone crocodile, or makara. In Indian art, the makara is an emblem
of the waters. It serves as a pedestal for Ganga and as her signature,
distinguishing the river goddess from other figures. From here the
stream divides—one part, Yamuna, leading to an unadorned basin
called Prayag (the ancient name for Allahabad and the place where
Ganga and Yamuna meet) and the other, Ganga, to a tank named
Manasarovar, which contains, in miniature, the story of Ganga's
descent from heaven.

The small stone pool—less than eight feet square—contains an
elaborate filigreed niche sheltering the god Vishnu seated in a cross-
legged yoga pose *(ardha-padmasana)* (Figure 11) and bearing his
special emblems: the conch shell, the fiery wheel, the club, and the
lotus, or padma. A stream of water issues from a pipe concealed
beneath his left foot, which extends over a narrow channel. From
here the water is carried to a smaller shrine containing five con-
torted faces whose disheveled hair marks the image as Shiva.
Water flowing over the hair continues along the channel, flowing

Figure 11. Vishnu, Shiva, Jahnu, and Mount Meru, in a Pool at Ganjam, Depicting the Descent of the Ganges. Courtesy of The Asiatic Society.

under the bearded figure of Rishi Jahnu, another irascible sage, who swallowed Ganga as she flowed past his hermitage, overturning his pots and pans and disturbing his meditations. Eventually the Rishi acceded to Bhagiratha's plea and released the river. After passing beneath the statue of Jahnu, the tiny stream turns a corner and enters a decorated semicircular stone that represents Mount Meru (Figure 12). At its base are three jets of water—Ganga, Ya-

Figure 12. The Pool at Ganjam. Courtesy of The Asiatic Society.

muna, and the river Sarasvati—that empty into the pool of Manasarovar. Atop the stone, a tree houses several small figures, probably yakshas (genii).

Brahma, Vishnu, and Shiva

By the Gangavatarana theme, the river is connected with the great gods of the Hindu trinity. According to the early texts, Ganga originated in the heavens; her home was in the Milky Way. The site itself is described by the *Vishnu Purana,* an encomium to Vishnu: the space between the Seven Sages (Ursa Major, the Great Bear) and Dhruva (the Pole Star), the third region of the sky, is the splendid celestial path of Vishnu, the home of those who have surmounted every form of pain and pleasure, spectators of the world, incandescent, clothed in light. Here are interwoven all that is and ever will be—animate, inanimate. From this region flows the stream whose benediction graces all it touches. The Seven Sages, unmoving, perform austerities within her waters. [12]

It is told that whenever the world is overwhelmed with evil, Vishnu returns in one of his ten incarnations (avataras). One such appearance is Trivikrama, god of the three strides. The demon *(asura)* Bali, so the story goes, acquired great power by his austerities and eventually deposed Indra, Lord of Heaven. Vishnu, entreated by the gods, agreed to overthrow the demon and, descending to earth, changed himself into a dwarf child. He then approached Bali with a request to grant him a gift marked by three paces. Though he knew the identity of the dwarf, the demon could not but agree. Then Vishnu swelled to gigantic size and, with one step, paced off the entire earth. With a second he reached the heavens, and with a third he pierced the roof of the universe, intruding into Satyaloka, Brahma's Realm of Truth. And from that crevice flowed the divine Ganga itself, poured out by Brahma in reverence for the mighty deed of Vishnu. [13]

We have already seen Shiva's role in the descent of Ganga to the earth. This reveals but one aspect of their primordial relationship: he as lord, she as mother and child, of the mountain; he as the organ of generation (lingam), she as the liquid essence of life; he as the mystery, she as the door to the mystery; he as the tomb, she as the waters of life. They are never far apart and occur together both in ritual and in several of Shiva's manifestations. Their conjunction reaches its fulfillment, as we will see, in the later development of the Hindu temple by the sixth or seventh century A.D.

The Mother Goddess

In the plains and down along the Bengal delta, the river is known as Ganga Mata, Mother Ganga, bringing life in the form of water. This image of Ganga echoes throughout her history, and many tales are told of her generative powers: giving birth, restoring life, conferring immortality. The most famous legend, of Ganga and the Vasus, elucidates her descent from heaven.[14]

One day a king named Shantanu was walking by the river when he saw a lovely woman, ripe, with long dark hair, and skin like the inside of a seashell. Unknown to him, she was the goddess Ganga. Completely enchanted, he asked her to be his wife, and she accepted. "But on one condition," she smiled. "You must not interfere with anything I do, no matter what. I will be your wife, but the moment you reproach me, I will leave you."

The king gladly agreed and returned to the palace, where he was greatly pleased by her beauty and her knowledge of love, by her gentleness and dance and her devotion to his comforts. In this way, years passed unnoticed. "And the king, while enjoying himself with his wife, had eight children born to him who in beauty were like the celestials themselves." But at birth each child was thrown into the river by Shantanu's wife. The king remained silent for fear of losing her. Still, neither fate nor human nature would countenance such things. And with the birth of the eigth child, Shantanu could restrain himself no longer. "Why have you done these terrible deeds, murdering your own children?" he demanded.

"There is no blame in what I do," she replied demurely. "I am the goddess Ganga. And these children I have borne to you, they are the Vasus, celestials who were cursed to appear in human form as punishment for their misdeeds against the sage Vasishtha. It is a terrible fate to live as a man once you have known immortality; and out of compassion, I agreed to bear them here on earth and restore them to paradise the moment they were born. And now, according to our compact, I must leave you." She then disappeared, leaving Shantanu alone and miserable except for the eighth child, who remained with him and was called Gangadatta, for he was the son of Ganga.

The story is told in stone on the four sides of a pillar at the Virupaksha temple (ca. A.D. 740) in Pattadakal, southwest India.[15] Strands of the river extend behind the figures from one panel to the next, providing a visual continuity that is repeated in the sinuous movements of the actors. At the left of the first panel is Bhagiratha, doing penance to the gods in the hope of gaining salvation for his ancestors; to his right is Ganga seated before the eight Vasus (Figure 13). As often happens over a long tradition, the artist has here confounded the Bhagiratha story with Ganga and the Vasus, unless the eight celestials are added as a sculptural coda, reminding the viewer of the other reason for Ganga's descent to earth.

The remaining sculpture follows the Bhagiratha narrative. To the left of the next panel, moving clockwise around the pillar, we find the river goddess beside a stern Kapila, who sits meditating (Figure 14). In the center we see a young man with his arms raised in anger, advancing on the sage and the sacrificial horse. The young warrior probably represents the sixty thousand sons of Sagara, for nearby stands Diggaja, the celestial elephant, waiting to accept the prince's ashes in the underworld.

The third panel (from right to left) shows Ganga flowing down from heaven. Resting on the bull Nanda, and with his wife Parvati beside him, Shiva receives the force of the river in a leisurely fashion, holding out one or two locks of hair to accommodate the waters which he then releases on the other side. And we find Bhagiratha praying for Shiva's favor (Figure 15).

From here the stream bubbles off into the next panel, there to be imprisoned in the water vessel of Rishi Jahnu. Once more Bhagiratha must perform austerities until the Rishi agrees to release the river (Figure 16). At last Ganga has been tamed and follows Bhagiratha demurely to the underworld, thus returning us to the first panel. In all Bhagiratha has undergone four long penances: to Brahma for releasing Ganga from heaven, twice to Shiva for cush-

Figure 13. The Story of Ganga at Pattadakal. Bhagiratha, Ganga, and the Vasus. Courtesy of *Oriental Art* and C. Sivaramamurti.

ioning the fall of the waters and then for releasing them, and finally to the angry Jahnu.

Indirectly, Ganga is also the mother of Skanda or Karttikeya, god of war and the planet Mars. At one time, the gods were powerless against the demon Taraka, who, it seems, could be destroyed only by a child of Shiva born without aid of a woman. Acceding to their

Figure 14. Ganga, the Sage Kapila, the Sons of Sagara, and the Elephant Virupaksha. Pattadakal. Courtesy of *Oriental Art* and C. Sivaramamurti.

pleas, Shiva finally released his seed, first to Agni. But even the god of fire could not contain it and cast it into the Ganges. From this union sprang Karttikeya, sometimes called Gangaputra (son of Ganga).[16]

Other legends attest to Ganga's life-giving properties. In the

Figure 15. Bhagiratha, Shiva, and Ganga. Pattadakal. Courtesy of *Oriental Art* and C. Sivaramamurti.

Buddhist *Jataka* stories, we read of a parrot-king who lived in a fig tree on the banks of the Ganges, eating the fruit of the tree and enjoying its shelter. In the sodality of all life—recognized by many early cultures—the parrot felt gratitude to the tree for its beneficence. This feeling sent a tremor through the kingdom of Sakka (Indra), and the ruler, to test the bird's loyalty, magically withered the tree. But, out of friendship, the bird remained. Finally Sakka

Figure 16. Ganga, Bhagiratha, and Jahnu. Patradakal. Courtesy of *Oriental Art* and C. Sivaramamurti.

granted the parrot-king any wish he desired. Whereupon the bird asked that the tree be restored to its old vigor. Then Sakka "took up the water from the Ganges in his hand and dashed it against the fig-tree stump. Straightaway the tree rose up rich in branch and stem, with honey-sweet fruit, and stood a charming sight, like the bare Jewel-Mountain."[17]

This restoring quality of Ganga is further revealed in the *Mahabharata,* where at the end of the great war Vyasa, the legendary author of the epic, calls the slain armies from the depths of the river for a final reunion:

> Then Vyasa entered the sacred water of the Ganga, and summoned all the warriors. . . . Immediately there was a deafening roar from within the waters, and the kings . . . with all their armies, arose in their thousands from the waters of the Ganges . . . free from all animosity and pride, anger and jealousy . . . and purged of every sin, the heroes met with each other. All of them were happy of heart. Son met with father or mother, wife with husband, brother with brother, and friend with friend. . . . All the warriors . . . reconciled with each other, renouncing enmity and becoming established in friendship. Thus they passed that night in great happiness.
>
> When the day dawned, they embraced each other and took their respective places. Thereupon, Vyasa, the foremost of ascetics, dismissed them. Within the twinkling of an eye, they disappeared in the very sight of all. Plunging into the sacred river Ganga, they proceeded to their respective abodes.[18]

After two thousand years, the goddess is still worshipped as a source of life and generation. Even today in Bihar, at the start of the plowing season, before the seeds are sown, farmers put Ganga water in a pot and set it in a special place in the field to ensure good harvest. Among those who live along the river, a newly married woman unfolds her sari to Ganga and prays for children and the long life of her husband.

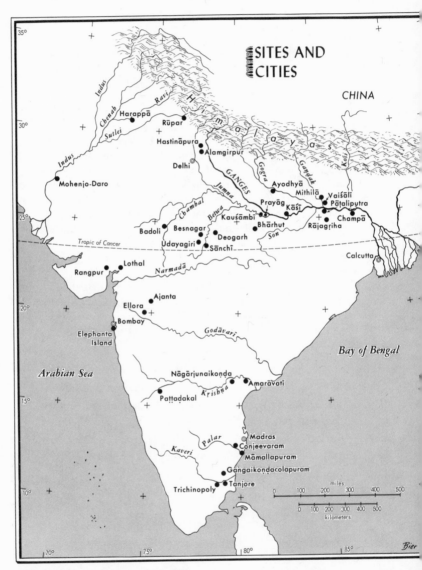

Map 2. Cities and Archaeological Sites.

3
The Indus Legacy

THE FIRST CIVILIZATIONS are known by their rivers. The Nile, the Tigris and Euphrates, the Indus, and the Ganges all fix the cultures they created with a certain likeness in society, religion, and economic structure. In one sense, the Ganges Valley—with its heavy monsoon rain—differs from the others.[1] But throughout the year, it is the river that answers the people's pervasive needs: for sanitation and ritual, for drinking and irrigation. To appreciate the role of Ganga, we must first understand the institutional forms imposed by the great rivers, especially the Indus, which gave rise to the first true Indian civilization. We will also find in the Indus legacy startling antecedents of the Ganga image as it appears over two thousand years later in Indian art.

The Indus civilization flourished roughly 2300–1800 B.C. in an area slightly larger than modern Pakistan. Over and above the many smaller sites, the kingdom is marked by its two great capitals of Mohenjo-Daro and Harappa, 350 miles apart but joined by a major river. (See Map 2.) In spite of the devastating floods—at least three at Mohenjo-Daro—the cities were not abandoned until the end. Faced with such dangers, the inhabitants must have had compelling reasons for retaining the river site. With few exceptions, urban centers in the ancient Near East were built on rivers. Those deserted settlements that now seem far removed reveal a proximity to some early riverbed long since smoothed away by time.[2] The reasons are clear enough: sanitation, trade, the many needs people have for water. From 2000 B.C., the metropolis of Ur presents a massive rampart along the Euphrates, with a large harbor at the western end. Already in the fourth millennium B.C., boats appear on cylinder seals; from a king's grave of the third millennium a silver model of a ship is recovered.[3]

A similar plan unfolds on the Indus. At Harappa, a twenty-foot-high retaining wall runs along the old riverbed. Beside the wall we find a range of barracklike dwellings, rows of work platforms (apparently for pounding grain), and a double range of granaries, all within easy reach of the river.[4] A similar configuration seems likely at Mohenjo-Daro, though all the evidence is not yet in. At one end of the ruined city, a wall of burnt brick thirty feet deep contains a gate opening out on the riverbed. Further along the wall, a little fortlike structure reveals a series of rooms on a platform, with a flight of stairs leading to the river.[5]

The implications are clear: two large urban centers with their major food supply grown along the river and brought down by boat. This picture is strengthened by the agricultural pattern of the Indus period. In areas of negligible rainfall, flood irrigation alone affords a limited extension of fertile land. Mesopotamia produced a dozen city-states in a region no more fertile than the Indus Valley.[6] There, however, the system was based on canal irrigation, which is lacking in the Indus culture. Thus grain would tend to be sown in narrow fields along the river. It is difficult to gauge the volume or extent of river traffic. Traces of sandy material on the lid of a Harappa coffin were identified as deodar, a cedar which grows chiefly in the Himalayan foothills.[7] Though wheeled vehicles existed, they would have been less efficient for the long-distance hauling of grain, especially with the lack of roads. The river offered far easier transport.

While we find only three representations of boats on Indus seals and pottery, the external evidence for Harappan shipping is impressive. Archaeologists have found more than thirty Indus sites in Gujarat, on the west coast of India north of Bombay. Of these, at least nine were ports. Lothal, the most famous, dates to 2000 B.C. and represents the earliest Harappan settlements in the region. In all likelihood, Indus settlers in the subcontinent came chiefly by sea.[8]

Points of Contact

The sites in Gujarat plus several settlements on the upper Ganges carry the Indus horizon deep into the subcontinent. From here it permeates the Ganges Valley and has remained part of Indian culture ever since. The chief line of transmission is Gujarat, an area of low rainfall close to the original Indus conditions. Here, from the eighteenth or nineteenth century B.C., the Indus settlements began to mix with the indigenous people. By 1750 B.C., the cities of Harappa and Mohenjo-Daro were dead, but the synthesis proceeded in Gujarat, stimulated by settlers who had abandoned their original homes, extending the Harappan culture south and eastward from the Indus basin.

In Gujarat and eastward along the lower reaches of the Narmada River, the Indus pottery blends gradually into several other ceramic traditions. The total picture reveals a transplanting of Indus technology and culture to the region of Saurashtra and Gujarat, where it is absorbed by people of several traditions and eventually brought into contact with the Ganges Valley by groups following the Chambal River northeast toward the Yamuna and by others along the Narmada into southern Bihar.

The Genesis of Cities

The earliest Gangetic settlement of any dimension was Hastinapura, which contains pottery remains from a period before 1200 B.C. Located sixty miles northeast of Delhi, it was once on the banks of the old Ganga. Through the millennia the river has shifted eastward, leaving the ruins of the city five miles from its present course. In succeeding ages, Hastinapura was to become a cultural and commercial center, capital of the great Kuru dynasty in the *Mahabharata*. But above all it marks the first efforts at urban life in the Ganges Valley.

In addition to Hastinapura, we find the ancient city of Kausham-

bi, located on the Yamuna thirty-two miles southwest of Allahabad
and along the trade route running west-southwest toward the Narmada. From the tenth century B.C. there appear massive defenses
closely resembling the Harappan plan. Here the chief excavator
G. R. Sharma has found major architectural features "with proto-
types for each . . . in Harappan architecture."[9] The defenses also
employ baked brick, a common feature of Indus construction. It is
significant that both cities lay along the two routes followed by
earlier Harappan traditions.

The later Aryan invaders were nomads with little use for cities
and no experience in building methods: the knowledge of brick-
making, town planning, and the thousand subtle skills requisite to
urban life. We must look elsewhere for the first impetus. The only
other source is from the Indus legacy, with its highly developed
traditions of wide streets and evolved sanitation. However far removed in time, the Harappan influence leaves the impress of its
forms. And with its technology goes its vision of the world, for as
archaeologist S. C. Malik reminds us: "Both the metaphysical and
the 'material' world are interrelated and neither can exist without
the other."[10] Several features of that world are central to our understanding of Ganga and her image in Indian civilization.

Of Trees and Goddesses

The language of the Indus people is still obscure. Its script exists
in fragments of the faces of a thousand tiny seals—seldom more
than one or two inches high—used for religious or commercial purposes. These seals are the first documents of Indian culture and
offer secret access to a world still all its own. By counting backward
from historical times, we can begin to understand the genesis of the
goddess Ganga and those qualities that have been drawn to her
from the dim reaches of prehistory.

The tree—as the vegetal essence of life—figures prominently in
the image of Ganga, who is usually depicted beneath a tree and,
later in her evolution, beneath a parasol or other canopy. This association of the goddess and the tree dates from the Indus civilization. Time and again the tiny Indus seals portray a female figure in
the branches of a tree. On one seal, for example, she is being wor-

shipped by a devotee while a hoofed animal looks on from behind (Figure 17).

Often the Indus seals confront us with what we might call "interpenetrating forms": a common rhythm flowing throughout the range of portrayed objects, human, animal, and vegetal. Notice the seal of a horned animal, a female, and a tree depicted in Figure 18. The branches of the tree duplicate the animal's horns and the pigtail extending behind the raised arm of the female. The animal's tail corresponds to the female's, whose feet end in birdlike claws. The lower part of her body—from the waist down—is distinctly nonhuman, an impression immediately revealed by covering the top half. Such composite figures occur in later Indian art and usually indicate mythical beings like yakshas or gandharvas, creatures part human, part immortal, halfway between men and gods. So it

Figure 17. Antecedent of Ganga. Tree Goddess from an Indus Valley Seal. Courtesy of The Archaeological Survey of India.

Figure 18. Female Figure, Indus Valley Seal, Revealing Common Rhythm of Animal, Tree, and Human. By permission of Arthur Probsthain; © Government of India.

is with our superhuman figure on the tiny seal. By assimilating human, vegetal, and animal qualities, she becomes part of nature itself, no longer bound by the human mode. As we will see later, on the great Buddhist monuments of Bharhut and Sanchi, the yaksha image contributes certain sculptural and religious values to the Ganga theme.

Several seals stress the relationship between vegetation and woman. One (Figure 19) marks the connection unmistakably: it depicts a female, a kind of Mother Earth, giving birth to a tree.

Yet, throughout the ancient world, the tree also retains its primacy as a source of creation. In Mesopotamia, the sexual property

Figure 19. "Mother Earth." Indus Valley Seal. Courtesy of The Archae-ological Survey of India.

of plants was known by 2327 B.C. On two tablets from the great library of Nineveh, we read about propagation of the date palm "in which male and female flowers grow on separate trees and must be brought together artificially to assure abundant fruit."[11] The conjunction of goddess, fertility, and tree is common in the Middle East: the ancient Egyptians, for example, depicted certain gods as living in trees. It seems likely that at some time the two symbols coalesced, the goddess and the tree jointly affirming the mystery of creation. In Crete, the sacred tree was above all the emblem of the goddess. In Babylonia, the Divine Lady was called the goddess of the Tree of Life. A hymn from Eridu (near the Persian Gulf) mentions a tree whose foliage served as a couch for the primeval mother.[12] As Eric Neumann observes: "The Great Mother who brings forth all life from herself is eminently the mother of all vegetation. The center of this vegetation symbolism is the tree."[13]

Along with the goddess and the tree, water may also have assumed a sacred character in the Indus civilization, especially in its religious ritual. This is inferred chiefly from the Great Bath, located in a prominent position on the citadel at Mohenjo-Daro. Near the 39-by-23-foot pool were several other smaller facilities, all of which may have served a sacred function. "It seems likely," says Ernest Mackay, one of the chief excavators, "that ceremonial bathing had its part in the religious observances of the people of Mohenjo-Daro . . . and that the large bath was the place where the people performed this ritual."[14]

In later or better-documented cultures, we find an unmistakable relationship of water to the goddess and the tree. The goddess and the waters are one in their prime value of fertility and birth. This is especially true in those ancient culture areas—Egypt, Mesopotamia, the Indo-Gangetic plain—where the life-creating waters are embodied as a goddess. We have seen this with Ganga. In chapter 5, we will find it again with the Vedic river Sarasvati. Similarly Isis, the great goddess of Egypt, begins as a river spirit. In the *Papyrus*

Figure 20. Goddess, Tree, and Vase. Egyptian Sixth or Seventh Century B.C. Courtesy of Situle de Pa-sheri-Hor—Louvre N908.

Ani (bk. 59), her mother, Nut, is portrayed in a sycamore tree, pouring water from a vase (Figure 20).

In their legacy, the Indus people bequeathed a series of numinous objects drawn into a matrix of equivalent functions: the goddess, the tree, and the waters, all representing life in its increase. As we will see in the next chapter, this relationship grows among the Vedic settlers of northern India (ca. 1000–700 B.C.) and comes to fruition on the great Buddhist stupas of the first and second centuries B.C. As the Ganges Valley becomes the heartland of Vedic culture and the seat of empires, the river increasingly reflects human experience with the land—an experience perceived, in slightly altered circumstances, by the Indus people a thousand years before.

4
The Settlers

ABOUT THE THIRTEENTH OR FOURTEENTH CENTURY B.C., there began a southeastward migration of people across what is today Iran, Afghanistan, Pakistan, and on to India. It may have been caused by political upheavals or ecological changes such as the drying up of grazing lands, for the wanderers depended chiefly on flocks and cattle in contrast to the more sedentary agriculturists of the river cultures. Primarily for linguistic reasons, these pastoral people were called Aryans.[1] For the most part, the record of their movement into India and the Ganges Valley has been literary. Certain artifacts—pottery types and iron tools and weapons—are tentatively ascribed to the Aryans, but the archaeological record is still far from complete.

The Aryan Vision

The settlers arrived from the west, descending the passes of the Hindu Kush and traveling ever eastward. In the Rigvedic period, from 1200 B.C., the river remains a distant dream and is mentioned only twice in this, the earliest Hindu scripture. Gradually the immigrants cross the Punjab and the Indus, dwelling for a while on the Sarasvati, which figures prominently in the *Rig Veda,* and eventually moving into the Ganges Valley, at this time thick with jungle. For a long while Ganga must have been their chief means of communication with older communities in the Punjab, their only highway, inviting them toward some unknown fulfillment. Early settlements sprang up on its banks, and the newcomers soon assimilated the ways of the indigenous people.

There are no reliable estimates on the number of Aryan invaders that entered India let us say between 1200 and 700 B.C., the period that saw the formation of the early scriptures, the Vedas and the Brahmanas.[2] We can readily assume small bands of pastoral tribes, in tens, occasionally hundreds, rarely in thousands, settling among an often hostile population with unfamiliar modes of life. The first stage of such contact is usually withdrawal from the unaccustomed, the first reaction one of violence, unless one party is somehow accepted as "superior."[3] The *Rig Veda* rings with such violence in its descriptions of Aryan battles with the indigenous people: the destruction of forts, the slaughter of alien gods. Isolation was impossible, however, especially as the Aryans moved eastward through the jungles of the Ganges Valley, which were clearly unsuitable for grazing. Adaptation to local conditions became necessary for survival. Such adaptation brought with it increasing culture contact, which must be regarded "not as a transfer of elements from one culture to another, but as a continuous process of interaction between groups of different cultures."[4] Historians long assumed the primary influence of Aryan customs on the earlier people, but certain lines of inquiry reveal an even stronger flow in the opposite direction.

Responses to such culture contact tend to follow three patterns: syncretism, acceptance, and reaction. Usually all three occur. The remarkable thing is the speed with which the indigenous values—those of the Indus civilization and the earliest inhabitants of the Ganges Valley—find their way into the Hindu scriptures, starting from the Vedas. Such a rapid process is usually induced by incorporating slaves into a society, but even more so by taking native wives. This practice seems likely among the Aryan settlers, despite its limited acknowledgment in the Vedas.[5] One sign of prolonged intimate contact is the indigenous retroflex sounds in Vedic Sanskrit, which were probably acquired in the Ganges Valley and the region immediately south.[6] Mutual impact resolves itself in different ways. Experience from other cultures is instructive. Due to intermarriage, the Normans in France and Sicily, for example, actually lost their language, although they came as conquerors. At the same time, "the continuity of an appellation or even a language in no way warrants racial individuality."[7] The Aryan settlers of India were a primitive warlike people. Their wealth and sustenance lay in cattle. By taming the horse and developing the war chariot, they were able to conquer those who lived along the route of their eastern migration. Our general knowledge of Aryan culture is reconstructed largely from the existence of words for an object in the different Aryan (or, more properly speaking, early Indo-European) languages. For example, the absence of words for hunting and fishing suggests little reliance on these sources of food.

The most prominent artisan was the carpenter, who was called upon for a wide variety of products. For the highly prized wheeled vehicles, there exists such detailed terminology that orientalists have reconstructed its shape down to the finest detail. In the *Rig Veda* rivers subside, allowing the wagons to pass across. "I will bend and yield myself as a woman to her lover," says the river. To which the poet answers: "Soon as the Bharatas have crossed, then let your stream flow on. So may the pins and thongs and pair of bulls not waste away."[8] The *Rig Veda*—often praising the artifacts most essential to its people—compares the chariot to the house.[9] In the metaphors of a sedentary race, a man's home is his castle; to wanderers, that castle becomes a chariot.

Terms for the house and its parts are widely distributed among the Indo-European languages. Words for door, door frame, and pillar indicate something more substantial than a temporary shelter. The Sanskrit word for door is *dvara*. As we will see later, the goddess Ganga appears in sculpture chiefly as a *dvarapala* (door guardian) at the entrance of Hindu temples. However, this role emerges only as a transmutation of Aryan and indigenous values, resulting in a new vision of life and the forms that sustain it.

The carpenter also served as shipwright, since we find the word for boat in many Indo-European languages. The vessel itself may have varied from a small river canoe to a modest seagoing craft. The Vedic people may have learned something of shipbuilding from early contact with Mesopotamia before their dispersal eastward.[10] Yet there seems to be particular need for such knowledge in the Punjab—Land of the Five Rivers—with the great Indus flowing to the sea; and it is likely that the settlers gained a considerable amount from the natives of the region.[11] This knowledge must have served them well as they traveled further east. For at this time the Ganges Valley lay thick with jungle; the river would have offered a far more accessible route to those with skill in handling boats.

In contrast to the widespread use of pastoral terms, the Indo-European languages contain few words dealing with agriculture. We find only three seasons: winter, spring, and a hot summer.[12] Of the more than ten thousand verses in the *Rig Veda,* only twenty-five refer to agriculture.[13] Yet, as we are about to see, by the time the Aryans reached the eastern limits of the Ganges Valley, agriculture and the religious significance of plants had attained a primary place in sacred texts.

Above all, the Aryans are a martial people. The *Rig Veda* sings of arms and the hero. Its chief god is Indra the warrior, drinker of soma. For a western counterpart, we would have to choose the elder Ajax of the *Iliad:* strong, aggressive, valiant; but also vain, impetuous, little given to reflection, and in the end rather simple. He excels in the arts of war; as a creator of peaceful institutions, he is found wanting. Typical of a pastoral people, Vedic society is strongly patriarchal and patrilineal, with families tracing their descendants through the male. The primary gods are overwhelmingly masculine, their realm the sky—*deva,* the Sanskrit word for god, means the Bright One. The goddess, as we will see in the next chapter, is more a product of agricultural and hunting societies. As the Vedic settlers blend with the farmers of the Punjab and the early inhabitants of the Ganges Valley, the goddess and her symbols of increase—the plants and the waters—become a centering vision of Hindu thought, often displacing the hard bright male gods of earlier times.

The Impact of Other Cultures, Other Worlds

The *Rig Veda* was probably composed in the Punjab and the Indus region. Even before reaching the Ganges Valley, the Aryans began to acquire more settled pursuits. There is limited mention of agriculture, trade, and units of exchange. "The cloud . . . shed sweet rain . . . for the merchant Aushija," it says,[14] a possible reference to dealing in grain. We read of a rich trading people, the Panis, who are non-Aryan and make no offerings to the Vedic gods or priests. Their name has given rise to a host of Sanskrit and later words relating to trade: *bania,* a trader; *pana,* a Sanskrit coin; *panya,* a word covering trade goods and commodities in general.[15] A rudimentary currency appears in the *nishka,* originally a gold ornament shaped like a necklace.

None of the Indus elements—especially the concept of interpenetrating forms, the vegetal essence of life—were common to the invading Aryans. Yet this new vision, the perception of an agricultural people, soon appears. It becomes prominent in the last book of the *Rig Veda.* But even before, plants are praised for their healing properties. They are addressed as objects of veneration equal to the gods themselves. By Book 10, the primacy of plants seems well established; they become antecedents "that arose in times of old, three ages earlier than the gods." The affinity of plants and humans makes its first appearance. Descending from heaven, the plants pronounce their benediction: "No evil shall touch the man who while we live we pervade." In a line recalling the Indus seals of the figure in the tree, the *Rig Veda* mentions Yama—the first man, the god of death—who dwells in a tree, drinking with the gods.[16]

Two hymns incorporate an alien vision of death: the human reversion to plant form, coupled with intimations of Samsara, the endless round of birth and rebirth common to agricultural societies: "The Sun receive your eye," sings the poet, "the wind your spirit. . . . Go, if it be your lot, unto the waters; go, make your home in the plants." A second hymn is addressed to the manas or spirit:

> Your spirit went far away to the four quarters of the world . . . away to the billowy sea . . . to the beams of light that flash and flow . . . to the waters and the plants . . . to the lofty mountain heights . . . into the All that lives and moves . . . to all that is and is to be.[17]

It may seem strange to us, the connection between plants and humans. But our habits of mind are sharply limited to our culture, and as our thoughts so our perceptions. We applaud the revelations of primordial people while accepting their limitations—such things, for example, as their ignorance toward the process of birth itself. For very simple reasons, early people often failed to associate birth with the act of intercourse. Among both humans and animals, the intervening time between the cause and its effect was too great. But in the vegetative world the act of creation becomes far more obvious. Here the enigma of birth is more readily comprehended: where the seed has fallen, there the plant will grow. The relationship is inescapable in tropical countries, where vegetation bursts out with an energy unknown to us. From the day that people first understood the unfolding of life from the seed into the plant, they seemed to see in it the origin of all beings.[18] At the root of it lies what anthropologist Lucien Levy-Bruhl calls "participation mystique," a feeling of mutuality between animal, plant, and human. It is the touchstone of the early planting societies and has been effaced more and more as cultures evolve and language succumbs to the rule of categories and contradictions. But this need for participation, as Levy-Bruhl reminds us, remains "more intense, even among people like ourselves, than the thirst for knowledge and . . . conformity with the claims of reason. It lies deeper within us and its source is more remote."[19]

The authors of the *Rig Veda*, stimulated by the impact of an alien culture, ranged far and wide in their attempts to understand the universe and the source of its creation. Their inquiries have been described as a "henotheism": each god or embodied force of nature worshipped in its turn. In a well-known line, the priest of the *Rig Veda* speculates on the beginning, where "everything was like a sea without light." As in many primal visions of creation, the waters "know the birth of heaven and earth; they beget all that stands and moves." Along with the Ionian philosophers, the *Rig Veda* contemplates heaven and earth, the archetypal male and female, as the agency of creation. "When Heaven and Earth were forced apart, the universe complained. Bring them together once again. Sweet be my going forth, sweet by my return." At times, the two are given equal recognition: "From Heaven and Earth," sings the Vedic poet, "have come the gods and all that lives and dreams of immortality." In a patriarchal culture, the father may give birth to the daughter and between them produce the universe. "I offer my song to the Great Father," chants the priest, "who with love conceived through his Daughter all begotten forms."

Now and then the poet questions the "official" values, glimpsing the ancient wisdom that flourished before the Aryan invasion and was to reclaim the subcontinent before a thousand years had passed: "Which one [heaven or earth] is older? How were they born? Who can speak of such things?"[20] Speculation on the female—as the primal source of creation—appears in the form of Vach, goddess of speech and firstborn of the waters. "On the world's summit," she explains, "I bring forth the Father: my home is in the waters. . . . From there I extend to all existing creatures."[21] While mentioned earlier in the *Rig Veda*, it is not until Book 10—one of the latest chapters—that the goddess is considered in this eponymous role. By then, the settlers had spent considerable time in the region of the old Indus civilization and had begun to acquire new values.

In the Ganges Valley

For the Aryans, the skills acquired during the Punjab prelude become more pronounced with arrival in the Ganges Valley. The development of trading and agriculture and experience in boat-building—these will enhance the first tentative efforts toward larger settlements, such as those at Kaushambi and at Hastinapura and Ahichatra on the upper Ganges. With the diffusion of ironworking techniques from the west, about 1000 B.C., the elements are present for the urban revolution in the Ganges Valley.

Following the Harappan and other intermediate remains on the upper Ganges, there appears a painted gray ware or PGW pottery identified with the Aryan settlers. At lesser sites such as Rupar and Alamgirpur, it occurs several layers above the Harappan remains, suggesting a lack of contact between the two.[22] Yet this PGW culture, as archaeologist Raymond Allchin indicates, "occupies almost the same area as the late or post-Harappan cultures in this part of India. Moreover, it extends from Harappa and a line of sites along the Ghaggar or Sarasvati branch of the Indus, eastward to the Ganga-Yamuna Doab," thus denoting a broad region of culture contact between the new settlers and the older indigenous population.[23] Although five hundred years separated the Indus people from the Aryans, conditions responsible for the Indus culture remained very much the same; in all likelihood, its descendants retained the old values. Artifacts unearthed at the PGW settlements correspond to the Aryan mode of life: iron tools and weapons, cattle, horses, wheeled toys, and temporary houses.[24]

Dense jungles prevented early exploitation of the Ganges Valley. Stone tools of the prehistoric people lacked the efficiency for clearing heavily forested areas; the river had to await a more advanced technology. The post-Harappan pre-Aryan settlers must have begun the transformation with their copper tools—copper axes appear at Hastinapura and Kaushambi. But the Rigvedic people know only copper. It was iron that accelerated the clearing of land and the number of settlements along the river. By the start of the Ganges period, the technique of iron smelting arrives from the west. The Iron Age begins in India around 1000 B.C. and leaves its record among the formative centers of Hastinapura, Atranjikhera, and Kaushambi. Iron is first mentioned in the *Atharva Veda,* the last of the four Vedas but containing material from the earliest, most primitive, levels of Indian culture. The distribution of iron tools led to clearing roads through the forest and to considerable quantities of land for cultivation, both of which stimulated river trade and communication. Together these events created the need for collection centers and more complex units of organization—in short, the need for cities.[25]

The first proto-urban site in the Ganges Valley is Hastinapura, whose beginnings date before the twelfth century B.C. Its second period of settlement, from about 1100 to 800 B.C., contains painted gray ware and the bones of horses, sheep, and cattle. Clearly the early settlers were not vegetarians. In the *Mahabharata,* written centuries later (ca. 400 B.C.–A.D. 400), Hastinapura is the great capital of the Kuru dynasty and was swept away by the Ganges several generations after one of its rulers, King Parikshit, who may have reigned in the ninth century B.C.[26] The archaeological record reveals that Hastinapura was abandoned after a devastating flood around 800 B.C., thus lending support to some of the *Mahabharata* narrative. The city of the epic is a dazzling affair, with King Duryodhana's pleasure palace on the banks of the river, decorated with rich fabrics and tapestries. In honor of Krishna's visit, the city streets are decked with jewels. People throng to see the god-prince. High mansions seem ready to collapse beneath the weight of eager spectators. And though Krishna's steeds were like the wind, "yet they moved . . . slowly through that dense mass of human beings." The city is endowed with broad streets and public squares.[27]

Other towns emerge along the river. The *Yajur Veda,* third of the four Vedas, mentions Kampilya, almost midway between Hastinapura and Kaushambi,[28] while east of the Doab the enormous clay rampart of Rajghat (Banaras) dates from about 800 B.C. Thus even in the Vedic period we begin to find growing river settlements in the Ganges Valley. Their development, as historian D. D. Kosambi remarks, "can be explained only on the basis of still earlier navigation of these powerful rivers that followed swiftly through impenetrable forests and swamps."[29] For, as a rule, rivers played a more important part than roads in the ancient valley civilizations.[30]

River commerce is further implied by the nature of these communities. In a classic article, Gideon Sjoberg observes that "preindustrial cities depend for their existence upon food and raw material obtained from without; for this reason they are marketing centers."[31] The sites mentioned here were apparently not chosen for their proximity to mineral deposits, and since the extent of surrounding peasant cultivation could not have been especially large, these early riverside cities must have relied on commodities carried by ship. In all likelihood, colonization and urbanization proceeded inland from along the chief rivers, creating small towns that served as economic and administrative units. These units extended from the Nepalese Terai on the north to the Vindhyan foothills, but they were ultimately oriented toward the large, growing river centers.[32]

The archaeological record yields no information on ships during this period; even the *Atharva Veda* confines itself to metaphors and religious symbolism.[33] We do find increasing dependence on fish and fishing, however, with mention of several specialized jobs such as fisherman and fish vendor. We read a growing commerical sense from the list of occupations in the *Yajur Veda.*[34]

Indra, the great warrior of the *Rig Veda,* becomes a patron of trade. "I stir and animate the merchant Indra," says the *Atharva*

Veda. "May he be our guide, chasing wild beasts and highwaymen; may he bring me riches." In a hymn worthy of a good Calvinist, the trader prays: "Let us find favor in selling and bartering, may this exchange of goods enrich me."[35]

As the settlers move further down the Ganges Valley, vegetation and the produce of the soil acquire greater importance. Rice and barley are compared to the very breath of life, even becoming part of the sacrifice.[36] As plants become the sustenance of life and water the source of that sustenance, these two elements loom larger in the speculations of the Hindu scriptures. The priest addresses "plants whose soul is water." He invokes the plants and the waters as the essence of all living things: "In the sea is your heart, within the waters; let the plants and the waters enter you." In a metamorphosis of the gods, the priest calls: "Let the Waters bless us; may the Plants be auspicious." He confers on the new benefactors the qualities of the older gods. So plants are endowed with a semblance of immortality—the Veda addresses "all Plants that hear my speech, and those that have departed far away." In like manner, the sap of plants is equated with all life-sustaining liquids: "Rise up with life," says the *Atharva Veda.* "Unite yourself with life, rise up with the sap of plants."[37]

The vision revealed in these lines is a far cry from the Aryan herdsmen we first encountered in the Punjab, with their chariots and war gods. It has been a while in coming; the transformation extended over half a millennium, from roughly 1200 to 700 B.C. No doubt the process was accelerated by the greater preponderance of indigenous people absorbed into the Hindu fold as the new settlers moved further east toward Bengal.[38] In the end, people grow to worship the things they need. In India, above all, these things included water and the sustenance of the fields. Just as the early Aryans praised the wheeled vehicles which served them so well, we begin to understand how the Ganges, which now served them in so many ways, assumes the form of a goddess, a living thing.[39]

Besides assimilating their beliefs to the new environment, the Aryan settlers carried over certain others in their totality. One of these is the myth of the Sarasvati, the great Vedic river whose image lingers in the minds of the immigrants as they continue their journey east.

5

Ganga and Sarasvati: The Transformation of Myth

Time and again, the *Rig Veda* refers to the mysterious river Sarasvati, which has long since ceased to exist. As we have glimpsed from the archaeological evidence, pottery associated with the Aryans has been found all along the Ghaggar River—regarded by some as the ancient Sarasvati—and we can assume that the river provided a center for early Vedic culture.

Leafing through the endless offerings of Indian literature—sacred and secular—one becomes aware that a significant number of tales and qualities later associated with the Ganges also describe the Vedic Sarasvati. And after careful analysis it is hard to resist the conclusion that the image and sanctity of Ganga have evolved from that of the Sarasvati—as a mythological projection of the ancient Aryan river.

The Lost Sarasvati

The actual location of the Sarasvati and the myth of its disappearance have long tempted geographers and orientalists and is still not completely resolved. Nothing is said in the *Rig Veda* of the Sarasvati's disappearance, but by the time of the *Mahabharata* and the *Laws of Manu* (ca. first to third centuries A.D.), it has lost itself in the sand. There are two main theories of the lost Sarasvati. The first regards the original river as the Harahvati (Arachosia), located in the Helmund Valley of southwestern Afghanistan.[1] The second regards the modern Ghaggar River, east of the Indus, as the original Sarasvati.[2] The two theories are not essentially incompatible, however. The evidence of myth and geography points to a third interpretation: that the name Sarasvati did refer to the Arachosia in the Helmund Valley and was later applied by the Aryan settlers to a river of considerable size, the Ghaggar. The process of mythological projection simply carried the qualities of the river further east to Ganga.[3]

It is difficult to determine when the Sarasvati was reduced to an insignificant stream, if this indeed was the case. Arab historians of the eighth century speak of "two great rivers flowing through the land: to the west the Indus, to the east the great Mihran, also known as the Hakra."[4] But there is little in the sacred literature to bear this out. While praises of the Sarasvati are sung well into the period of the Puranas, religious texts from the first seven centuries A.D., the river itself has long become but a memory. In all likelihood, the Sarasvati once flowed through a region of considerable Aryan settlement. With migration eastward, we find intimations of leaving its protective shelter. The Rigvedic poet offers his friendship and allegiance to the river and prays that he may stay forever on her banks.[5] But gradually—under pressure from other Aryan tribes arriving from the west—the migration continues. By the time of the Upanishads (ca. 700–400 B.C.), the geographical horizon of the Aryans extends from the Indus to the Ganges. But even before, according to the texts, the river had disappeared.[6] It may have dried up after losing several of its feeder streams.

Numerous Rigvedic descriptions of Sarasvati are later applied to Ganga. Sarasvati's home is in the heavens. She fills "the realms of earth, and that wide tract, the firmament." The worshipper hopes that the river will descend from heaven and, from the mountains, hear his prayers.[7] We have already observed the significance of Ganga's descent from heaven and the prevalence of the theme in art and myth. In later literature, Ganga is described as "the path of heaven," a river "flowing through the sky."[8] We may recall her home among the stars, in the realm of Vishnupada, the Path of Vishnu, between Ursa Major and the Pole Star.

The Sarasvati, with her strong waves, bursts the mountain ridges.[9] In the Puranas, Ganga too falls from on high, sweeping the mountain crests before her.[10] Both rivers flow from the mountains to the sea.[11] Once, the Sarasvati and her sister streams all used to bear gold—the *Rig Veda* speaks of the divine Sarasvati, "terrible with her golden path"; later the precious metal is found only in the Ganges.[12]

We have seen how from earliest times a relationship existed between the tree, the goddess, and the waters. The Sarasvati is described as originating in the Himalayas and flowing from a fountain at the foot of a plaksha or fig tree.[13] Significantly, several legends describe Ganga as originating from a tree. On their journey north to Mount Kailasa, the five Pandava brothers—heroes of the *Mahabharata*—came upon the hermitage of Nara and Narayana (twin forms of Vishnu), filled with celestial trees and flowers. And they beheld "the rounded trunk of a great jujube tree. It was fresh and shining. . . . And hard by the gigantic jujube tree . . . the Bhagirathi of graceful descent, with stairs of rubies and corals."[14]

In several texts the two rivers arise from the same source and appear at the same locations. The Sarasvati is described as issuing from the water jug or kamandalu of the god Brahma; then, starting on its downward course at the fountain of Plaksha, it passes through Kedara, as we have seen, one of the three most famous sources of Ganga.[15] Like Sarasvati, Ganga also issues from a kamandalu.[16] The *Mahabharata* describes the lake where Ganga descends, dividing into seven streams, including the Indus and the Sarasvati. As for the Sarasvati, "in some parts [of her course] she becomes visible and in others not so. The celestial sevenfold Ganga is widely known over the three worlds."[17] Thus the Sarasvati, once covering the universe, now appears sporadically, but Ganga has assumed her role. The later literature, now and then partial to the Sarasvati, describes the ancient stream as flowing through Hardwar as well as Kedarnath.[18]

Sarasvati is sometimes known as Vach, goddess of speech and related arts such as poetry and music. This role evolves slowly from the *Rig Veda,* where she is "enriched with hymns," an "inciter of all pleasant songs, inspirer of all gracious thoughts." She has many other qualities, but by the time of the Brahmanas she becomes, above all else, the goddess of speech,[19] perhaps because Vedic culture and poetry flourished there:[20] indeed, one of the early texts describes her as the mother of the Vedas.[21] Several of these qualities later adhere to Ganga. She, too, becomes "mother of the Vedas." She is "identical with the Word or Speech." "She engages herself in grammar . . . she gives pleasure to the ears."[22]

For the burning of the dead, prayers and offerings were addressed to Yama—god of death—and to Sarasvati. After the ceremony, the mourners departed to wash themselves and offer libations of water for the dead. As late as the seventh century A.D., the *Harshacharita,* a long poem about the Emperor Harsha (A.D. 606–647), describes the death of Harsha's father, whose body the people carried to the Sarasvati, "and there upon a pyre befitting an emperor solemnly consumed all but his glory in the flames. . . . Thus the prince passed on to the Sarasvati's banks, and having bathed in the river, offered water to his father."[23] But long before, by the fourth century A.D., the religious texts are advising the use of Ganges water for funeral services. After cremating a dead relative, the mourners are instructed to immerse themselves in water. Then, on the fourth day after the ceremony, "they should collect the bones. . . . And they must throw them into water from the Ganges."[24] Philosophically, the ritual offers the adherents symbolic participation in this phase of the cosmic cycle: returning to the undifferentiated *(pralaya)* state. As Ganga gradually replaces Sarasvati in matters of sanctity and ritual, it becomes the goal of every pious Hindu to die at Banaras and mix his ashes with the Ganges.

In Indian tradition, water is renowned for its life-producing properties, and couples eager for children would invoke the rivers for their blessing.[25] Like Ganga, Sarasvati also gives birth to a child herself. We read of the sage Matinara, who performed a sacrifice lasting twelve years on the banks of the Sarasvati. At the conclusion of the sacrifice, the river appeared before him in the form of a beautiful woman and together they produced a son named Tansu.[26] Through a long line of descendants, Tansu was an ancestor of King

Shantanu, who, as we have seen, married Ganga and had children by her. The rivers gave birth in another way. Indian literature often tells of great ascetics who accidentally come across lovely wood nymphs (Apsarasas) while wandering in the forest. Such was the case with the hermit Dadhicha, who, as often happens under such circumstances, could not contain himself. His semen fell into the Sarasvati, the river nurtured it with care, and it developed into a fetus. When the time came, Sarasvati brought forth a child.[27] We have already read the tale of Karttikeya, born of Shiva's seed cast into the Ganges.

While Ganga receives many of her features from the Sarasvati, the two rivers are sometimes directly connected in several ways. The sanctity of Ganga, for example, is promoted by association with the Vedic river. The great epic mentions several places on the Sarasvati where Ganga bathed to wash away the sins accumulated by countless numbers of pilgrims.[28] Furthermore, the two rivers sometimes blend together in place-names, such as at Bhera Ghat, a famous bathing site at the confluence of the Narmada River with a smaller stream. At the old city, the river is called the Banganga; but where it joins the Narmada, it becomes the Sarasvati.[29] In the mythical geography characteristic of Indian thought, we find a passage from the *Mahabharata* in which the Yamuna—in addition to Ganga—is drawn into physical proximity to the Sarasvati. The epic describes a tirtha (bathing site for religious purposes) called the Fountain of the Plaksha Tree, located on the Yamuna:

> Here is the beautiful and sacred river, Sarasvati, full of water; and here . . . is the spot . . . where it disappeared. . . . Yonder is the visible region of Vishnupada [the realm of Vishnu from which Ganga descends] . . . yonder is the gate of Manasarovar [the lake into which she falls].[30]

The Temple of the Serpent King

Stories like these serve as a prelude to the Sarasvati's union with Ganga and Yamuna at Allahabad (ancient Prayag), for it is said that the three rivers meet at Prayag—Ganga and Yamuna visible to all, Sarasvati only to the spiritually enlightened. The idea does not appear until the later Puranas.[31] But myths are often cumulative, building on earlier conceptions. As early as the *Rig Veda* we read of three mighty rivers, two in this case concealed from sight.[32] Though Ganga is mentioned only twice in the *Rig Veda,* it is one time coupled with Yamuna and Sarasvati.[33] The *sangam* or confluence at Prayag joins two themes. One is the myth of the three rivers that flow in the three realms of space: in heaven, on earth, and in the underworld. We will examine this theme in the next chapter. The other is the story of Naga Vasuki, the serpent of the deep, who dwells in the underworld. Vasuki's home is on the river Bhogavati, a name sometimes referring to the Sarasvati.[34] The serpent also has a bathing site (tirtha), named Bhogavati, located at Prayag.[35] Vasuki's pond near Prayag is known from the time of the epic as a tirtha famous for its spiritual benefits.[36] Some time later,[37] the name Bhogavati is applied to Ganga's course in the underworld, and a temple to the serpent king is built not far from the original pond. Thus, as the Sarasvati fades into memory, the legend of Vasuki, the tirtha, and the river are transferred to this newer setting.

Ganga's relation to the serpents is basic. Each contains the life-increasing power of the waters. As a result, we often find them together in myth and art. Ganga herself sometimes acquires a serpent form—for example, at Darasuram, a twelfth-century temple in South India, where the lower half of the goddess is rendered in a series of wavy lines indicating her watery or mermaid quality.[38] The figure recalls the female naga rising from the central fissure at Mamallapuram. In sculpture of Shiva Nataraja, Lord of the Dance, Ganga rests in the hair or jatas of the god, her figure below the waist of a watery or serpent quality (Figures 21 and 22). At Prayag, the serpent king's temple still exists, housed in a grove of trees overlooking the Ganges. It is well maintained. During my visit to it in 1972, a priest and several worshippers were attending. An Indian scholar, writing in 1873, reports that the massive building, on its elevated terrace, looked quite new, having been repaired but a hundred years before. Over two feet high and carved in black stone, the image of Naga Vasuki hovers as if enraged. To the pilgrim, "the merit of bathing at the sacred confluence of Ganga and Yamuna is not complete until he visits the temple of the King of Ser-

Figure 21. Ganga and Shiva Nataraja. Thirteenth Century. Photo Darian. Courtesy of the Madras Museum.

pents.''[39] On his lonely journey, Kalidasa's cloud messenger describes the Ganges at the place where the river meet:

> If like some insubstantial elephant of the sky
> you would tumble from heaven
> and taste the crystal stream,
> so would your darkened shadow swell her

Figure 22. Ganga in Shiva's Jata. Photo Darian. Courtesy of the Madras Museum.

> as the Jumna does at Prayag,
> lending substance to a dream.

The Cloud Messenger 51

In this place, where the mythical Aryan river joins the real Ganga, one tradition flows irrevocably into another. Possibly for this and other reasons, the confluence provides the site for the most famous religious festival in all of India.

The Kumbha Mela at Allahabad

Allahabad is known chiefly for the Kumbha Mela, the great religious bathing fair that occurs every twelve years at the place where the rivers meet. The Mela of 1954 attracted upwards of six million people. In their fervor, hundreds were injured and trampled to death by the surging crowds eager to perform their religious duties at the confluence.

The Mela draws an incredible spectrum of humanity: yogis from the Himalayas, peasants and businessmen, sannyasins and bureaucrats, sages and charlatans. Some of the renowned holy men give audience in great billowy tents erected by their followers. Others sleep in the sand under the cold January sky. The most dramatic moments occur when the Akharas, guilds of sadhus, move in sizable numbers toward the *sangam*. Their processions spring lifelike from a canvas by Bosch or Brueghel: horses, camels, elephants draped in silver brocade and surmounted by sadhus brandishing iron tridents; kettledrums and trumpets, blaring with the urgency of judgment day (Figure 23).

It is an ancient custom, the Kumbha Mela, for it is described by the Chinese pilgrim Hiuen Tsiang, who witnessed the event during his travels through India in the seventh century A.D. He reports a gathering of half a million people, which suggests a tradition begun considerably earlier. Hiuen Tsiang relates that every day a large number arrived at the *sangam,* hoping to drown in the sacred

Figure 23. The Kumbha Mela at Allahabad. Courtesy of the Northern India Patrika, Allahabad.

waters and be reborn in heaven,[40] a practice that continued at least through the reign of Akbar in the sixteenth century.

According to legend, it was from out of the Milky Ocean—during the creation of the world—that the divine healer Dhanvantari offered the cup of immortality to Jayanta, regent of paradise. The precious drops falling at Prayag, Hardwar, Nasik, and Ujjain sanctified these places and made them centers of pilgrimage for all times. Since Jayanta took twelve days on his return to paradise, the pilgrims gather every twelve years according to a simple equation: one day of the gods equals a year of human time.

In its entirety, the myth contains a hodgepodge of themes and offers little in the way of rigorous interpretation. We have seen how water and the rivers are regarded as the source of life in a tangible and in a mythical sense. Throughout the tradition, Ganga is thought to confer immortality on her devotees; indeed, the *Mahabharata* exclaims: "As amrita is to the gods, so Ganga water is to the world of men." Thus it is not unreasonable to equate Ganga with the deathless liquid (amrita) fallen from the kumbha, the cup of the gods. (The kumbha itself, as we will see in a later chapter, becomes one of Ganga's distinguishing features.)[41] Yet it seems highly unlikely that the pilgrims at Allahabad draw any such connections. The reasons for the greatness of the *sangam* may be more down-to-earth but no less exalted, for the confluence provides a meeting place of India's two greatest rivers,[42] each with a long tradition. As a result, the site has been sanctified from early times.[43]

A small Mela—held in other years—better serves the tempered rhythm of pilgrimage. Some are drawn there from a sense of religious duty. Others attend out of mourning for a dead relative. At such times, people have their heads shaved; for hair, much as trees and vegetation, represents life in its increase. In this way, shaving the head marks a cessation of growth, a return to the earth.

To derive the full benefits of the pilgrimage, one should remain for a month, bathing in the *sangam* at prescribed times of day. Few people stay the entire period. Some who do may build small thatched huts on the strip of land between the rivers, performing their ablutions, meditating, trying in whatever way they can to glimpse the invisible Sarasvati where it joins Ganga and Yamuna. Prayaga, says the *Mahabharata*, is the "foremost of all tirthas in the three worlds . . . let not the Vedas or the opinions of men dissuade your mind from the dream of dying at Prayaga."[44] The three worlds of the epic exist in space (heaven, earth, the underworld) and in time (past, present, future). It is the goal of the spiritual seeker to shed such distinctions by experiencing time as a continuum, by realizing the realms of space as one. During her long tradition, Ganga is constantly referred to as mistress of the triple world. While essentially a religious concept, the goddess of the three realms represents the accommodation of pastoral and planting societies throughout the ancient world. The assimilation occurred in India as it did in Greece. Contrasting the different reactions to this fusion in the two culture areas will enhance our knowledge of Ganga and help us grasp the meaning behind some of her many legends.

6
Ganga and Artemis: Two Versions of a Single Theme

THROUGHOUT HER HISTORY, Ganga appears as a triple goddess: flowing in three regions or three directions. As with other cultures, the number three has particular sanctity in India and has drawn to it a bright constellation of ideas on space, time, and immortality. In the west, it has never failed to color people's thoughts—from the beginnings of philosophy in Mesopotamia, in the Christian Trinity, even in the triadic formulations of Freud and Hegel.

In the classical world, the triple goddess also figures prominently in the cults and legends of Artemis, Hecate, and, to a lesser degree, Demeter and Hera. A comparison of Ganga with her Mediterranean counterpart deepens our understanding of the river goddess, her genesis, and primordial affinities. The point of comparison— simple at first—soon extends to significant themes that react in unlikely and revealing ways upon the goddesses who have summoned them. As a triple river, Ganga is said to flow on earth, in heaven, and in the underworld. In heaven she is called Mandakini; on earth, the Bhagirathi; and below, Patala Ganga or the Bhogavati.

Though often mentioned as flowing in the three worlds, the triple river is seldom portrayed in sculpture. The best-known example is found at the cave temples of Elephanta (sixth century A.D.) on an island off the coast of Bombay. There the darkened hallway of Cave I reveals a standing image of Shiva; and balanced on his head is a bowl containing the triple goddess (Figure 24). Many figures cluster around the scene: to the left a bearded ascetic shelters a young girl. Who can say that in the sculptor's mind this was not Bhagiratha reverently accepting the youthful goddess in his charge?

We find another well-known formulation—the shrine of the river

Figure 24. Ganga as the Triple River. Elephanta. A.D. 550. Courtesy of The Archaeological Survey of India.

goddesses—at the eighth-century Kailasa cave in the great complex at Ellora, Central India. Here on high platforms and in separate chambers we find standing images of Sarasvati, Ganga, and Yamuna, each beneath an elegant arch or torana (Figure 25). The goddesses are distinguished by their identifying pedestals: Yamuna on

Figure 25. Shrine of the River Goddesses. Elephanta Cave XVI. A.D. 750–850. Courtesy of The Archaeological Survey of India.

a tortoise, Sarasvati on a lotus, Ganga on a makara or crocodile. The makara is an ambivalent figure, a creature of the waters in both their life-increasing and life-enveloping role. We will explore him more fully in a later chapter. At the center of the three figures stands Ganga with an aureole behind her head (Figure 26). Like the other goddesses, she wears a crown, a necklace, and other jeweled

Figure 26. Statue of Ganga in the Shrine of the River Goddesses. Courtesy of The Archaeological Survey of India.

ornaments. Of the three pieces, Ganga is the most sober and serene. The abundant hips, drawn in tightly at the waist, combine with an upper body that is tapered but only slightly idealized. The parts of the body fuse to create a perfectly balanced image that is saved from a certain heaviness by the tension of the arms.

As the most prominent goddess of Greece,[1] the triune Artemis suggests the perfect contrast. Like Ganga, she is acknowledged in heaven, on earth, and in the underworld.[2] But within the like paradigm we find surprising inflections, growing chiefly from the impact of the later settlers and invaders on the original prehistoric cultures of India and the Aegean and from the different reactions of those cultures in the course of time.

With this inquiry, we enter the realm of the great goddess, whose first symbolic function in prehistory is one of mother; the distribution of Aurignacian "Venus" figures—from sites in the Pyrenees to north of the Black Sea—leaves little doubt of this.[3] The early hunting societies contain a strong matriarchal flavor. The pursuit of animals was a full-time occupation that left men little time for other activities.[4] Although Paleolithic cave temples depict animals and reedy male figures, sculptural remains are almost exclusively female.[5] Weaving, making pottery, preparing food, rearing children—all were the domain of woman. This pattern lasted several hundred thousand years and established the primal symbolic value of woman as mother. All other values are derivative or are attempts to harmonize male-oriented conceptions with the primeval vision.

This female world view was overturned—at least in Greece—by the pastoral Indo-European invaders from the north who drifted down through the passes and across the plains early in the second millennium B.C., bringing with them an exclusively patriarchal outlook universal among pastoral people.[6] As we have seen, the same invasion later occurred in India. But while the maternal horizon was eventually restored in India, it never fully recovered in Greece. These contrasting responses may account for many otherwise unintelligible episodes in myth and religion, especially in our theme of the great goddess.

The Greek Artemis evolves from earlier figures in Crete and the

Near East, where their signification of human fertility is central—for example, the Lady of Ephesus. But while the Homeric Greeks reject the mother goddess, her primal image cannot be effaced. As a concession, her role in fecundity is expressed in partial and inconsistent ways. In legend a virgin, Artemis is the patron of childbirth. She dwells in forests and mountains; yet, as she explains in a hymn of Callimachus: "When women in the pain of parturition call to me from the cities, I must hurry to them. So it was ordained at my birth that I should be their comfort."[7] To protect an expectant mother, certain herbs were placed beside her, and at Athens her bedclothes were removed and dedicated to Artemis Brauronia.[8] The myth contains no plausible explanation for the chosen virginity of the goddess. But the reason may well be a rejection of the eternal feminine in her eponymous role as mother.

Not so in India, where the goddess reclaimed her supernal influence after brief eclipse in the Vedic period and the Upanishads (ca. 1200–600 B.C.). Ganga, as a manifestation of the archetypal female, fully retains her maternal nature. In the legend of the Vasus, she gives birth to eight children fathered by a mortal, King Shantanu. We have also seen her indirect maternity of Karttikeya, as well as her other life-giving properties.

Another aspect of the great mother is her connection with the underworld. This role develops, by extension, from her primal association with birth. It is an expression of the agricultural revolution and the increasing importance of grain, sedentary farming, and the gradual development of paternal institutions. It reflects the belief that human fertility and fertility of the soil are in some mysterious way, bound together, that death must precede the coming of grain, that out of death—in the barrenness of nature—issues life in all its fullness. To us moderns, the idea strikes a dissonant chord. For its truth balances on a metaphor: the equation of woman with the earth, of the womb with the dark cavern from which all life flows. Nonetheless, even a brief glimpse of man's first written speculations confirms that metaphor is not a literary refinement but one of the earliest modes of thought. In all likelihood, such an equation was made. And the connection, once drawn, offered people a palpable, numinous intermediary with the earth and its bounty.

At the same time, it coupled the mystery of life with the impenetrable chthonian forces of the underworld. In Greece, the life-engendering value was appropriated by Demeter and Kore; it was the sepulchral quality that constellated around the figure of Artemis. Already in the Middle Minoan period (ca. 2100–1700 B.C.) her Cretan prototype appears in the dual role as goddess of fertility and mistress of the nether regions.[9] She is also pictured standing between maned lions, a motif derived from Asia Minor, where the great animals guard her entrance to the other world.[10] Artemis is famous as huntress and as protector of animals. These apparently conflicting themes may be pre-Homeric. The Lady of the Bow confers a talismanic blessing on the hunt, while as protector she reaffirms her maternal quality.

We may still be troubled by woman as copula in the equation of life and death. This is but natural, given our submission to the linearity of time, which presses upon us like a tourniquet. To understand the "primitive" perception of causality, we must feel our way into the oscillation of the pendulum: we must accept the equal reality of a film run forward or in reverse. Only then can we know, as one, the mystery of birth from the darkness and return into an endless night.

In India, the destructive connotations are assimilated to the goddess Kali-Durga; and Ganga, while following the triadic formulation, serves in the dark regions the role of redeemer. We have seen how, in religious ritual, a person's bones were thrown into the Ganges to ensure rebirth in heaven. This ritual, the story of Sagara, the incident of Vyasa summoning the dead warriors from the river—all make the same point. In the *Mahabharata,* the hero Yudhishthira and his brothers are found wandering in hell. Eventually they are met by the god Indra, who leads them to the river of the nether region. "Here is the celestial Ganga," he explains, "sacred and sanctifying the three worlds. Enter it, and you will find your rightful place."[11]

With most of the triple goddesses, Greek and Indian, their chthonian affinity is a gloomy one. This is expected among such figures as Hecate, who presides over the place where "three roads meet."[12] But in Greece even Demeter, goddess of corn and abundance, has her morbid nature and is sometimes called Erinys, "Angry One," or Melaina, "Black Demeter."[13] Under Spartan law, a sacrifice to Demeter followed twelve days of mourning for the dead,[14] who according to Plutarch were "Demeter's People."[15] In India, the animal sacrifices to Kali-Durga, as well as their other mortuary associations, are too well known to need elaboration. Almost alone among the triple goddesses of India and the Aegean, Ganga retains her beneficence in both realms. This may well be due to her primal image as the great river. For while she fits easily into the triadic formulation of the eternal feminine, her physical role as bringer of life (water for irrigation, silt for the fields) quite overshadows her destructive nature, although her floods and shifting course have ruined many towns and cities.

From all that has been said, we may judge the early conception of the earth goddess as twofold: fertility and death. With the ascendance of patriarchal people in the Indo-Greek culture area, we are introduced to a third realm—sky and heaven.[16] To reflect this new dimension, a third celestial aspect is added to the dual goddess, thus relating her to the masculine god—god the creator—whose realm is the sky. Accordingly, Artemis is provided a genealogy as a daughter of Leto by the Great Olympian himself. And the Mistress of the Bow is pictured as a child seated on her father's knee, requesting her domain on earth.[17]

This celestial affinity of the great goddess is adumbrated in her primeval form. We have seen antecedents of Artemis in Crete and the Near East, where she is pictured as the Lady of the Mountains. In Mesopotamia, the celestial mountain was represented by the ziggurat, where, on a moonlit night, a priestess would ascend the long flight of stairs to the pinnacle and invite the god to partake of her.[18] And through their conjugation, the earth would swell with abundance. In Mesopotamia, the mountain, in Henri Frankfort's words, "is the place where the mysterious potency of the earth, and hence of all natural life, is concentrated."[19] It is the closest point to heaven, to the weather god with his vivifying rain. It possesses, as Jung says of the mountain and the mountain cave,[20] the same chthonian value of woman as the fertile darkness of creation, but here transposed to another plane. The prototype of Artemis as

Mountain Mother is most evident in Cretan seals and signets, where she appears on a summit, flanked by two adoring lions. Her association with the mountain provides an effortless transition for the Lady of the Animals to her new role as child of Olympus.

Throughout her history, Ganga is undeniably a child of the mountain. Her home is in the Milky Way, where "through the darkness she sheds her silver light."[21] She descends from heaven, mingling in the matted hair of Shiva and flowing from the golden peaks of Himavat.[22] "On the summit of Mount Meru," explains the *Vishnu Purana,* "is the vast city of Brahma . . . enclosed by the River Ganges, which . . . falls here from the skies, and after encircling the city, divides into four mighty rivers flowing to the ends of the earth."[23]

We may be troubled by the presence of disparate traits among the Indo-European goddesses. Aside from the cultural synthesis explored above, there took place what Gilbert Murray calls a "Sunoikismos" or settling together,[24] in which a wide variety of pre-Olympian female figures are later reduced to four or five individual types. Due to the tenacity of local cults, certain of these goddesses remained, but in forms partly accommodated to the new religion. To judge by numerous appearances in later texts, there existed in pre-Aryan India as well as great variety of female spirits: yakshas, gandharvas, vidyadharas, kinnaras, goddesses of fertility and terror, some continuing in a light, nearly disembodied state while others pass through the screen of Vedic personification to assume individual names and qualities.[25]

In our comparison, we have seen how both the Greek and the Indian goddesses are associated with birth, but Artemis' role is indirect and contradictory (as the patron of childbirth, yet herself a virgin) while Ganga is fully acknowledged as a source of creation and abundance. In the underworld, Artemis projects a dark enveloping image. Nothing about her reassures the traveler on this, his final journey. In contrast, Ganga serves in the nether regions as redeemer, restoring the *Mahabharata* heroes and the sons of Sagara. In their celestial affinities, both goddesses are children of the mountain. But Ganga's relation to the celestial realm is more as an equal, not a subordinate like Artemis.

These contrasting qualities represent Ganga's primal image as a river and the traditional values of water. They also represent two different responses—of the prehistoric cultures in the Indo-Aegean areas—to the Aryan invaders, who tried to impose their vision of the universe on the new worlds they settled. As we have seen throughout this study, they not only failed to do this in the subcontinent but were themselves absorbed by the new ethos. Several reasons may account for the different reaction in India: the greater size of the indigenous population, the greater suitability of the land for agriculture, and the previous existence of an advanced society already embracing these values. By the sixth century B.C.—and the rise of Buddhism—the synthesis was nearly complete. It remained only for the alchemy of culture to transform experience and geography into a new vision of art, religion, and philosophy.

7
The New Vision

IT WAS IN THE GANGES BASIN and the region immediately to the south—as far as the Narmada River—that the Aryan and indigenous world attained its final fusion. The new world was set in a form that drew its rhythm from rain and rivers and the dry heat of summer and drew its sustenance from trees and plants and the harvest of the earth. This fusion—tentatively begun in the Punjab and carried forward with early settlement of the Ganges Valley—now reaches fruition. In addition to the blending of Aryan and indigenous values, we find a general coalescence underlying a wide variety of philosophical speculations. Gradually the new values permeate art and religion.

In the Upanishads—from the seventh or eighth century B.C.—several seemingly unrelated lines of thought begin to converge, providing a philosophical rationale for the belief in interpenetrating forms. One is Brahman, the unitary substance possessed of consciousness or spirit—much like the Stoic concept of Logos and matter—and encompassing the universe. All organic things are born from the same Brahman material and contain the same spirit.[1] Another formulation is Samsara, the perpetual round of birth and rebirth.[2] Combined they reveal the possibility of continuous permutation: the vital energy passes in unending cycle from the heavens, through the waters and plants into the born and dying shapes of life—men and beasts and birds, the very gods themselves—at last returning to the waters, the tangible form of Brahman.

By the time of the *Mahabharata* (ca. 400 B.C.–400 A.D.), Brahman and Samsara have become fundamental to Indian thought. Along with them grew up several other ideas that reinforced a single source of generation. One of these is Shakti, the property in a substance that produces an effect.[3] It is the Stoic Logos, the power in the deity enabling him to produce diverse shapes from his own essence. As a non-Aryan perception, it has probably existed in India since the beginning and was slowly brought into the Vedic texts.[4] We first perceive it in the power of Agni, dwelling in the earth, in the plants, in the waters. "He is in the stones and within men. He lives in cattle, in the horses."[5] With the fading of the Aryan vision, Shakti is transformed into a feminine principle, becoming a goddess. Eventually this Shakti combines with Maya, the belief that all forms are but an inflection of the Formless.

Still another notion effacing the difference between human and nonhuman, animate and inanimate, is the existence of Agni and Soma qualities. All things are thought to contain both properties; and the nature of any being is determined by the preponderance of one substance over the other. This distinction applies not only to living and inanimate objects but also to "abstract notions like colors, senses, natural phenomena, seasons, professions, theoretically all that exists or can be imagined."[6] A figure is classified by its inner nature—for example, its fiery or gentle quality—or its physical appearance, or both. Thus the Agni animal *par excellence* is the lion because of its fierce countenance as well as its fiery nature. In the same manner, apparently random objects are associated with one another. Due to their slow gentle movements and their association with water, elephants are related to clouds. By this hidden affinity, they were originally thought to have wings and dwell in the sky.[7] In this way, diverse things—animal, human, vegetal, mineral—are related to one another by Agni or Soma similarities of an internal or external nature.

Thus Ganga is one with Soma (the immortal drink that fell from the kumbha at Allahabad), with the feminine qualities and all the life-giving liquids, including semen, with the moon, the lotus, and the serpents. By contrast, the force of Agni dwells in the masculine—in blood. It is felt in the sun and in Garuda, the sun bird of Vishnu. It is in Yamuna as the sister of Yama, the god of death. (In this way, Yamuna is the river of the underworld in its traditional foreboding image.) It is Shakti, who, while now a goddess, manifests the essentially masculine creative power (the contradiction revealing an unresolved accommodation of the two previous cultures). The distinction appears very early, even from the time of the Brahmanas in the eighth century B.C. "What is dry," say the texts, "that relates to Agni; and what is moist, that relates to Soma." The comparison is strongly reminiscent of the Chinese Yin-Yang. At the same time Indian thought, in its ceaseless effort to achieve a unitary principle, states: "Water is female and fire is male; life is born of their intercourse."[8] This conjunction, as we will see in chapter 10, underlies the relation between Ganga and Shiva in the figurative architecture of the Hindu temple.

Literature offers a striking example of the mutuality between human and plant in the figure of Mankanaka, the mythical sage who once cut his finger by accident. But instead of blood, vegetable sap flowed from the wound. Seeing this, "the sage was filled with joy and danced about his hermitage," knowing he was free, finally on the plane of indifferentiation. "And seeing him dance, all creatures animate and inanimate began to dance."[9]

The "historical" birth of Indian art occurs in the third century B.C. with the appearance of the Mauryan dynasty, the first distinctly Indian empire, whose kings concerned themselves with palaces and building in the grand manner. Their legacy has bequeathed an imperial architecture little concerned with the urgent calling of the earth. But the deeper native traditions, reflecting the new vision of life, emerge with the Buddhist art of the Shunga period—from about 185 B.C.—which draws upon the wealth of indigenous customs. The Buddhist stupas were giant hemispheres of brick and clay constructed over some relic of the Buddha, at once a commemoration and a reminder of the Great Teacher. Years after the original structures, stone gateways and railings were built by pious kings or groups of individuals. These additions contain a wealth of sculpture depicting mythological events and the primordial beliefs of the people. They also provide a starting point from which to trace the continuous development of the goddess Ganga as she evolves in Indian art.

Of the three great cenotaphs, only the stupa of Sanchi remains in place: the others, Bharhut and Amaravati, exist as fragments in the galleries of dimly lit museums. Sanchi lies at the top of a hill, at the end of a long winding road leading up from the dust-devoured town. The great stupa overpowers the smaller buildings nearby. Its pink stone railings, blackened by age, seem to glow in the morning sun, their sculptured figures still straining eagerly for a glimpse of the Enlightened One. On a stone medallion, a centaur hurries past with a lady on his back. From atop the north gateway or torana, a carved lion crouches in hushed anticipation. Here, as on the other stupa railings, the vegetal rhythm is felt everywhere. On the south gateway, one can see vines and plants growing from the mouths of yakshas. On Stupa II, at a lower level, we are suddenly back in the world of 2000 B.C., as the Indus seal of the tree growing from a woman reappears in the female figure giving birth to a sinuous lotus root (Figure 27).[10]

The plant style reaches full development on the railings of the Bharhut stupa, its reliefs interlaced with lotus vines that seem to generate all the other living forms. One panel depicts a clump of mangoes to the left of a woman seated before several cats and dogs (Figure 28). The noses of the human and animal figures are repeated in the tips of the mangoes, which bend toward them and seem ready at any moment to break open revealing the animals inside. Another frieze depicts several jackals observing a woman in a tree (Figure 29). So attuned are the components that the woman's limbs, the jackals' ears, and the branches of the trees are all sustained by a common rhythm.[11] As in literature, Indian art is concerned with the concept of Dhvani or reverberation, the repetition of a theme in subtle and unstated ways. Aside from the plant motif, we find that Agni, the god of fire, is often portrayed as a jackal because of his rapacious nature. Like Agni, the giant fig tree is called *vanaspati*—Lord of the Jungle—from its habit of growing on other

Figure 27. Vines Growing from a Yaksha. Sanchi. Stupa II. Courtesy of The Archaeological Survey of India.

trees and eventually strangling them. In this way, Agni's flamelike quality provides a secondary association between the jackals' ears and the tips of branches.

In another line of development, the yaksha figures found on the stupas offer a prototype for the later image of the river goddess. Ganga's role as a source of fertility and birth is further enhanced by her identification with the yakshas, spirits of primeval India who

Figure 28. Woman, Dogs, and Mangoes. Bharhut. Courtesy of The Archaeological Survey of India.

lived in trees. As the imagined source of life, the tree was a treasure to be protected, since nothing of great value is had for the asking. Its guardians are drawn from pre-Aryan deities who were dethroned by the Vedic settlers, only to be reinstated as followers and guardians.[12] Surprisingly, they are assigned this role as early as the *Rig Veda.*[13] The connection between yakshas and the waters may be seen in the makara or other aquatic animals often used as their vehicles.[14] They were worshipped as the keepers of amrita (soma) and appeared in sculpture holding a vase in their left hand. The *Atharva Veda*—a text representing the earliest stratum of Indian culture—depicts the great-bodied yaksha who dwells in the golden vessel (kumbha) in the city of Brahma.[15] At this early time, the yaksha itself was the center of devotion; already the relationship existed between the yaksha and the kumbha. It was only later that the yaksha as a guardian was removed from the center of the sanctum. From earliest times, female yakshas (yakshis) were known for their powers of granting fertility to women and are worshipped even today in remote villages, especially in South India.[16]

By and large, the tree spirits from Bharhut and Sanchi were conceived as yakshas (Figures 30, 31). One figure from Bharhut is standing on a makara, which, as we will see in chapter 9, becomes a defining emblem of Ganga. Another is supported by a small elephant, a symbol of Lakshmi, goddess of fortune. The combination is instructive, for it enables us to understand the yaksha idea as a matrix giving rise to diverse Indian goddesses of abundance. The only thing necessary for the transfer of sculptural details was the intersection of two religious complexes, a process clearly delineated on the great stupas, where the primordial value of the tree is absorbed by the Buddha realm. At first the brethren hesitated to portray the Buddha in physical form. In early art, the Master was often indicated by a tree—the Tree of Life—in much the same way as Jesus was not originally represented in human form. The tree was a natural alternative, since trees had been worshipped in India from earliest times.[17] A similar transference may have begun between Ganga and the tree spirit, for even at this early stage we may

Figure 29. Woman and Jackals. Coping Stone. Bharhut. Courtesy of The Archaeological Survey of India.

Figure 30. Tree Goddess at Sanchi. East Gateway. First Century B.C. Courtesy of the American Institute of Indian Studies.

glimpse the veneration of the river goddess, at Sanchi and Bharhut, by short dedications containing the name Ganga.[18] In addition to the yaksha named Sudarshana, who appears with Ganga's emblems of the tree and the makara, we find the name Gangita applied to another yaksha figure at Bharhut.

Figure 31. Tree Goddess at Sanchi. Courtesy of the American Institute of Indian Studies.

From the dim past of the Indus civilization, we have glimpsed the undefined image of the goddess, the tree, and the sacred function of water. By the time of the Vedas and early Aryan settlement of the Ganges Valley, the plants and the waters have acquired specific meanings, existing separately and reciprocally as the source of

life. Several centuries later the goddess reappears, providing a human valence for these disembodied forces. The goddess and the
waters find a natural affinity in the obvious association of water with
nourishment and the birth of vegetation. As early as the fourth century B.C., prayers were offered to Ganga as a remedy for drought.[19]
Furthermore, the goddess of the waters finds her antecedents in a
pre-Indian context. Even before their arrival in the Punjab, the
Aryans came upon the lady of the waters during their migration
through Persia. For the old Zoroastrian texts mention a goddess
who descends from heaven, flowing from a mountaintop and
bringing life to barren women.[20] In all likelihood, this image was
carried over to Sarasvati and then to Ganga.

From the sixth century B.C., a whole new cultural ethos came to
dominate the subcontinent, much as the Indus civilization had
done almost fifteen hundred years before. Though the new values
radiated throughout the country, the Ganga-Yamuna Doab—the
land between the two rivers—was regarded as Aryavarta, the home
of Hindu civilization, later becoming the political epicenter of the
great imperial dynasties: Mauryan, Gupta, the Delhi sultans, even
the Moghuls. Above all, these empires were associated with the
Ganges Valley. Their political and commercial life was oriented
toward the river. The cultural dominance of the region must have
enhanced the fame of the Ganges, which provided its most out-
standing physical feature. In art, Ganga figures prominently from
the sixth century A.D. as a door guardian of Gupta temples. By this
time Ganges civilization had attained maturity and the name of
Ganga was known in varying degrees from Southeast Asia to Rome.
To deepen our impressions of the river, let us now reconstruct the
pattern of trade and travel along its banks from the rise of Buddhism through the classical period of Indian culture.

8
The Rise of
Ganges Civilization

IN THE EARLY BUDDHIST PERIOD of the fifth and sixth centuries B.C., most of the Ganges Valley remained largely jungle. Small settlements promoted independent development; gradually, such settlements proliferated into village communities of landowners and peasant proprietors. With the growth of population, specialization evolved, and people formed themselves into guilds for producing and distributing goods. The existence of guilds and the increasing use of money must have accelerated the growth of trade. And with the abundance of navigable waterways in northern India, we can assume the early development of river commerce.

Buddhist records mention river traffic as far east as Magadha—South Bihar—or Champa as its farthest point, while the existence of Champa, a great commercial port, suggests the possibility of trade with Bengal. The city of Champa was a sacred place for Buddhists and Jains. Gautama himself visited it several times, and it was frequented by Mahavira, the founder of Jainism.[1] At the time of the Buddha's death, it was one of the six great cities of India.[2] Beautiful and prosperous, Champa became a center of trade and commerce in the sixth century B.C. Long before the start of the Christian era, its merchants sailed to lower Burma or the Malay peninsula.[3] Hastinapura was rebuilt early in the sixth century B.C.

and Kaushambi was flourishing. In Jain texts, Kampilya, Banaras, and Champa are counted among the ten ancient capital cities of India.[4] The three are conveniently located on the upper, middle, and lower Ganges, while Champa lay within coasting distance from the ocean port of Tamralipti at the tip of the Bengal delta. Such a distribution of ports, evenly placed along the river, would well have suited the needs of merchants and their cargoes.

Not only the Ganges but several of its tributaries served for trade and travel. Buddhist texts from the fifth century B.C. mention boat travel from Vaishali on the Gandak River, which descends from the Nepalese Terai and enters the Ganges just below Patna.[5] According to Megasthenes (ca. 300 B.C.), Greek ambassador to the Mauryan court at Pataliputra (Patna), the Gogra River—also flowing from the north—was navigable throughout the year and was probably used for trade.[6]

By the fourth century B.C., Pataliputra had come to dominate the entire Ganges basin. Even before the Mauryas, boats may have set out for Java and Ceylon. The city was founded around 487 B.C., the year of the Buddha's death. Later texts relate the apocryphal words of the Buddha predicting the future greatness of the city: "As far . . . as Aryan people dwell, as far as merchants travel, this will become the chief town, the city of Pataliputra."[7]

The third archaeological level of Hastinapura, from the early sixth to the early third centuries B.C., contains artifacts rich in their suggestiveness. Jadeite, also found in the ruins of Harappa, indicates a link with the region beyond the mountains: Pamir, Tibet, or East Turkestan. The *Mahabharata* speaks of celestial silks from Manasarovar sent for a king's coronation.[8]

At this time, metal currency begins to appear throughout the Ganges Valley.[9] Coins were issued by government mints and by authorized guilds of traders and bankers. Perhaps the clearest indication of commerce and communication is the distribution of a new pottery type called northern black polish ware, found at major sites along the river from Hastinapura to Tamralipti and as far afield as the Punjab in the northwest and Amaravati far to the south.[10]

Buddhist literature contains the most numerous references to traffic along the Ganges. In the *Jataka* stories we find a great patter of activity: a village of carpenters traveling down the river to build houses on its banks, a large ship arriving in port with merchandise from a far country. In another story, the Buddha instructs his disciple Ananda: "Take 300 shipwrights, go to the upper Ganges, procure timber, build 300 ships, make them cut stores of wood for the town, fill the ships with light wood, and come back soon." Elsewhere we find a group of carpenters who sail down the river and out to sea to escape debt.[11] Many Buddhist sources refer to ocean voyages and shipwrecks.

The Mauryan Empire (ca. 322–183 B.C.) brings with it the unification of the Ganges Valley. From the time of Ashoka or before, the region from Hardwar to Tamralipti had fallen under one rule. The Greek ambassador Megasthenes comments on the growth of urban life: "Of their cities it is said the number is so great that it cannot be stated with precision." The most famous by far is Pataliputra, capital of the Mauryan universal state. From here the emperor Ashoka sent his Buddhist missionaries to the farthest reaches of the known world. From beyond the Hindu Kush, the great highway from the Near East and Persia brought to Pataliputra a commerce in goods and ideas: Greek and Persian influence were felt at the Mauryan court, in the train of a Greek wife sent to the emperor Chandragupta by Seleucus, successor to Alexander in the eastern satrapies. The city, according to Megasthenes, extended for nine miles along the Ganges and was surrounded by high wooden ramparts fitted with gates and military emplacements.

Several sources tell of constant activity on the river. Excavations at Kumrahar, near Patna, have revealed a Mauryan pillared hall fronting a canal forty-three feet broad by ten feet deep. The canal leads to the Ganges by way of the Son. The huge monolithic pillars are made of sandstone brought from the quarries of Chunar, twenty-five miles southwest of Banaras and almost two hundred miles from Pataliputra. In all probability, the pillars were transported by barge from Chunar along the river and directly to the hall.[12] A Jain text mentions a wealthy potter who distributed his wares throughout the Ganges Valley in a fleet of his own boats.[13] The *Artha Shastra,* a manual of statecraft presumably from the

Mauryan era, describes a vigorous economy actively engaged in domestic and foreign trade. The commercial traveler fell under the jurisdiction of at least two government offices. The superintendent of ships examined accounts relating to navigation on oceans, rivers, and lakes and was instructed to pay special attention to battered ships arriving at port. Among other things, the superintendent of commerce was responsible for certain aspects of foreign transactions. He was instructed to remit the trade taxes for those who imported foreign merchandise.[14]

From this picture, we begin to understand the role of Ganga in what was at this time the center of Indian civilization. We see great port cities strung out along the river, serving as entrepôts for an ever-widening hinterland, quickening the commercial and cultural life with their exchange of goods and their reports of new lands and people beyond the ocean. These cities ranged from Hastinapura, north of Delhi, to Tamralipti on the Bay of Bengal.

At the end of the Mauryan period, northern India falls prey to the instability of contending powers; not until Chandragupta II, in the latter part of the fourth century A.D., do the entire reaches of the Ganges Valley know political continuity. But there is reason to believe that, despite the political disruption of the region, internal and ocean trade continued. We still find mention of a seafaring merchant of Banaras who crossed the ocean and returned after a prosperous voyage.[15] Chinese records note an itinerary of the first or second century B.C. from the Gulf of Tonkin that includes the names Ganga and Tamala (probably Tamralipti). Several texts from the early centuries of the Christian era express concern for maritime trade. The *Law Book of Manu* fixes the legal agreement for rates in ocean commerce, referring as well to the cost of hiring boats for varying distances along a river. The region of Vanga (lower Bengal) is mentioned as a place where ships gather for the purpose of trade.[16]

The classical writers also shed light on the period. Now and then we find reference to a longer journey down the river: the *Periplus of the Erythraean Sea* (ca. A.D. 80)—a firsthand account of a mariner in the Indian Ocean—traces a silk route from Northwest China which divided in Bactria. One segment branched off toward Barygaza, a west coast port of India, while in the easterly direction silk was "exported to Damirica (land of the Tamils) by way of the river Ganges." In the *Periplus,* the word *Ganges* applies to lower Bengal, its chief ocean port (probably Tamralipti), and the river itself. "On its banks," says the anonymous author, "is a market town which has the same name as the river Ganges. Through this place are brought malabathrum and Gangetic spikenard, pearls, and muslins of the finest sorts, which are called Gangetic." Both malabathrum and spikenard grow in the Himalayas and were carried down via land routes or along navigable tributaries of the Ganges. The trade of Tamralipti must have been considerable even at this time, handling as it did exports from the Ganges Valley and the Himalayan regions. It also served as a center for goods coming from the south. The mariner of the *Periplus* comments on the numerous east coast ports "where ships put in from Damirica and from the north (Bengal)." The ships "which make the voyage to Chryse (Malacca) and to the Ganges are called *colandia* and are very large."[17]

These passages from the *Periplus* and elsewhere point to a well-developed maritime tradition in northern India throughout the early centuries of the Christian era. A collection of Buddhist stories from the second century A.D. mentions a village of mariners (sailors, raftsmen) located near the city of Shravasti, far north on the Gogra River, not far from the Nepalese foothills. It describes a merchant of the city who goes off to sea with five hundred other traders; similarly, his son hires a boat, fitting it out with sailors, a cook, a helmsman, and a pilot. Political conditions must have inhibited the normal pattern of trade along the river. It seems that ships no longer sailed directly from Banaras to the sea. For we read of a merchant from Banaras who invites a group of five hundred traders to join him in an ocean venture. "Those of you who have the determination, come with me," he urges. "Bring with you merchandise suitable for sea trade, and we will avoid the constraints of paying duties for export, cargo, or passage." Arriving at the seacoast, he hires a ship and signs on a pilot, a helmsman, and deckhands. In another passage, a group of five hundred Banaras merchants who want to engage in sea trade take an overland route and, passing through several countries, finally reach the sea.[18]

Toward the end of the first century A.D., a considerable part of the Ganges Valley came under control of the Kushanas, warriors from Central Asia who migrated southeast through Afghanistan and the Punjab. The extent of their occupation remains uncertain. The main southern capital was at Mathura—on the Jumna—which became a great cultural and commercial center. Banaras may have served as a provincial capital further east. Pataliputra was also included in the empire. Commerce must have been considerable, judging by the scope of the Kushana dominions, which extended from Afghanistan to the central Ganges Valley. This commerce was stimulated by the growing needs of Rome for spices and luxury goods, though much of this trade was carried on through west coast ports. In the mid–third century, the Kushanas were overthrown in the northwest and their empire in the Ganges Valley fell to a more obscure but related tribe, the Murundas, whose influence seems to have spread quickly throughout the region.

We hear of a Murunda king at Kanauj, on the upper Ganges, and of another at Pataliputra whose envoy travels to Peshawar on what is today the Afghan-Pakistan border.[19] Chinese sources shed some light on Ganga during the period. We read that shortly after A.D. 225 the king of Fu-Nan (the region of Cambodia) sent an embassy to India. After reaching the mouth of the Ganges, it sailed upriver to the Murunda capital either at Pataliputra or Vaishali. After traveling in the kingdom, the embassy returned with a present of horses. The Chinese records also indicate earlier shipments of horses by Kushana merchants to the kingdom of Kia-ying (southern Malaya) in the third century A.D.,[20] probably through the port of Tamralipti.

During the half millennium from about 200 B.C. to A.D. 320, the political map of the Ganges Valley forms and dissolves several times. The period of greatest instability includes the 150 years from roughly 70 B.C. to A.D. 80, when no one power extended its control along any considerable distance of the river. This insecurity is reflected in the story of the Banaras merchant who traveled overland to reach the sea. Otherwise, commerce on the river seems to be flourishing throughout the period, stimulated by the near insatiable Roman market and by the Pax Kushana, which opened up trade with Central Asia and the northwest frontier.

With the rise of the Gupta Empire in A.D. 320, the Ganges

Valley settles down once more to peace and plenitude. Gradually the empire expands westward, reaching to the Indus. Pataliputra is flourishing. We read from Fa-hien, the Chinese pilgrim who traveled in India from A.D. 405 to 411, that "the royal palace and halls in the midst of the city, which now exist as of old, were all made by spirits . . . in a way which no human hands of this world could accomplish."[21] Banaras maintains its age-old reputation for silks, though the Pundra region in Bengal also acquires a growing importance. The poet Bana describes Pundra silk: "pale as the corner of a peacock's eye."[22] Along the Gogra tributary of the Ganges, Kalidasa pictures the royal city of Ayodhya with its prosperous markets, its boats, and its pleasure gardens.[23] Literature often refers to merchants away in distant countries. In a play called *The Toy Cart,* an actor comments on the folly of loving a merchant, for they are always doing business in foreign lands.[24] Traders and merchantmen appear here and there throughout the literature of the times. Furthermore, the number of foreign merchants was great enough for the law books to stipulate that the king should preserve the goods of those who died in the country until an heir comes forward.[25]

The Gupta Empire disintegrated by the middle of the sixth century. For almost another fifty years (606–647), those parts of the fallen Gupta Empire in the Ganges Valley were held together by the Emperor Harsha from his capital at Kanauj on the upper Ganges. Prayag, Banaras, and Tamralipti are thriving. In his journey, Hiuen Tsiang comes upon Hardwar, which has a large population and is "attracting many thousands of people." He also mentions Champa, which seems to be fairly active, but his details are only fragmentary. The pilgrim's journal provides a good description of activities along the river as the age of classical Indian culture draws to a close. He mentions, for example, numerous boats on the Ganges at Kanauj[26] and describes the great fleet of Bhaskaravarmin, Harsha's ally, as it proceeds upriver to Kanauj, all the way from Rajmahal on the border of Bengal.[27] We follow Hiuen Tsiang on his boat trip south toward Prayag; we experience the terrifying moment en route when he is captured by robbers who nearly sacrifice him to their patron Durga.

Aside from commerce and transport, the Ganges was used for

warfare. Kalidasa describes Rama's attack on the Vangas of lower Bengal, who opposed him with their naval force. After his conquest, Rama "planted the pillars of victory on the islands of the Ganges delta."[28] We find an inscription commemorating a military campaign and a king's forces: "invincible through its equipment of great ships, elephants, and foot-soldiers."[29] Harsha's inscriptions also refer to the emperor's victorious camp, with its division of ships, horses, and elephants. In the eighth century, the Palas of Bengal deploy a fleet of boats that lie strung out along the Ganges like a series of mountain peaks.[30] The later Sena kings continued to use the river for military purposes. One inscription tells of a naval expedition that traveled the entire course of the Ganges.

With the collapse of Harsha's empire in the middle of the seventh century, the Ganges Valley once more splinters into many pieces. They are not to be reassembled for another five hundred years. Throughout the medieval period and up to the nineteenth century, the river continues to serve as a main highway of long-distance trade and transportation. Several English travelers from the early seventeenth century have left vivid descriptions of commerce along the river. John Jourdain, a servant of the East India Company, had this to record in his journal of 1611: "There is yearlie carryed from Agra to Bengala above 10,000 tonnes of salte in great barges of 400 and 500 tonnes apeace."[31] Peter Mundy, who traveled in India from 1628 to 1634, tells of barges plying between Agra, Allahabad, and Patna. Some of these great boats, he reports, contained "several rooms [and were] able to carry a pretty village with all their inhabitants and goods; such is their hugeness."[32]

9
Ganga, Shiva, and the Hindu Temple

The Temple

TOGETHER GANGA AND SHIVA ILLUSTRATE a primordial relationship prefigured in the Vedas and hinted at as early as the Indus civilization. We have seen them together in myth and art. Ultimately their relationship underlies the spiritual architecture of the Hindu temple as it evolves from its primitive antecedents. For this reason, it is necessary to trace the development of the temple—and its exemplar the Shiva shrine—from the beginnings.

The Temple as Cave

Gertrude Levy makes it abundantly clear that the earliest religious enclosures were the prehistoric mountain caves of northern Spain and southern France, which served as both tombs and shrines.[1] The inaccessibility of its sacred pictures suggests that the sanctum was not a place for people to gather but a repository of potent forces designed to ensure the fortunes of the tribe. In this sense, it is closer to the Hindu temple than to the western cathedral.

The Temple as Tomb and Memorial

The Vedic literature demonstrates the evolution from tomb to temple. The original burial place served the dead ''as a house or as a monument."[2] The site was marked with a stone slab, a mound of earth, or both. "Over thee," says the priest in the final ritual, "I place this piece of earth. . . . Here let the Fathers keep this pillar firm for thee, and there let Yama make thee an abiding place."[3] We need but recall "the tree where Yama drinks with the gods" to perceive a correspondence between the tree and the stone pillar. This correspondence was strengthened by the indigenous custom of planting a sapling over the grave.[4] The tree as cenotaph becomes a home of the departed spirit. In the *Mahabharata* and the *Jataka* stories, we read of malign spirits who wait in trees for unsuspecting passersby. The mound of earth, with its contents, also duplicates in miniature the mountain cave. "Here I build this rampart for the living," sings the Vedic poet. "May they survive a hundred autumns, and may they bury Death beneath this mountain."[5] Thus the tree, the pillar, and the mountain all come to mark the center of the site.

The stone element serves both as center and as circumference of the entire configuration. After constructing the funeral mound, the priest encloses it in a ring of stones, which is regarded as a womb.[6] It is not surprising that stone, the least perishable material, was first reserved for the dead. As Siegfried Giedion observes, its enduring qualities made it the ideal substance from which to build a perpetual resting place for the dead. It was the grave, in fact, that gave birth to the first stone architecture.

The Vedic fire altar—a more highly structured antecedent of the Hindu temple—combines the functions of tomb and temple. In the ceremony, a golden image of a man and a golden disk representing the sun are placed above a lotus leaf. The sacrificer then places the leaf at the bottom of the fire altar, "for the lotus leaf is a womb."[7] And we find the lotus, a distinctly non-Aryan vegetal symbol, giving rise to the sun, to humankind, to the entire universe. According to the scriptures, the tomb is fashioned after the fire altar: "For when a Sacrificer builds a fire altar he thereby constructs for himself a [new] body for that distant world; but that sacrifice is not complete until the making of a tomb."[8] The fact is implicit in the ritual itself: the universe is created anew by sacrifice of the Great Purusha (the original inchoate being from which the world was fashioned and who later evolves into the impersonal Brahman substance); and man, the little Purusha, by identifying himself with the cosmic act, becomes reintegrated with the universe. The point in any such ritual, as anthropologist A. M. Hocart explains, "is to make one thing equivalent to another so that by acting on one you can act on another. . . . Without these equivalencies there would be no point in the ritual. . . . The participants are deliberately seeking to establish an identity between man and the ritual objects, between ritual objects and the world, and so between man and the world."[9]

The relation between tomb, tree, and monument is equally apparent in the evolution of the stupa, which has the same origins as the Hindu temple. The earliest stupa mounds, which may date to pre-Mauryan times, reveal a post running vertically through the center of the structure as a representation of the Tree of Life.[10] The Vedic literature describes the structures of the ungodly (the easterners, the Asuras), who make their sepulchers round, while those who are godly make theirs four-cornered.[11] The "ungodly" refers to the indigenous people who had not accepted the Vedic ritual but followed the age-old enchoric patterns of the subcontinent. These patterns continued undiminished until the second century B.C., when they burst out in the fully developed form of the Buddhist stupa.

The Life within the Pillar

The little mountain—rock or pillar—was a numinous object throughout the ancient world. In the Near East and in Mycenaean religion, it is interchangeable with the sacred tree as a dwelling place of god.[12] It occurs in the Old Testament (Gen. 28) representing Yahweh: "And Jacob rose up in the morning, and took the stone he had put for a pillow, and set up a pillar, and poured oil upon the top of it. . . . 'And this stone, which I have set for a pillar, shall be God's house.' " The Vedas contain frequent references to the pillar or stambha as a cosmological principle, and various gods are identified with the power in it. Perhaps because of his column of fire—see Exod. 13.21: "And the Lord went before them in a pillar of fire"—the chief association falls to Agni, whose column of flame supports the vault of heaven.[13] In a long hymn, the early thinkers search for the god behind the symbol: "Who out of many, tell me, is that Stambha to whom the pathways lead . . . to whom the Waters make their way with longing?"[14]

Certain passages in the Vedas indicate the generative properties of the stambha. We read in a hymn to Agni: "He who knows the Golden Reed that stands in the sea, he is the Lord of Life." The Sanskrit word *vetasa* signifies both "reed" and "phallus."[15] This correspondence between phallus and reed (or stambha) suggests affinity with Shiva, who is sometimes portrayed as a column or pillar. It is Shiva in his stambha form that Bhagiratha worships for the gift of Ganga (Figure 8). Furthermore, Shiva is characterized as Lord of the Lingam, a word popularly translated as phallus. Although Vedic orthodoxy condemns those who worship the phallus, the very force of their imprecations suggests its popularity. In one passage, Indra is urged to keep them far from the sacrifice. In another he slays them after storming their castle.[16]

But whether as lingam or pillar, worship of the stone column undergoes the same tendencies as other numinous objects, absorbing the values of the indigenous people. The *Rig Veda* addresses itself "to him even in the rock and in the house: Immortal One, he cares for all mankind."[17] Like the tree, the pillar develops from a burial marker into a dwelling place of god, charged with the powers of life. Similarly, as the tomb of earth is a mother, so its circle of stones becomes a womb, propitious to birth and its renewal.[18] Accordingly a bracelet—shaped like the female organ—is invoked for its power of fertility.[19] At the same time, the pillar is equated with the organ of generation. Prajapati the creator, desiring increase, "stretched out for himself that stone which projects. With that he impregnated [woman]. Her lap is a sacrificial altar."[20] Due perhaps to its generative association, the pillar evolves from burial marker to stambha to lingam, the main object of worship in the Hindu temple.

The relation between the lingam and Shiva—or what archaeologists call the Proto-Shiva—extends to the Indus Valley civilization, where several remains, such as the round stone caps at Harappa (Figure 32) and the well-known seal of the polycephalic yogi, have led scholars to attribute a primordial native origin to the Lord

Figure 32. Harappa Lingam. Courtesy of The Archaeological Survey of India.

of the Lingam. Despite Vedic condemnation, the lingam as stambha retains its generative quality, which in the *Mahabharata* becomes Shiva's mark, acknowledged by all the gods.

The Lord of the Burning Ground

Aside from his association with the lingam, Shiva fills several other roles as the temple archetype. One is his strong connection with the burial ground, which first gave rise to the temple idea itself. In the epic, Shiva declares: "I do not see any spot that is more sacred than the crematorium . . . of all abodes, the crematorium pleases my heart most."[21] Yama, god of death, receives his stewardship from Shiva.[22] At times Shiva temples were built upon the graves themselves. This custom may well explain why the architectural treatises specify their construction outside the village precincts.[23] A ninth-century inscription of the Chola king Rajaditya records the construction of a Shiva temple, built on the spot where the king's father was buried. The practice exists today in the south, but only for the more affluent; the less fortunate still set up modest lingams on the site.[24] Mrs. Sinclair Stevenson mentions a small Shiva temple in Kathiawar built on the spot where a local raja had been burned and his bones buried. The shrine contained a lingam, an image of Shiva's wife Parvati, and a statue of Ganga.[25]

Shiva and the Mountain

Shiva, as a god of death and emblem of fertility, is also associated with the cosmic mountain. This identity is seen in his epithets, such as "he who dwells in the mountains." He is known variously as lord, protector, or friend of the mountain. The relationship is expressed in the names of his wife—Parvati and Uma Haimavati—both signifying the daughter of the mountain; it is visually portrayed by the image of Ganga that accompanies him and who is also called Haimavati. In a world of endless permutation and equivalence, lingam and mountain coalesce. In the Himalayas, the lingam is called *dhruva*, fixed or unmoving, a term describing the primordial unmovable lingam and the great mountains themselves.[26] In South India, whole mountains are regarded as lingams.[27] The conjoint theme of lingam and mountain corresponds to the Greek *omphalos,* which may incorporate the three functions of grave marker, fertility, and sacred mountain.[28] Thus, like Ganga, Shiva becomes a god of the triple world, his symbol the trident often carried by his devotees.

The Temple of the Mountain

The notion of mountain as a home of god, a common theme throughout the ancient world, culminates in the mountain built by human hands, the ziggurat (ca. 2000 B.C.). Its long flight of stairs was designed to receive the god, who descended from the summit. The names of different ziggurats—Home of the Mountain, Mountain of Storm, Bond between Heaven and Earth—leave no doubt of its prototype.[29] Moreover, it seems likely that ideas related to the mountain also served as a model for the Hindu temple. In the architectural manuals, Meru and Kailasa appear as names for the most prominent types of temples.[30] Both literary evidence and inscriptions compare the temple to a mountain. In his search for Rama's wife Sita, Hanuman the monkey king comes upon "a splendid temple white as Mount Kailasa . . . supported by a thousand pillars . . . and of such height that it seemed to kiss the sky." And again: "The temple was as high as the peak of Meru, and . . . resembled a mountain."[31] In a fifth-century inscription, a king's minister directs his sons to build a temple to Vishnu resembling the peaks of Kailasa. Elsewhere Mount Meru itself is described as the king of temples.[32] The temple ritual of circumambulation is sometimes performed about a sacred hill or mountain. Madras State, for example, has several hills ringed with prescribed paths for the pilgrim. They serve on a larger scale the same ritual purpose as the temple.[33]

Some people claim to find a linear resemblance between the magic mountains and the temple—for example, if "the side elevation of the Kailasa Temple at Ellora is compared with the actual skyline of Kailasa . . . it will be obvious that the temple designer was not relying upon his imagination only. He himself must have performed the greatest of all pilgrimages and his intention was to reproduce the exact build-up of the holy mountain."[34] While such thoughts hover in the realm of speculation, the mountains have undoubtedly exerted their influence on the Indian mind since Vedic times, when they were already the home of the gods and the source of soma.

With the Aryan movement southeast into the Ganges Valley, the mountains are left behind; but their significance remains. Such conditions are favorable to both literary and architectural mythology, and there may be certain truth to one writer's statement that "Kailasa temples were built everywhere in order to carry the Himalayas into the smallest villages."[35] However, since the *Rig Veda* reflects Aryan experience west of the Indus and nearer the Hindu Kush, Kailasa may later have come to represent more "a Himalaya of the mind" than an architectonic model. The temple as symbolic mountain reflects Levy-Bruhl's contention that myth remains poorly developed when the cohesion of a social group is strong, for then participation in the group is actually lived. Myth arises when the group "endeavors to realize a participation no longer directly felt."[36] To the extent that Levy-Bruhl is correct, the temple represents a fusion of Vedic and non-Vedic sources, since the Vedic mountain and the abode of Shiva are two diverse perceptions. Ultimately Mahadev (Shiva) predominates, as the temple ritual is chiefly non-Aryan.[37]

At the core of these ideas is Shiva. His association with the funeral ground, the lingam as an emblem of death and symbol of life, his identity with the mountain, his connection with the waters—all provide a blueprint for the symbolic and ritual design of the Hindu temple. According to the Puranas, the temple "should be contemplated as filled throughout with the essence of Shiva."[38] In terms of symbolic architecture, the primary units of the temple include the building, the altar, the door, and the guardians.[39] As we have seen, the building may be conceived as a mountain. Though various sects have different summits—Kailasa for Shaivites, Vaikuntha for Vaishnavas—Shiva's mountain serves most often for comparison. The sanctum of every Shiva temple, and many others as well, contains a lingam and *yoni,* stylized representations of phallus and vulva, which evolve from the slab and ring stones placed above the funeral mound. In literature the lingam is sometimes pictured as rising from a lake, an image that reflects the place of water in the structure and rites of the temple. In addition to the yoni, the water element is emphasized by the door guardians—especially Ganga and Yamuna—and the role that Ganga water plays in the temple ritual itself. We will examine these features next.

The Guardians and the Sanctum

The Parts of the Temple

In unassembled form, the parts of the Hindu temple can be seen as early as the Indus civilization—for example, lingams and ring stones with probable fertility values, the tree spirit as prototype for the door guardian, and a seal showing a god in yoga position (Shiva is considered the great yogi) surrounded by two nagas and two kneeling human figures (Figure 33). Since one of the serpent's chief associations is with water, we may attribute—however tenuously—some water significance to the figures surrounding the god. Such a relationship, as we are about to see, underlies the entire temple concept.

Formally the Indian temple serves as an icon, each part in meaningful relationship to the others, the whole designed as an aid to contemplation *(dhyana)* and realization *(samadhi)*.[40] As such it possesses the Dhvani quality, the literary term describing the resonance or suggestion of the major theme throughout a work of art. The theme of the Hindu temple is stated and repeated in the rela-

Figure 33. Snakes Worshipping a Yogi. Mohenjo-daro. Courtesy of The Archaeological Survey of India.

tionship between lingam and yoni, Shiva and the guardians (especially Ganga and Yamuna), the mountain (building) and the rivers (waters).

The Door and the Guardians

The indwelling deity of trees and pillars made them objects of worship in the Mediterranean world. With the evolution of structural architecture, first one and then the other came to be used as a building support throughout the temple and at the entranceway.[41] With the development of iconic images, the door pillars—with their anthropomorphic quality—were transformed into guardians. The change occurred slowly: at Eridu in Mesopotamia, for example, sixteen levels of settlement (from about the fifth millennium B.C. to the rise of the ziggurat around 2000 B.C.) disclosed no human sculpture.[42]

The first guardians, like the genii and fabulous animals standing at the gates of Assyrian palaces, were terrifying figures. Even the cherubim at the Garden of Eden may have been minatory and foreboding.[43] Aside from the mystery religions, the Mediterranean world viewed the doorway as an entrance unto darkness. To the ancients, the Pillars of Hercules signified the farthest limits of the known world. Samson's pulling down the temple pillars (Judges 16:30) reaffirms the Old Testament vision of redemption through death. Some of the Indian door guardians present the same fierce aspect.[44]

The gateway as a passage to life also pervades the ancient world. We find it in Odysseus' perilous journey through Scylla and Charybdis and the vision of paradise that awaits him in the golden island of Scheria.[45] "The feminine principle of the dolmen and the gate is always connected with rebirth through the woman's womb."[46] Christ's statement "I am the Door" (John 10:9) refers to the door of metaphysical understanding that one may enter while still alive. In Indian architecture, sculpted temple guardians have existed since early times in Buddhist and Hindu art and have served different purposes: to ward off evil spirits, to beautify the entrance, to suggest the devotional holiness of the structure, and to distinguish the temple from domestic architecture.[47] But most important, they contribute directly to the temple idea itself.

The image of the door appears as early as the *Rig Veda* in a speculation on the origins of life: "Ancient will be those creatures, whatsoe'er they be; with moons, with autumns, doors unclose themselves to you." It is the portal of good fortune: "Agni bestows a blessing on each pious man, and opens wide the doors for him."[48] Even at this early time, the door was associated with the waters ("Agni and the Waters, the first door to divine order") and with the goddess ("Wide be the doors, the goddesses, throw open, easy to pass, invoked through adoration").[49] The guardians, the waters, and the goddess are drawn into the same compass. The First Principle (Atman) reflects on his labors: " 'Here are now worlds. Let me create world guardians.' Right from the waters he drew forth and shaped a person."[50]

We also glimpse the Agni-Soma nature of the entrance and the guardians, with its implication that *moksha* (spiritual enlightenment) is only achieved by the reconciliation of opposites: Agni (fire) and the Waters; "Day and Night the two doorjambs, the Year the roof."[51] In the temple scheme, Ganga is associated with the left side (looking toward the temple), Yamuna, the other guardian, with the right.[52] Hints of the desired reconciliation occur as early as the *Rig Veda*: "Lull thou to sleep, to wake no more, the pair who look upon each other." Similarly: "Neither the right nor the left do I distinguish, neither the east nor the west."[53] The union of opposites, stated first by Ganga and Yamuna at the entranceway (and in their union at Prayag), is repeated in the sanctum as the metaphysical blueprint of the entire temple. Recall the earlier line: "Water is female and fire is male: life is born of their intercourse."[54] The Sanskrit name for the sanctum, House of the Womb *(garbha-grihya)*, establishes its primary meaning.

Just as India possessed a "spiritualized architecture," so it displayed a "spiritualized physiology." The *Hathapradipika,* a yogic text from the fourteenth to sixteenth centuries, explains the portal of ascension: "The goddess Ganga is Ida [referring to the Soma qualities], the river Yamuna is Pingala [of the Agni traits]. Between them lies the Kundalini [the untapped source of spiritual energy resting at the base of the spinal cord]." To attain the sanctum, "the poor young ascetic widow [Kundalini resting between Ganga and Yamuna] should be caught by force [by the yogi]. That would be the highest stage.''[55] Among the many yogic exercises recommended, this "brings about the confluence of the three currents [flowing in the three channels: Ida, Pingala, and the center channel, the *Sushumna*] and carries the mind to Kedara [Kedarnath, the Himalayan shrine marking the confluence of the Alakananda and the Mandakini, two of the three original tributaries of Ganga].''[56] Here, in altered form, reappears the image of the *sangam* at Prayag, the point of mystical consciousness where the three rivers meet.

So important was the entranceway in South India that by the twelfth century monumental gateways (gopuras) became the largest and architecturally most significant structure of the temple.[57] In South Indian ritual, the priest may begin a ceremony by asking permission of the Guardian of the Field (often himself a manifestation of Shiva) to enter the temple and worship Mahadev (Shiva). He then sprinkles water over the door as well as upon the guardians on either side.[58] In worshipping Shiva, one should first adore Ganga, Yamuna, and Sarasvati among the other gods and celestials.[59] After worshipping the river goddesses, the priest addresses the door, whose ultimate meaning is known through Vedanta, who has the shape of all the worlds and is omnipresent.[60] The ritual relation between temple and water—especially water from the holy rivers—existed elsewhere in the ancient world. A ceremony at Babylon resembles the one described here, down to the mention of the two rivers. The priest is directed to draw water from the Tigris and Euphrates in two separate cisterns and with these sprinkle both the temple and the sanctuary.[61] The ceremony resembles the pouring of Ganges water on the lingam, a rite in Indian tradition that duplicates the descent of the rivers from the holy mountain. We will now examine both these themes.

The Mountain and the Waters

In the *Rig Veda*, the mountains are the home of water: of rivers, of rain, of soma—all forms of the life-conferring liquid (amrita). At that time the mountains were portrayed as holding back the water-laden clouds which lay hidden among them. Gradually the theme recedes and the mountains—notably Himavat (Himalaya)—are characterized as the home of the rivers. Chapter 5 described Vedic Sarasvati and its close association with the mountains; likewise the relation between Ganga and Himalaya, mentioned throughout the epics and Puranas. Frequently in Indian literature Ganga is specifically connected with Kailasa, Shiva's mountain, and with Meru, where he sometimes dwells.[62] Along with other rivers, Ganga, Sarasvati, Sindhu (Indus), and Yamuna are described as flowing from the slopes of Himavat.[63] In fact, several Puranas mention the entire river system of Asia as rising in the region of Meru and flowing from there to the corners of the earth—after first separating from Ganga.[64] Sometimes Ganga falls directly on the head of Shiva before dividing into its several streams.[65] From this wealth of mythology emerges the further correspondence between Shiva and the mountain—conjointly the origin of the rivers, with Ganga the foremost.

Ganga and the mountains were regarded as a source of life and sustenance. The *Arthashastra* (late fourth to early third centuries B.C.) recommends that in time of drought one should worship Indra, Ganga, the mountains, and the sea.[66] Ganga's relation to Shiva evolves naturally from Ganga and Himalaya, especially with the emergence of the Shiva-lingam as the embodiment of the magic mountain. Thus the ritual of pouring water on the lingam duplicates the river's descent from Himavat and the semen (amrita) flowing from Mahadev's endless powers of generation. Seen in this light, Shiva's two consorts—Ganga and Uma-Parvati—become declensions of the archetypal Himalayan river, since Uma and Parvati, along with Ganga, are often described as daughters of Himavat.[67] In his poem *The Cloud Messenger,* Kalidasa fuses the image of Shiva and the mountain. The poet points the direction of the cloud across the high peaks (Gauri is another name for Parvati):

> Fly then where Ganga on the king of mountains
> Falls like a flight of stairs from heaven let down
> For the sons of men; she hurls her billowy fountains
> Like hands to grasp the moon on Shiva's crown
> And laughs her foamy laugh at Gauri's jealous frown.

The Cloud Messenger 50

The relation between the mountains and the waters is further reflected in the image of the lotus. "The lotus is the waters," says the Brahmana.[68] From it rises Meru, the primeval mountain. This theme underlies the custom of surrounding the temple with an artificial body of water (as at Martand and the Golden Temple at Amritsar). The lotus as the womb duplicates the yoni, the foundation of the lingam.[69] Thus the sanctum is founded on the waters. Its name *garbha-grihya* (House of the Womb) is embodied in the yoni and ritualized by the pouring of Ganga water.

The Lingam and the Waters

The delightful *Kathasaritsagara* (Ocean of Story) from the tenth or eleventh century relates the tale of a woman who stood beside a lake, praying to Mahadev. "And Shiva rose from the lake . . . in the form of a linga."[70] In the *Ramayana,* the demon Ravana emerges from a bath in the Narmada River and leads a ceremonial procession. "Wherever the Lord of the Rakshasas went, a golden Shiva-linga was borne before him."[71] The relationship between the lingam (mountain, pillar) and the waters already appears in the Brahmanas, where the stones encircling the burial mound are equated with the water. The sacrificer "thus surrounds this world with water."[72] We glimpse it again in the Upanishads, where "he who was born of old from *tapas* [austerities] was born from Water."[73] Although the Upanishad is referring here to Atman, it is Shiva who later becomes the ideal *tapaspati,* Master of Austerities.[74] The lingam and its effluents are coextensive. "Who is it whose semen was offered in the sacrifice in the beginning of the world? . . . Is the golden mountain [Meru] made of any other semen? . . . See how the world bears everywhere the signature of the lingam and the yoni."[75] We come upon the story of Rama, his brother Lakshmana, Sita, and the monkey king Hanuman, crossing Rameshvara Island (near Sri Lanka) after defeating the demon Ravana. There they stopped to worship and adorn the well-known Rama lingam "that Hanuman had brought from the Ganges."[76] The story may represent a local legend, since it is not attested by any Rama lingams on early South Indian temples. If so, it further emphasizes the association of Shiva with the river goddess, at this point far distant from the source. At all events, the connection between Ganga and the lingam has become inseparable, as indicated by the modern guidebook issued to pilgrims at the Rameshvara temple. The instructions are worth quoting extensively:

> Ganges water must be brought in a metal vessel. . . . Gentlemen wishing to have the Ganges water poured on the God but who are unable to take it to Rameshvara can send the same metal vessel by parcel from any part of the country with . . . a money order of two Rupees for each vessel, but if they want *abhisheka* [ritual pouring]to be done on a particular day . . . they should take particular care to send them at least two weeks in advance. Pilgrims bringing Ganges water will have to . . . go to the priest in charge of the temple, who will have the water poured on the God. Such pouring of Ganges water takes place daily from early morning almost continually till the sandal anointing during the . . . night. . . . For the convenience of those who do not bring Ganges water with them, it can be had from the *Peshkar's* [caretaker's] office in the temple.[77]

One of the public rituals in the South Indian temple involves a ceremonial bath in which Shiva is taken to a sleeping chamber outside the sanctum. During the procession, Ganga, who lives in the god's matted hair, flees at the sight of Shiva's wife Parvati. From that hour, all sacred water places or tirthas become Ganga's abode and for that reason are considered holy. "In order to bring her back to Shiva's hair, she is made to enter a vessel filled with river water. The vessel is then decorated . . . and carried on the head of an elephant or . . . a temple servant" to the accompaniment of music.[78] It is brought to the lingam and poured over it. The water falling on the lingam is collected in the yoni, then carried from the shrine through a small channel that sometimes ends in a makara or cow's head.[79] Inside, the wall above the water drain may contain a figure of Ganga, which is worshipped during temple ceremonies.

Still another theme connects the waters and the temple. A long Bengali poem about the goddess Chandi describes the building of a temple. "In the course of a single night, the temple was constructed by Vishvakarman [the celestial architect]. . . . The waters of the river Bhogavati [Ganga in the netherworld] oozed up to fill the tanks." The same event is mentioned by the poet Bharatachandra of the Patala-Ganga, filling the tank or pool of a newly created temple.[80] The tradition is difficult to interpret. It may express the same relationship as the burial marker and the womb of the waters, the reciprocity of death and life. It also bears some resemblance to the Vedic hymns in which the cleft mountain releases the waters. In this respect, it may represent a ritual designed to ensure the flow of the river for agricultural purposes.

Both texts mentioned above are Bengali, and as we will see in chapter 11, the life of Bengal has been shaped by Ganga and her tributaries. In interpreting the myth, Near Eastern parallels are instructive. Hebrew tradition mentions the stone placed over the deep to hold in the waters of the deluge. Eventually the stone is housed in the sanctum of the temple. When the waters had sunk too far beneath the earth, David (according to the Babylonian Talmud) uttered the Songs of Ascent to bring them nearer the surface.[81] The waters of the deep are also encouraged by the festival of water libation, which was performed at the temple of Hierapolis with water brought from the Euphrates and at Athens in a shrine near the temple of Olympian Zeus.[82] A limestone plaque from Ur depicts a priest pouring a libation from a vase onto an altar before a temple or ziggurat.[83]

The Merging of Dualities

With the rise of the Gupta dynasty in the fifth century, the age of temple building begins. As we have seen, the Hindu temple evolves from several different antecedents reaching back to the origins of Indian civilization. The sapling, the tumulus, the stone slab, and the pillar—announcing the place of the dead—come to house the departed spirit and eventually the deathless god himself, embodied in the lingam. This mark of potency stands at the center of the temple, the center of the world mountain. Surrounding the central point is the ring of stones—the shape of mother earth, the lotus, the waters—evolved into the yoni that ultimately gives birth to the creator. The parts of the temple are conceived in apposition and embellish this single theme—the merging of dualities: male and female, fire and water, left and right, Ganga and Shiva. As the contrast to Mahadev, the river goddess appears as a door guardian;

Ganges water poured on the lingam often flows from the temple
through an opening shaped like a makara (Ganga's vehicle) or a
cow (the river begins at Gomukh, meaning the mouth of the cow).
Above the drain may be found an image of Ganga herself.

In art, the goddess is portrayed in freestanding statuary and in
several other forms. But her best-known representation is at the entrance to the temple, where her life-conferring image is enhanced
by the sculptured ornaments that normally accompany her. Let us
now examine this image.

10
The Image of Ganga in Indian Art

IN HER ROLE as guardian of the sanctum, the river goddess displays several distinguishing emblems: the makara (crocodile), the kumbha (vase of plenty), and the various coverings that shelter her. All these features amplify the meaning of Ganga. As in most aspects of religion, mythology, and art, this final statement reflects centuries of experimenting with forms and themes. We have touched upon the significance of the kumbha and the tree in their relation to Ganga. Let us begin then with a new element: the makara, that strange creature of the waters.

The Makara

In art, the makara provides a pedestal for the image of Ganga. Apart from identifying the river goddess, it also serves as a vehicle or *vahana,* an animal counterpart of the god. Older by far than any statue of Ganga, it is portrayed in art since ancient times: on a temple pot, on rare pre-Kushana coins,[1] as a sculptured waterspout, on bracelets and earrings.[2] It confronts the pilgrim time and again on stone medallions from the great stupas.

The makara is usually regarded as a Soma animal: an emblem of the waters, the plants, the entire vegetal substratum of life; and in this connection it provides the vehicle for the river goddess.[3] Yet its acknowledged prototype is the crocodile, an animal that has been an object of fear and a symbol of the unknown sea since the beginnings of Indian civilization. Throughout its long evolution, these somber values surround the makara and influence its role in literature and art.

Fearsome and Talismanic Qualities

The makara may have first appeared on the Indus Valley seal of a boat sharply upturned at both ends, with a makaralike figure at the prow.[4] The construction—probably of bound reeds—suggests it was used chiefly for river traffic along the Indus and its tributaries.[5] Of the two species of Indian crocodiles, the larger and more dangerous is found in the river deltas and along the seacoast,[6] and it seems likely that the makara figure on the boat serves as a talisman against the crocodile and the terrors of the sea. The unknown author of the *Periplus* (first century A.D.) describes the dangers awaiting the sailor: "The Sinthus [Indus] is the greatest of all rivers that flow into the Erythraean Sea. . . . Now as a sign of approach to this country to those coming from the sea, there are serpents coming forth from the depths to meet you" (*Periplus* 38).

Several Puranas mention rivers with makara as part of their names. A fresco from the Ajanta caves—depicting a naval force landing in Sri Lanka—shows makara heads on the prows of the invaders' ships. The Bengali poem *Chandi* mentions ships with prows shaped like makaras. Even today, makara handles are often found on the oars of country boats in Bengal.

By Buddha's time, Indian sailors had probably traveled great distances across the sea, reaching as far as Malaya and Indonesia.[7] But the fear of such journeys always remained. Passages from the Jatakas, the epics, and the Puranas describe the dangers of sea voyages. In one story, a makara overturns a ship and the hero reaches shore by clinging to a plank.[8] Another tells of an ill-fated traveler who is caught in a storm: his ship is sunk and his companions are devoured by sea monsters.[9] A distaste for the ocean was compounded by the growing religious belief that foreign travel was polluting to the Hindu. More and more maritime trade fell to foreign merchants, and as knowledge of the sea diminished, people's fancies increased. In a story reminiscent of the Old Testament, we read of a minister who is swallowed by a whale after his boat overturns but eventually escapes by cutting through the creature's belly.[10] The eleventh-century Muslim traveler Alberuni reports the following information, presumably gleaned from a native:

> In the rivers of South India, there is an animal called by various names. . . . It is thin, but very long. People say it spies and lies in wait for those who enter the water and stand in it, whether men or animals, and at once attacks them. . . . A man who had seen the animal told me that it has the head of a dog and a tail to which there are attached many long tentacles.[11]

The makara's fearsome nature is emphasized in literature, where its name is used for a battle formation.[12] The makara is also a dark star that colors people's destinies. We read of the Nidhis (demigods who influence human propensities): "The Nidhi who is composed of darkness [ignorance, *tamasa*] is named Makara. And a man that he looks upon is indeed born characterized chiefly by ignorance. . . . He gathers together arrows, swords, spears and bows . . . and he finds pleasure in buying and selling weapons and in nothing else."[13] In a statue from Mathura, the Kushan emperor Kanishka is shown holding a war club decorated with a makara (ca. first century A.D.).[14]

We hear of Ganges crocodiles and the terrifying practice associated with them. The Roman historian Aelian (second century A.D.) reports that the Ganges

> breeds also two kinds of crocodiles, and of these one is quite harmless, while the other devours all sorts of flesh and is unsparingly cruel. They have an execrescence on their snout like that of the horned serpent. The natives employ their services in inflicting the supreme penalty on malefactors, for they throw to them those who have been found guilty of the most heinous offences, and so they do not require the services on an executioner.[15]

Evidently the custom persisted. Abul Fazl, the sixteenth-century Muslim chronicler of the Emperor Akbar, records a sacrifice in which a human was offered to crocodiles at the confluence of the Ganga and Yamuna. Portuguese travelers also report a trial by makara "in the River that runs from Cochin to Cranganor, where is the Pagod of the crocodile. The Bramenes, by their sorceries bring one of them [crocodiles] to the shore, the person accused leaps upon his back; if he is carried over safe, they account him innocent, if devoured guilty."[16]

Fear of the crocodile reaches its height in the Bengal delta, with its swamps and endless streams. The next chapter, on Ganga in Bengal, describes a firsthand report of the makara's ferocity and of rituals designed to appease it.

Symbol of the Unknown

As a symbol of the unknown, the makara provides the vehicle (vahana) for Varuna, lord of the waters and guardian of the western quarter, the region of Yama, darkness and death.[17] We find certain equivalencies between the god and his vehicle: Varuna as lord of the waters and darkness, the makara as creature of the sea and the unknown. Given these correspondences, their coalescence is but natural, considering that the vahana provides an animal counterpart of the god it serves.[18]

It is as symbol of the unknown that the makara may have first appeared on gateways (toranas) (Figure 34) and beneath the architraves of doorways, especially since the sanctum of the temple—notably of Shiva temples—evolves from associations with the dead. The earliest Ganga image atop the door frame occurs in Cave VI at Udayagiri, Central India (about A.D. 400); there two goddesses, still undifferentiated, balance on makaras. In the Hindu zodiac, the makara signifies Capricorn, Door of the Gods.[19] In art the makara often appears with a small human figure *(gana)* at its mouth (Figures 35 and 36), signifying the abiding tendency toward involution *(pralaya, nivritti)*. The motif is not uniquely Indian. Initiation to the underworld is often symbolized by a consuming monster.[20]

The subject of a Chausa bronze sculpture now in the Patna Museum is the Chakra, above all a symbol of time in its endless round of emanation and return. The makaras and human figures beneath serve the philosophical function of vahanas: reflecting the essence of the god, or here the main figure, the Chakra. In this case, the human figure indicates growth and development, the makara those forces inhibiting it (Figure 36).

Figure 34. Makara Torana. Bharhut. Courtesy of *Revue des Arts Asiatiques.*

In diverse cultures, the crocodile or dragon is often depicted about to consume people, especially children. Eliade notes that in certain African tribal initiation ceremonies, a boy may be sequested in a cabin representing the maw of a water monster or crocodile.[21] In emerging from its mouth, the boy is freed from the "uroboric" pull toward envelopment and reabsorption. Thereafter he may assume his place in the tribe.[22] An essential feature of the young boy or child motif is its futurity. The child represents development *(udbhava).* Mythically, the various fates that may befall the child, signify—in Jung's words—the powerlessness and helplessness of the life-urge; more especially the threat to one's inmost self from dragons.[23]

This life-threatening quality has characterized the dragon from the time of the *Rig Veda,* where Indra slays Vritra and sets the rivers free. In the Vedas, the dragon (Vritra, Ahi) dwells exclusively in the atmosphere and on the mountain tops. Only one hymn refers to the dragon in the depths of the sea. As the Vedic settlers enter the Ganges Valley, the sky dragon gradually fades; and in one ritual, a priest offers "to the offspring of the waters a fish; the crocodile, the dolphin . . . are for the ocean."[24]

Figure 35. Ganga, Makara, and Gana. Besnagar. A.D. 500. Courtesy of the Museum of Fine Arts, Boston; Charles Amos Cummings Bequest 26.26.

The makara retains Vritra's habit of holding back the waters, an act restraining life in its increase. This value is indicated by the makara's threat to the child. Given the negative cast of Vritra in the *Rig Veda,* and the inhibiting role of the dragon in Near Eastern mythology, it is not surprising that the makara should have a similar connotation.

Both the makara and the small human figure, or gana, emerging from its mouth occur frequently as a pedestal vahana of the goddess

Figure 36. Chakra, Makara, and Child. Patna Museum. Courtesy of The Archaeological Survey of India.

Ganga. Traditionally, the makara has been thought to embody the fructifying powers of the river. This seems likely when the animal in its vegetal form is found without the child. But judging from our inquiry, the appearance of the gana may alter that meaning radically. Conjointly with the makara, the gana's life-affirming role may be seen to emphasize the dual nature of the river goddess herself. For while Ganga is portrayed in benevolent terms throughout Indian literature, the river has often caused great hardship, destroying countless settlements large and small along its banks, and this aspect could not be overlooked. A friend from Patna, for example, relates that his family farm ninety miles from the city had been washed away six times in the previous forty years.[25]

The Makara's Dual Nature

As a creature of the waters, the makara is also an affirmative symbol, producing life in its endless convolutions, as witnessed by its great floral tail and vines growing from its mouth (Figures 37 and

Figure 37. Ganga and Makara. Ellora XXI. Photo Darian.

38).[26] Though this value is primary in its role as Ganga's vahana, the darker meaning remains. The ambivalence is inescapable, since in the Indian tradition the waters create and dissolve all of life.[27] This dual meaning is reflected in the *Mahabharata* story of a crocodile that is dragged from the water and transformed into a beautiful girl decked with ornaments.[28] We find it in the modern worship of the Gujarati crocodile god Mogra (makara) Dev. "The mouth [of the wooden crocodile] should always point to the sunrise," explains a villager. "If it has turned and points to the north or the sunset-side, then . . . something bad is going to happen."[29] Thus, a solar disk surrounds the Egyptian crocodile-headed god Sebek.[30] Jung's story of the *quaestio crocodilina* illustrates the widespread ambivalence associated with the makara,[31] as does the Tarasque, the dragon of Tarascon (Provençe), that both devoured and protected the flocks.[32] Likewise, Orphic cosmology pictures a dragon arising from the waters of creation, and growing from the head of a lion.[33]

In Indian art, the union of lion and makara is illustrated by a tree goddess from Nagarjunakonda (third or fourth century A.D.), standing on a composite figure that is half-makara, half-lion (the solar animal par excellence) (Figure 39).[34] Eventually, the fierce or Agni quality is assimilated to the *Kirttimukha,* literally the "face of glory," while the gentle traits are absorbed by the makara. But the distinction is never final, and in the protean world of Indian art, a correspondence once established allows different forms to assume each other's qualities at will. This, of course, happens with the Kirttimukha, which often acquires a vegetal shape.[35] In the Hindu art of Indonesia, the joint figure is known as the Kala-makara; the lion—with its voracious nature—representing the sun, that consumes all things, in its role as an instrument of time. In Indian thought, Kala—the word for time—becomes a synonym for death and thus a designation of Yama.[36]

From historic times, the makara is first portrayed in Indian art on the portal of the Lomas Rishi cave (around 350 B.C.) in the Barabar hills just south of Patna. Its form is a truncated crocodile. Thereafter it is widely adopted. At Bharhut and on a Jain stupa at Mathura, it is used as a base for female figures, thus creating a rudi-

Figure 38. Ganga and Makara. Baroda Museum. Courtesy of the Museum and Picture Gallery, Baroda.

Figure 39. Tree Goddess with Makara and Lion. Nagarjunaikonda Museum. Courtesy of O. Viennot.

mentary iconography for the later Ganga image. It is carried forward on the stupas of Sanchi and Amaravati, where it supports a river goddess on both sides of the door. After this, it becomes the common property of Indian art and undergoes a broad range of animal and vegetal permutations in the course of its existence.

The first unmistakable association of Ganga with the makara is at the Varaha Cave V at Udayagiri (around A.D. 400) (Figures 40 and

41), where a large cutting in the rock offers the central image of Vishnu in his incarnation as a giant boar, and on either side, at right angles to the huge figure, two sculpted panels. Both depict Ganga and Yamuna standing on their vahanas—the makara and the *kurma* or tortoise. Around them swirl the two rivers, converging at Prayag and then flowing to the ocean, where they are received by a deity with a vessel—possibly Varuna or perhaps Sagara, whose sons were redeemed by the river released from the vessel of Brahma.

The Kumbha

After the makara, Ganga's most distinctive sculptural feature is the full vase, first appearing with the river goddess on the same Varaha cave frieze from Udayagiri. Although not common in the early stages of the Ganga image, the full vase appears more and more frequently as the Ganga theme reaches maturity. It becomes obligatory for the goddess in her role as door guardian—for example, at the Dasavatara temple, Deogarh (seventh century) (Figure 42), the Trimurti temple, Badoli (Chittor) (Figure 43), and at Kharod, Bilaspur (ninth or tenth century), all in Central India.[37]

The kumbha expresses several values, mostly related to the generative and purifying power of water. The full vessel, as an object of worship even today, represents the deity and may be understood as an expression of the formless Brahman. We have mentioned the vast-bodied yaksha inhabiting the golden vessel in the city of Brahman.[38] Similarly, the Upanishad states: "The face of god is hidden in a golden vessel."[39]

More significantly, the vase and water serve as both symbol and vehicle of initiation, promoting strength, youth, puissance, and immortality. The regenerative property of water is illustrated by the story of the Rishi Chyavana, who is restored to youth after his wife takes him to bathe in a pool.[40] Ganga water in golden jars is provided for Rama's consecration at Ayodhya.[41] Of all sacred water, Ganga is the holiest. "As Amrita to the gods," says the *Mahabharata*, "even so is Ganga water to human beings."[42] One of the earliest descriptions of a religious bath is found in the *Matsya Purana* and is common to people of all castes. If possible, one should bathe with water drawn in a vessel from a well or stream. He should invoke

Figure 40. Ganga and Yamuna on Their Vahanas. Udayagiri. Fifth Century. Courtesy of the American Institute of Indian Studies.

Ganga to be present there. Then, uttering the names of the great sages, he would be encompassed by Ganga flowing in the three worlds.[43]

But the most important value of the kumbha is as woman, as womb, as birth. We may recall the birth of Sagara's sixty thousand sons from a gourd. Similarly, the epic warrior Drona is born from a pot.[44] Both Ganga and Sarasvati are born from Brahma's water jug.

Figure 41. Ganga and Yamuna on Their Vahanas. Udayagiri. Courtesy of the American Institute of Indian Studies.

The equation is stated specifically at the ceremony performed in the sacrificial shed prior to building a temple. The sacrificer "shall carefully excavate a hole in the center . . . and place the pitcher in the midst thereof, the hole with the pitcher in it, standing as it were, for the impregnated womb. . . . Worship the earth-goddess in a lotus-shaped copper receptacle."[45]

The goddess and the vase have strong Near Eastern antecedents.

Figure 42. Ganga with Vase and Chatra. Deogarh. Seventh Century. Courtesy of O. Viennot.

By itself, the vase with flowing water appears on the well-known Telloh bas-relief from the twenty-first century B.C. It is found, together with the goddess, on a fragment (also twenty-first century B.C.) now in the Istanbul Museum.[46] Another piece from Mari (eighteenth century B.C.), now in the Aleppo Museum, shows a vase held by a female figure—a goddess of the waters, to judge by the fish and wavy lines inscribed on her skirt.[47] An Egyptian bronze

Figure 43. Ganga with Vase and Lotus Chatra. Badoli. Courtesy of O. Viennot.

vessel from the sixth or seventh century B.C. combines the three themes of woman, tree, and vase (Figure 20). It may be the goddess Nut, pouring water from her sycamore. In hieroglyphics, the vase—part of Nut's signature—is also the symbol for woman and womb.[48] In the Near East, the flowing vase developed into a vessel of vegetation, which is how we sometimes find it with Ganga, for example at Bajaura and Badoli (Figure 43).

Evolution of the Covering

In her earliest role as door guardian, Ganga appears beneath a tree. The long association extends from the tree spirit of the Indus civilization, through the Vedic texts that help to bridge the gulf of archaeological evidence, to the flowering of stupa art under the Shunga dynasty. From there the motif remains a permanent feature of Indian art. One of the caves at Udayagiri provides the first example of Ganga as door guardian, accompanied by the tree and the vehicle. Since both female figures stand on a makara, they are not yet clearly distinguished from the generalized form of river goddesses. The separation seems imminent, however, to judge from the makara and tortoise vehicles on the nearby Varaha cave (Figures 40 and 41).

A new stage in Ganga's iconography appears in the seventh-century Dasavatara temple at Deogarh (Figure 42). Above the door-jambs, the river goddesses stand on their respective vehicles, but in the space of one or two centuries the tree covering has evolved into a chatra or umbrella. We may speculate on this evolution. The change may simply reflect Ganga's status as a deity—though presumably this would have occurred before the seventh century— or it may have other significance. Traditionally, the white umbrella is a symbol of kingly power in Buddhist and Hindu art. The chatra makes its appearance with Ganga from the seventh century, when the Gupta Empire had disintegrated and Harsha was struggling to recreate central dominion. Ganga represented such a dominion. And the white umbrella, joined to an established symbol of imperial unity would not have been an unwarranted gesture.

The temple at Kharod, Bilaspur (ninth or tenth century), also shows the goddesses under parasols, each carrying a water vessel. But here the chatra begins to assume a lotuslike quality. The transformation is complete in the Trimurti temple at Badoli (Figure 43), where no trace of the parasol remains. The reason for such a change is impossible to determine. It is tempting to compare the symbolic paradigm of the lotus and the parasol against the backdrop of events. While the chatra has strong religious overtones in early Buddhism, it later signifies political dominion, an emblem conferred at the coronation of a king. The lotus, by contrast, is always the same: in Hindu thought it remains the spiritual ground of nonbeing. It dismisses all temporal forms—wealth and kingdoms, all shapes differentiated from the primal Brahman. It is a symbol of involution, of what is potential but not yet manifest. Not by chance, perhaps, in the ninth and tenth centuries northern India sees the crumbling of empire, the rise of small feudal hegemonies, and, soon after, the nightmare of foreign invasion. It is a time for turning away from the things of this world, a time for withdrawal. Such comparisons are highly speculative and cannot be pushed too far. Nonetheless, a relationship exists—often hidden—between people's experience and the symbolic forms they choose.

A final shape of Ganga's lotus-chatra appears on the Shiva temple at Pali, near Sagar in Central India (tenth or eleventh century). Here the covering unfolds in great spirals recalling vines and nagas; the entire piece is surmounted by small human figures (Figure 44). The image of threads and spirals is mentioned as early as the *Rig Veda*[49] and represents, according to Coomaraswamy,[50] the prolongation of life: the idea that the end of any journey is death and that the endless convolution of the spiral serves to extend the journey.

Throughout the Middle Ages—even after the Muslim conquest—the two goddesses are carved on temple doorways, but now only in remote, inaccessible places. From the twelfth century, the invaders devastated thousands of temples and made new Hindu building efforts impossible in the Doab and in the Ganges Valley. Moreover, after the death of Harsha in 647, the center of political power shifted toward the periphery, and the image of Ganga as a symbol of imperial unity held little attraction for distant rulers. At times she rekindles ancient dreams of empire: to commemorate his advance up the Ganges, the southern king Rajendra Chola I built a capital named Gangaikonda, south of Madras (around A.D. 1025). Here he constructed an irrigation tank filled with water from the river. According to legend, Ganges water was the only tribute he exacted from conquered kings. Ganga and Yamuna continue to appear as guardians on later temples, but they are never again to know the sculptural devotion experienced during the fifth to eighth centuries.

Figure 44. Ganga with Naga Chatra. Pali, Sagar, Central India. Courtesy of O. Viennot.

Figure 45. Ganga. Bengal. Twelfth Century. Courtesy of the Varendra Research Museum, Rajshahi, Bangladesh.

Ganga in Crafts and Sculpture

Aside from her appearance on temple doorways, Ganga figures as a motif in minor crafts and isolated pieces of sculpture, especially in the Gupta period: from Jaipur come several Gupta drinking vessels with handles fashioned in the shape of the goddess.[51] She is found on several Gupta coins.[52] In Bengal, unbaked clay images of Ganga are still thrown in the river after ceremonies, especially by peasants, whose crops are bound to the plenitude of the stream. The gift of Ganga is reflected in a twelfth-century sculpture from the Varendra Research Museum in Rajshahi (Figure 45). As a main source of transportation and of water to nourish the fields, the Ganges is the bearer of life and wealth to the people of Bengal. Its bounty is reflected in the statue: by the jeweled tiara, by the necklace falling over the ample breasts, by the rich ornament of the girdle, by the very size itself—five feet seven inches.[53]

More than elsewhere, the fortunes of Bengal are determined by the river. There the Ganges works its greatest power for good and ill. It is only natural that Ganga figures prominently in the literature and religion of the delta.

11
The Ganges in Bengal

BENGAL IS LITERALLY A CHILD OF THE GANGES. At one time, the delta lay beneath the water and the river touched the sea in one unbroken stream in the region of Gaur.[1] Gradually the silt, carried down from the Himalayas and along the Ganges Valley, began building up the land, dividing the river again and again. Through the ages the silt continued, and slowly the delta began to firm, filling out the 24-Parganas (south of Calcutta), Hulna, and the Sundarbans, all a gift of the river. From that time until today, the fate of the delta has been tied to Ganga and its intersecting streams. Cities and entire regions have come and gone in response to the changing course of the river, to its giving and withholding silt. The total water supply of the 24-Parganas, for example, is drawn from the Ganges and its distributaries.[2] Further south, in the Sundarbans, the remains of temples, buildings, and settlements all attest to the fluctuations of the rivers and the drying up of fresh water.[3]

The Life of the River

The Bhagirathi, the older of the two main channels, contains the great traditions and the relics of ancient cities. To Hindus there is little sacred about the Padma. The most fertile lands once lay along the Bhagirathi, from the area of Murshidabad southward. Originally the most active channel, it brought down the greatest quantity of silt and the most water for irrigation. It enriched the land and created a prosperous agriculture. At this time, the eastern parts of the delta were a wilderness of swamps and jungle. Gradually but ineluctably, the more vigorous flow of the river shifted southeastward, and along with it the rich silt. The new area began to flourish, leaving behind it decaying regions subject to famine and disease. One writer describes the process vividly: "No doubt it takes some time for the deterioration of the rivers to exercise their full effects. After the deterioration of the river system is completed, the anopheles takes possession of the land and finds in the . . . low-lying pools and depressions . . . and even in the hoof-marks of cattle, an ideal breeding place."[4]

Bengal reveals the Ganges at its most contradictory. The silt, necessary for healthy agriculture, also chokes the tidal rivers, drawing seawater further up the delta and reducing irrigation. It is the silt that makes the rivers more and more unfit for navigation.[5] At the same time, a rapid current often overflows its banks, leading to disastrous floods. The earliest inscription of Bengal, from Mahasthan (third century B.C.), remarks on the danger of floods and the need to store grain against such emergencies.[6] Almost two thousand years later, the Englishman Ralph Fitch, while traveling through the same region, observes in his notebook:

> [The city of] Tanda standeth from the River Ganges a league, because in times past, the River flowing over the bankes in time of raine, did drowne the Countrie and many Villages, and so they doe remaine. And the old way which the River Ganges was wont to runne, remaineth drie, which is the occasion that the Citie doeth stand so farre from the water.[7]

The river's fluctuations remain unpredictable over any short length of the delta. The history of Rajmahal illustrates Ganga's power over the people of the littoral. In medieval times, the Muslim rulers moved their capital to Rajmahal. In the seventeenth century it was filled with people and every kind of merchandise. Its port was jammed with vessels.[8] Toward the end of the century, the river shifted its course three miles eastward, whereupon the government and merchants abandoned it for Dacca, almost two hundred miles away.[9] During the next century, the Ganges resumed its earlier course, and Rajmahal sprang to life once more. Again, in 1863, the channel shifted further east, and the city became "a mere aggregate of huts surrounded by ruins."[10] In 1880, the river returned to its old bed and the city regained its prosperity.

Throughout the nineteenth century, British efforts to maintain a steamer channel from Calcutta north beyond Rajmahal met with repeated failure. We read in a surveyor's report of 1835:

> The extraordinary deviations annually occurring in the course of the Ganges, affecting as they did all the streams that flowed from it, rendered it impossible to lay down any fixed rule of guidance or plan of operations by which the navigation of Nadiya rivers could be permanently maintained.[11]

H. T. Colebrook, writing in 1803, observed incredible changes. He states that "there are few places where a town, or village, can be established in the Ganges with any certainty of long retaining the advantage of such a situation."[12] Colebrook reports that:

> In one part of the channel . . . where I expected to have met with the first shallows, I found from twenty to sixty feet in the very place where there had been a ford but two years before.[13]

In less than two years:

> A considerable portion of the main channel, which . . . had contained nearly the whole stream of the Ganges, was at the time I saw it so completely filled with sands that I hardly knew myself to be in the same part of the river. The sands, in some parts, rose several feet above the level of the stream; and the people had already begun to cultivate . . . rice, in the very spot where the deepest water had formerly been.[14]

Some of the islands were almost ten miles long and two or three miles across. L. S. O'Malley, who served as a district officer at the turn of the century, reports that during the rainy season an acre of land might be swept away in half an hour. As if to mock its image as an eternal river, some of the islands in the Ganges "become inhabited, cleared, and cultivated; the population increases, large villages start up; the land revenue is collected for ten or twelve years; and then the whole fabric will disappear within one rainy season."[15]

In the countryside, life is governed by the monsoon and its effects on the rivers. Plowing begins with the first rains. Rice fields are sown and their mud walls strengthened. Then comes the seemingly endless task of transplanting each stalk one by one—in one writer's words, "the result of bare backs bent to the task which starts at dawn and continues till dark, day after day, in mud and water until the monsoon ends."[16] During this time, and at certain other periods of the year, rivers replace roads as the chief means of transportation. To facilitate the interchange between village and village, or city and country, markets spring up along the waterways, endure for a short time, and disband.

This total dependence on the Ganges and its endless tributaries is reflected in the folk literature and religious ritual of Bengal. It is written in the names of the great cities that were called into being by the river, knew their hour of glory, and departed. The first and perhaps greatest was the fabled port of Tamralipti.

Tamralipti

Now an insignificant town on the Rupnarayan tributary of the Hughli, Tamralipti was once the chief trade emporium of the wide area between China and Alexandria. Ships touched the port from Ceylon, Southeast Asia, western India, and the Near East. By gradually displacing the port functions of Champa and Pataliputra, it also became the center of goods shipped from northern India. By the third century B.C., it was probably connected by road with the major cities of the north.

Its origins are obscure. Though several historians date it to the seventh century B.C., we find little but Neolithic remains below the level of Mauryan settlement. Several times the *Mahabharata* mentions the soldiers of Tamralipti, who fought bravely in the great war.[17] While the region was not "Hinduized" until later, the location was held sacred by virtue of its position on the Ganges and its proximity to Sagar Island, the holy site near the place where Ganga joins the sea.[18] Archaeologically, we find samples of northern black polish ware as well as gray ware similar to Hastinapura III (early sixth to early third centuries B.C.).[19] Two Egyptian vases found in a 1940 excavation may indicate early contact with the Near East, although the vase type had long been in use from about 2000 B.C. up to the Graeco-Roman period (ca. 200 B.C. to A.D. 200).[20]

The earliest detailed reference to Tamralipti appears in the Buddhist literature. One text tells the story of the mutual embassies exchanged between Ashoka and the king of Ceylon. We read of shells, pearls, and precious jewels sent by the Sinhalese king. Ashoka in return dispatched many treasures, including a diadem, a sword, rare garments, and water from the Ganges. Moreover, a cutting from the great Bodhi tree was sent by ship from a point near Gaya and then from Tamralipti to Ceylon. Ashoka, we are told, traveled overland to the port.[21]

With the quickening tempo of the Mauryan Empire, Tamralipti rose to international fame as the chief port of the entire basin, its ships, even before the Christian era, reaching Ceylon and further Asia.[22] Trade with China began as early as the second century B.C. and increased by the end of the century.[23] The *Periplus* and the *Milinda-panha* attest to the vigorous maritime activity in Bengal in the first century A.D. Commerce between China, Southeast Asia, and Bengal continued in the third century, as indicated by Chinese references.[24]

From the start of the fifth century to the end of the seventh, a succession of Chinese pilgrims provide a further glimpse of Tamralipti as the chief international port of call; Fa-hien and I-tsing, among the most illustrious, both sail from there on their homeward journey. An incident in *The Ten Princes*, a collection of stories by Dandin, reveals the harbor as a center of great activity in the late sixth century. We read of Mitragupta, who falls in love with a princess of Tamralipti. Secretly he is seized by the girl's brother and thrown in the bay to drown. In Mitragupta's words: "At daybreak I spied a kind of boat, manned by Greeks. They pulled me in. . . ." Soon after, "a galley, attended by numerous smaller craft, bore down on us. . . . The swift boats were about us in a moment."[25]

But gradually an expanding delta interposed itself more and more between Tamralipti and the sea. Some time after the eighth century, the Rupnarayan began silting up, due perhaps to the loss of an estuary from the Damodar River, which had helped sustain a forceful current. By the tenth century, the city's channel to the sea had become blocked, and the great port, famous for a thousand years throughout the ancient world, disappeared from mariners' charts and from the lips of men. To be sure, the name lingered on in story; the *Kathasaritsagara* (A.D. 1070) often mentions the wealthy merchants of Tamralipti. The city, in fact, continued as a commercial center for another half millennium, but its chief function was taken over by Satgaon, further up the Hughli. Today its modern counterpart, Tamluk, lies fifty miles from the sea.

In like manner, all the great riparian cities of Bengal have known the blight and benediction of the river. As we saw in chapters 3 and 4, the chief urban sites of the Indus and early Ganges civilizations lay along rivers for reasons of sanitation, transport, and travel. These considerations weighed especially heavy in the delta, where the rivers assume Venetian proportions for commerce and travel. The greatest of these cities was Gaur, the Muslim capital of Bengal from the early thirteenth century. The history of Gaur is a paradigm of man's relation to the river throughout the delta.

Gaur

With the invasion of Muhammad-i-Bakhtiyar Khalji in 1202, Bengal came under Muslim rule. The new kings and viceroys adopted the capital of the former rulers at Gaur (Lakhnauti). Strategically, the site lay above the bifurcation of Ganga into its two main tributaries, the Bhagirathi and the Padma or Meghna, thus allowing for water communication with all parts of the country. It was this position that probably determined its choice as a capital. The city itself abutted the Ganges, and a causeway extended eastward to the Mahananda River, which flowed into the Padma.

In its heyday, Gaur served as a busy port situated at the junction of the Padma, the Bhagirathi, and the Ganges proper. Among its ruins can still be seen oblong loading platforms surrounded by canals. Through connected channels, small boats transported merchandise to the center of the city.[26] Old Bengali manuscripts mention several Arab merchants who settled in Gaur and who spoke highly of its seaborne trade.[27] In Bengal, the chief passage to the city was along the Meghna from Chittagong, which traded with China and the Arab ports of Baghdad and Basra.[28] This was the route probably taken by the great traveler Ibn Batuta, who visited Bengal in 1345, and by the Chinese emissary Ma-huan in 1409. Ibn Batuta comments on the large number of boats used by the inhabitants in their battles against Lakhnauti (Gaur).[29] Ma-huan was impressed by the number of ships that the Bengalis built to carry on foreign commerce.[30]

Gaur remained the Muslim capital of Bengal intermittently between 1202 and 1575. During this period it was settled and abandoned several times, as the unstable bed of the Ganges often shifted westward, depriving the inhabitants of proper sanitation and laying the area open to swamp and fever. The city reached its height under Hussain Shah, who ruled from 1498 to 1520. During this time it was visited by several Europeans, notably the Venetian Ludovico di Varthema (between 1506 and 1508), who describes how from the city of Benghella (Gaur) "fifty ships are laden every year . . . with cotton and silk stuffs."[31] Portuguese merchants, visiting the city some time before 1540, describe it as extending three leagues along the Ganges, well fortified, and with a population of 1,200,000 families. The streets, though broad and straight, "are so thronged with the concourse of traffic and people . . . that they cannot force their way past one another."[32] In 1575, the Ganges deserted its banks once more, shifting westward. The abandoned riverbed soon turned to marsh and a breeding ground for malaria. This change, combined with the undisposed refuse, led to a pestilence that devastated the city. The following report appears in Hunter's *Annals of Rural Bengal:*

> Thousands died daily. . . . The living, wearied with burying the dead, threw their bodies into the river. This created a stench which only increased the disease. . . . The city was at once depopulated, and from that day to this it has been abandoned. At the time of its destruction it had existed for 2,000 years. It was the most magnificent city in India, of immense extent, and filled with noble buildings. It was the capital of a hundred kings, the seat of wealth and luxury. In one year, it was humbled to the dust, and now it is the abode only of tigers and monkeys.[33]

The Portuguese friar Sebastian Manrique, attached to the Bengal mission from 1629 to 1637, describes the ruins he came upon during a boat trip from Dacca up the Padma. Manrique's journal speaks of Gaur as "once the most famous of all cities in the Gangetic Empire." In his time, the fortifications lay a half mile from the river. "On reaching the great wall," he relates, "we passed through a fine, handsome, arched gateway of hewn stone, cut into rude floral decorations and leaves, supported by large, massive pillars."[34] From this point the friar was conducted through the ruins by a Moghul officer commanding a local troop of soldiers. "The Mirza [chief officer] joined me at once," he continues, "and taking me by the hand, showed me the great wall, which embraced . . . two of our leagues. These walls were 70 feet high, joined to 25 feet of width. This mighty edifice was constructed wholly of strong bricks, a fact which accounted for its being still intact, save for a turret here and there."[35]

Today the remains of the city extend eleven miles along the riverbank, its giant causeways and haunted palaces larger than life itself. At night kokila birds call among the ruins. In the cold season, the cotton trees run riot with crimson flowers and the whole scene is a reminder of the river's power—to give and take away.

A Hell Filled with Good Things

Through the centuries, the fortunes of Bengal have varied with the flow of its rivers, which dominate the ecological balance of the region. In the medieval period, foreign travelers were continually impressed by the abundance of food and manufactured goods, at the same time warning of the dangerous climate. Ibn Batuta in 1345 exclaims: "I have seen no region of the earth in which provisions are so plentiful."[36] At the same time, "the climate is muggy and the people from Khorasan [Persian officers and settlers] call it *Duzakhast bur ni' amat,* which is as much as to say, 'A hell filled with good things'!" To Varthema, 150 years later, the country was richer "in grain, flesh of every kind, in great quantities of sugar . . . ginger, cotton, than any other country of the world." In 1585, the Dutch merchantman Van Linschoten found Bengal the greatest storehouse of foodstuffs in all the east, remarking that ships came from considerable distances to purchase rice.[37] In his journey on the Padma arm of the Ganges, Manrique noticed "villages and country towns all along its fertile banks; every bit of land along the river . . . was cultivated, bearing fruit trees, wheat, and rice, and vegetables."[38] The image is confirmed in 1660 by the French traveler Francois Bernier, who notes that Bengal exports sugar as far as Arabia.[39] He further comments on the elaborate system of canals, from Rajmahal to the sea, used for transporting merchandise.[40]

Nonetheless, Bengal retained a certain evil reputation. Higher officers of the Moghul court were opposed to serving in the province, "as they fancied it not only fatal to human life but an actual haunt of demons."[41] The story did not end with Gaur. Other cities on the river were to know a similar fate. South of Murshidabad, on the Bhagirathi, lay Cossimbazar with a population of 100,000. The town was three miles long, two miles wide, and built largely of brick. It was said that one could do a circle of it by jumping from one rooftop to another.[42] During the eighteenth century, Cossimbazar flourished as a center for silk and cotton manufacturing, exporting goods to different parts of Asia. In the early 1700s, its climate was salubrious and the town was practically considered a health resort. In 1814, the Bhagirathi channel shifted three miles to the west, leaving behind swamp and stagnant water. Fever broke out and in a few years three-quarters of the population had died. Following the epidemic, the site was abandoned and before long reverted to jungle.

Satgaon

Some time after the tenth century, Tamralipti's economic role was taken over by Satgaon (Saptagrama). Though the city to dates Puranic times, it rose to prominence as India's greatest oceangoing port of the Middle Ages. At Triveni the river branches into three streams, the Bhagirathi, the Yamuna, and the Sarasvati, all navigable by large ships at one time or another. Satgaon lay on the Sarasvati, the main current of the Ganges until the middle of the sixteenth century.[43] Judging from Bengali literature, Satgaon was frequented by merchants from Ceylon and all parts of India. But the clearest reports are gained from European travelers.

The Venetian Cesare Federici, visiting the city in 1578, described it as the center where merchants gather for trade. He records a great patter of activity along the river during his four-month stay: "Whereas many merchants did buy or frait boates for their benefites, and with these barkes they goe up and downe the river of Ganges to faires, buying their commodities with a great advantage, because that every day in the week they have a faire, now in one place, and now in another."[44] But already in the mid-sixteenth century, the main western channel of the Ganges had begun to flow into the Bhagirathi, and silt accumulating in the Sarasvati forced larger ships to anchor at a point several miles below the city. Those that made the full trip to Satgaon had to row eighteen hours and berth until full tide.[45] Ralph Fitch in 1585 describes Satgaon as "a faire citie for a citie of the Moores, and very plentiful of all things."[46] But by 1600 the Sarasvati could not sustain an adequate current and Satgaon was abandoned.[47] Its place was taken by the town of Hughli, the new Portuguese settlement on the Bhagirathi which served as the chief port of Bengal up to the founding of Calcutta.

From earliest times, the Bhagirathi arm had provided the main channel for the Ganges through the delta. By the end of the fifteenth century, the major flow had been captured by the Padma with devastating results.[48] It was this change that contributed to the destruction of the Sarasvati and numerous other tributaries along the Bhagirathi. The ancient river has been slowly silting up ever since. Its reduced current further increases shoaling at the mouth of its larger feeder streams, such as the Damodar and Rupnarayan. English logs of the seventeenth century record chilling moments when their ships passed the dangerous bars near the river's mouth. The most treacherous of these is the James and Mary Sands, a constantly shifting silt deposit formed by the discharge of the Damodar and Rupnarayan. The name is taken from the *Royal James and Mary,* a ship sunk on this spot in 1694. Thomas Bowrey, who spent ten years as a merchantman in the Indies, leaves us the following reminiscence of his bout with these hazardous sands:

> Anno Domini 1676, in the Month of September, I was comeinge down the Hughly in a ship called the Santa Crux . . . and driveinge downe at a most Swift and violent rate, being timerous of driveing too farre down, upon the Shoals of the River Tamlook. . . . I lett

dropp our best bore anchor, veered forty fathoms of Cable out . . . and let fall our Sheet anchor. . . . It happened at that time for the Space of half an houre to be Slack water, but then the fresh came down . . . and hurried us away into a most impetuous Eddy, where, in a moment, our Ship turned soe often and quick withall that not one of us cold Stand to doe any thing. One cable broke, and the Other Swum like to a piece of wood. In the midst of this Extremity, when I thought our Ship wolde oversett with each Sally She took, it pleased God a very fresh gale Sprange Up, filling our Sailes . . . and runne her out of that Eddy.[49]

In 1823, the British inaugurated a steamer service which eventually ran from Calcutta to Allahabad. With the help of constant dredging, the Bhagirathi channel was maintained until the early twentieth century. Since then, however, the slowed current has created shallows all along the river, reducing navigation to a minimum in all but the rainy season. Even the country boats, requiring a draft of 2½ or 3 feet, often have difficulty between November and June. The process continues despite modern efforts to reverse it, and many fear that one day the harbor at Calcutta will become too shallow to receive large merchant vessels. At that time, its existence as a port will come to an end, and it will be replaced by a new city somewhere along a healthier part of the river.

The River of Life

In Bengal, the Ganges has bequeathed her greatest legacy for good and evil. As the magic of place is by some alchemy transmuted into culture, so the river invests the literature and religion of the delta.

Ganga in Poetry and Song

From earliest times, Bengal has evolved a unique civilization. With its ancient stock enriched by Mongolian people from Burma and the Himalayas, as well as Aryans and other settlers from the west, and stimulated by maritime contact with other cultures, it has often overflowed the bounds of caste and other formal limitations of Hindu society. It has created a deep fusion of Hindu, Buddhist, Muslim, and indigenous folk elements.

The earliest glimpse of this fusion appears among the Sid-dhacharyas, medieval writers of mystic songs who were believed to have attained great spiritual powers through yoga. Similarly the Buddhist Sahajiya sect and their modern reflection the Bauls. Like the Siddhacharyas, the Bauls regard the human body as a micro-cosm of the universe. They have little use for ritual but seek to realize god by knowing *maner manush,* the man of the heart. So the medieval poet Saraha exclaims:

> When the mind goes to rest,
> The bonds of the body are destroyed,
> And when the flavor of the Innate pours forth,
> There is neither outcaste nor brahmin.

> Here is the sacred Jumna and here the River Ganges,
> Here are Prayaga and Benares, here are Sun and Moon.
> Here I have visited in my wanderings shrines
>   and such places of pilgrimage,
> For I have not seen another shrine
>   blissful like my own body.[50]

Among the poets of Bengal it is natural that boats and rivers should pervade the imagery of religious understanding. In their desire to blur the distinction between opposites, the Sahajiyas often sought an outcaste woman as their partner. Dombipada sings:

> The boat sails on
> betweeen the Ganges and the Jumna,
> The Lady brings her children
> to the other shore.
> Steer my boat,
> oh outcaste woman,
> while time is far off in the sky.[51]

With the body as his vessel, the *sadhaka* (initiate) must steer toward the farther shore of understanding through the storms and deadly currents of his passions. The only mariner to guide him through the storm is God or Realization.[52] Bengali mystical songs such as Mar-fati, Murshid, and those of the Bauls, have little to do with ritual and with orthodox ceremonies. In such songs, Ganga finds a place not as something divine but as part of the simple imagery. Perhaps the greatest Baul poet was Lalan Shah (1774–1890), claimed by Hindus and Muslims alike, whose achievement soars beyond the faulted vision of denominations. "Who knows the Lord?" he asks:

> Like a small fish he is playing in the water.
> He encompasses the world.
> But you find him only
> in the mirror of your understanding.
> He swims within us,
> we who are like the Ganges.
>
> When the water dries,
> the fish will fly.
> Man is as deep as the Ganges.
> Only love can enter there.
> Lalan says: "I drowned to reach the depths."[53]

The body is described as a boat. It is built of love, and the shipwright lives within it. "Come to that boat, who is god," sings Lalan, "if you will cross the river. It is built with understanding and will never fail you."[54] The initiate must immerse himself in the river of love. "Only the diver knows the silent ecstasy of deep water. To the ignorant, the river itself cannot be seen. There, waves rise up without a wind, and that magic moment the river springs to life. In this river without banks, a great fish dwells in solitary splendor. He rises to the surface with the coming of the moon. Then is the time to seize him. Bathe in that river and your heart will lose all fear; the summons will not trouble you at all."[55]

The great fish, an emblem of the oneness beyond words, is waiting at Triveni, literally "the three braids," the place where three rivers meet. "Lay a snare to catch him at Triveni," Lalan says.[56] The great Triveni at Prayag is mirrored by the little Triveni in Bengal near Satgaon. It is also a place of the mind, a place where all distinctions disappear. The Baul poet Phatik Chand sings:

> On a river without water
> a lotus blossom floats,
> while gazelles leap silver,
> in the moonless night.
>
> Whoever can surmount the vortex
> of Triveni,

> where three rivers meet,
> will float forever
> on the waves of time.[57]

In Bengal, the folk gods have attained a permanent place in the tradition. By sanskritization they have become an accepted part of Hindu ritual. One of these gods is Dharma Thakur, whose worship is popular throughout the delta. In a ceremony called Vaitarani Par (Vaitarani is the river of the underworld), a pit is dug and then filled with fish and water. As a person crosses the river after death, so the worshipper is directed across the tiny pool while a priest recites verses appropriate to the ceremony.[58] A Dharma text, the *Shunya Purana,* describes the mind as a boat with Dharma himself as helmsman.

We find the same values in Ramprasad Sen (1715–1780), a devotee of Kali who was born at Halisahar, a little town on the Ganges near Calcutta. As with Lalan, "the pearl of Shakti lies at the depths, in the sea of knowledge."[59] But in his fascination with the goddess, Ramprasad rejects the boat of the body:

> The mind has freighted you across the waters,
> as a trader;
> buying, selling, gaining, losing.
> Bit by bit
> the boat is sinking.
> My mind, you have carried on your trade
> too well.[60]

Faith alone can save the devotee from the misfortunes of this world:

> The Tara boat cast its anchor
> at the landing place.
> O my mind! Come running if you want to cross.
> Set sail by Tara's grace and row it quickly,
> if you would cross the sea of suffering.[61]

To the end, Ramprasad embraced his morbid vision: "Afloat on the ocean of Samsara," he cries, "I journey back and forth, back and forth." At times, the disembodied Kali manifests herself in the image of Ganga: "When Kali is awake, then Ganga flows in your heart."[62] In his despair at not receiving the *darshan* of Kali (her appearance before him), Ramprasad reflects that the goddess is dead. As the co-wife of Shiva, along with Mother Kali, Ganga provides consolation for the poet:

> O mind! call "Mother" no more.
> Where will you find her, friend?
> Had She been alive, She would have appeared
> before you; all destroying Mother is not alive.
> Let me go to stepmother Ganga's banks,
> burn Mother's effigy of Kusha grass,
> offer rice-cakes to Her departed Spirit after mourning
> and go to Kashi [Banaras].[63]

At the moment of his death, that vision came to him. It is told that on the last day of the Kali Puja, when the Ganges at Hughli was filled with boats carrying images of Kali, Ramprasad suddenly rose from his boat. He began to sing of the goddess, and falling into the water was drowned.[64]

To the medieval Vaishnava poets, Ganga held a lesser appeal. They were devotees of Krishna, whose river was the Jumna. Nonetheless, Ganga appears now and then as a simple poetic image. Jayadeva, author of the most famous medieval poem, describes the lovemaking of Radha and Krishna:

> On the bank where her long braid lay undone,
> his black hair feels the sparkle
> of her necklace.
> There the cloud-dark Jumna
> meets the snowy Ganges at Prayaga.[65]

Among many legends told of Jayadeva, the Ganges is said to have changed its course, flowing near the poet's house so that he could bathe more easily in his old age.[66] The poet Vidyapati repeats the image of Radha in the act of love: "The broken garlands of her hair toss about like the waves of the Ganges in the water of the Jumna."[67] The images of river life take on a more erotic color. Radha recollects: "So long our world was new, we were one like fish and water. Such was our love."[68]

Ganga also flows in the love songs and ballads of the common people. So a young man says to the woman he adores: "You are the flower I set before me to worship. You are the water of the Ganges."[69] Another addresses his beloved: "I am an outcaste, and you are holy as the Ganges."[70] A husband describes his blind bride as "a waterlily floating in the stormy Ganges."[71] In another ballad, Prince Nanderchand says to Mahua: "What good is life [without you]? Let yourself be the river Ganges, and I will drown myself in you."[72]

In a river song from Bhagalpur (ancient Champa), Ganga is personified as a lovely woman called Gango. Kamla is another stream, whose presence means good harvest, while the sparkling adornments are the river's many tributaries. Tirhut is the upland region giving rise to two of these, the Gandak and the Koshi:

> East of the Kamla and west of the Koshi
> there is no woman like Gango.
> Where have you bathed, O Gango,
> Where did you comb your hair?
> Where did you find your sparkling adornments?
> In the Ganges I bathed,
> In Tirhut I combed my hair.
> Why did you bathe, O Gango?
> Why did you comb your hair?
> For grace I bathed.
> For the endless flowing of my braid,
> I combed my hair.
> And set in it these bright adornments.[73]

Ganga is likewise the answer to a riddle, an ancient vehicle of folk literature. The following comes from the village of Purulia:

> Who is that woman
> whose presence is a blessing,
> whose embrace redeems us,
> whose kiss can bring us immortality?[74]

Ganga in Religious Rites

In Bengal, from birth to death, Ganga plays a prominent role in the vratas or religious observances of the people. Though nominally Hindu, vratas have their roots in the folk culture and over the centuries became associated with the great tradition. At the morning or evening worship, a passage may be read from the *Bhagavad Gita* and a glass of Ganges water offered to the god.[75] At sunset, in a wish for well-being through the night, Ganga water may be sprinkled over the threshold or in the corner of every room, beginning with the Thakurghor or place of worship.[76]

In temple worship, the devotee would bathe in the Ganges, if possible, before proceeding to the temple. Ramprasad Sen worshipped both Shiva and the goddess Durga with bel leaves and Ganges water. For the installation of a god, the statue would be bathed in several different substances, then dipped in oil and washed in Ganges water.[77] In like manner, an image may be deconsecrated by immersing it in the water of the Ganges.[78]

If a woman is unmarried, her vratas are concerned with obtaining a good husband. So girls from their tenth to twelfth years may perform a Shiva Puja each morning in the month of Vaishak (April-May), fashioning a Shiva lingam from Ganges clay. At the end of the month, the lingams are immersed in the Ganges or some other body of water.[79] In the Bengali poem *Chandi,* a marriage is celebrated with kusha grass and Ganges water. The women of Bengal still perform a folk dance called "Gangavatarana" (the descent of Ganga), a ritual marriage dance in which the feet are barely raised from the ground but move from side to side. From the waist up, movement is free, and the motion of the hands describes the descent. Ganga also finds her place in the marriage songs of country people. A prospective bride praises Ganga and Durga, the two wives of Shiva:

> Hurry, O Durga, and let us be off.
> For the younger brother of Ramachandra
> has come to invite us.
> Hurry, O Ganga, and let us be off.
> For the younger brother of Ramachandra
> has come to invite us.[80]

The birth of a child brings with it several sacraments. A few days after the birth, a crowd of neighbors accompanies the new mother to the Ganges. There they make offerings to the river, proceeding to the temple of Shashti, goddess of children and the family.[81] In Bengal, for the *upanayana* or sacred thread ceremony, the young man may wear a yellow robe resembling the sannyasin's. For three days he remains indoors, taking nothing but bread and Ganges water.[82] The ceremony includes immersion *(abhisheka)*, performed in the Ganges if possible.[83] In times past, for initiation into studenthood a young man would go to the river just before sunrise and perform Shraddhas, rituals for a deceased relative. Along with Ganges water, he would present offerings to the god, at the same time doing honor to the Hindu goddesses.[84]

People in Bengal share the common wish of Hindus to die near the river. Village girls sometimes gather for a prayer to Vishnu, chanting rhetorically: "She will have vermillion on her head . . . and will not see the death of her husband or her sons. She will die in the waters of the Ganges, and will follow in the steps of Vishnu."[85] The poet Ramprasad exclaims: "Let my tongue utter Kali in the Ganges at the end."[86] In the following verse, the maharaja of Nator, a ninteenth-century contemporary, reveals the depth of his attachment to the river:

> When my mind is failing,
> then the name of Kali whispers in my ears.
> It calls me from my bed of sand.
> This body is not mine,
> but passion sweeps it on.
> O Shiva, grant me a rosary
> when I am floating in the Ganges.[87]

Travelers from Cesare Federici onward attest to the widespread acceptance of the practice. "When any is sicke," Federici observes, "he is brought out of the Countrey to the banks of the River [Ganges], and there they make him a small Cottage of strawe, and every day they wet him with that water."[88] Gautier Schouten, who visited Bengal in the seventeenth century, remarks that people "even carry the water of the Ganges to be made use of by the sick who cannot be brought to the River."[89] In modern times, during the period of mourning for a dead one, men will bathe in the Ganges and then be shaved on the riverbank by a barber.[90] If the deceased is a parent, a man will also have his head shaved, a sign of ultimate separation, of dying to the world.

In earlier times, people would swear an oath by the sanctity of the river. The *Calcutta Journal* of 24 January 1820 reports the following incident at a hearing of the Supreme Court:

> A native, in giving evidence on a case therein pending, refused to take the oath in the usual manner, viz., on the water of the Gunga. He declared himself to be one of the followers of Ram Mohun Roy [a well-known Bengali reformer] and in consequence, not a believer in the imagined sanctity of this river. He offered to be sworn by the *Vedas,* as a believer in these writings, analogous to the European method as it respects Christian scriptures.

The custom is an old one, for we read of it in the medieval *Dharmamangal* epic where the hero Kalu professes his love for his brother Kamba. "Here do I take the holy water of the Ganga in my hand," he says, "and take the vow that whatever you may demand of me I shall give to you, no matter if it be my head or all my property." The evil brother demands his head and Kalu complies. Similarly, in the eighteenth-century *Maharashta Purana* a Hindu emissary also swears an oath on Ganga for the safe conduct of Bhaskara, leader of the Maratha invaders. Ultimately the oath is broken and Bhaskara is slain.

As we saw in earlier chapters, men have praised the river's redeeming powers since the time of the *Mahabharata.* But for ablution the Ganges in Bengal was especially sacred.[91] Van Linschoten in 1585 observed that people came from all the countries of the east to wash away their sins.[92] According to Thomas Bowrey, the Brahmins round about Cossimbazar did a brisk export trade. They were held in such esteem that "the water and mudde of the Ganges Sent from them with their Choppe (signet) or Seale Upon it is accompted Sacred, even so farre as Persia."[93] The *History of Liang* records that in the fifth century King Ti Chen of Champa (Vietnam) abdicated his throne so that he might go to India. "A view of Ganga is a great joy," he said, "and left from here for the Ganges."[94]

Ganga in Festivals

Beneath the outer forms of Hinduism, religion in Bengal pulses with the indigenous gods and forces of the delta. In addition to Vedic ritual, there occur sacrifices of domestic animals to such terrors as snakes, crocodiles, tigers, and diseases like smallpox and cholera. Subject as they are to the caprices of the river, people do *puja* (a prayer with offerings) to Ganga as the Divine Mother. Her worship is more prevalent here than in any other part of India.

The most common form of worship is the snana or bathing festival, popular even among city dwellers. Bathing in the river while chanting mantras is an ancient and widespread custom. But worship of Ganga as an idol is peculiar to the delta. While Ganga dvarapalas (door guardians) appear throughout the country, it is rare to find a temple dedicated exclusively to the goddess. In Bengal, however, Ganga worship assumes an importance second only to the great religious festivals like the Durga Puja.

The Melas are a motley affair, with buying and selling, people bathing and reciting mantras, and a general air of celebration. In the West Dinajpur district, at least five prominent bathing festivals are held throughout the year. At auspicious times, especially during the month of Magh (January-February), Ganga on her makara is worshipped in an established shrine. On the full moon days, thousands attend a big fair, performing *tarpan* (an offering of water to the dead) and conducting special pujas to the goddess. In another village, a clay image of Ganga, with a thatched cottage to house it, is fashioned once a year. Surprisingly, the bathing festival is also popular in areas further removed from the river, such as Cooch Bihar. Here, in the village of Kachuban, we can glimpse the synthesis of Hinduism and folk religion. In the month of Chaitra (March-April), several thousand people gather on a site covering two or more acres, motivated by the belief that Ganga appears on the occasion of Baruni (worship of Varuna, god of the sea and rivers) and identifies herself with the local river Naya.

Other Melas are held for Ganga apart from the bathing fairs. The impact of the river's changing course is reflected in the annual fair at Azimganj on a seven-acre piece of land that was once a bed of the Ganges but is now raised due to the shifting current. In the village of Giridharipur, near Murshidabad, the fishing community offers a Ganga Puja in the month of Ashadha (June-July) or Shravana (July-August). The fishermen believe that the worship will bring them good fortune and improve their catch. It is an old festival; its origins cannot be dated. We can judge the primacy of Ganga from the festival Durghakhola in the Nadia district. The worship lasts for eight days in the month of Magh. There is no separate image of the goddess; instead the villagers prepare a clay structure called *mede*. On the top they place an idol of Vishnu, at the lowest part statues of Brahma and Shiva, and in the center an image of Ganga mounted on a makara. Thus the goddess appears as the central figure in the Hindu trinity. In the twin town of Berhampur-Murshidabad, the Mela features a clay model of Ganga on her vahana, with the sage Bhagiratha sounding his conch shell and conducting the goddess to the estuary where she will restore the sons of Sagara. Both banks of the river are thronged with women from all walks of life. They assemble in small groups for pujas and return with potfuls of Ganges water which is preserved throughout the year.

In Bengal, the "other face of the makara" becomes readily apparent. Here it is a fearsome thing, a force to be propitiated. Here it lacks any connotation as a gentle creature of the waters. In some festivals, people shape a large earthen makara. A baby, also fashioned out of earth, is placed near the mouth of the crocodile to placate its rapacious nature.[95] The *Calcutta Review* of 1859 provides the gruesome details behind such rituals. It explains that stakes are often driven into a riverbed at watering places, allowing people to draw water safely. But a crocodile incited by hunger may climb the bank and slip into the enclosure. The magazine reports the following incident:

> A young Hindu girl about fourteen years old came to get a pitcher of water, and had hardly put her feet into the water, when the crocodile, who had been lying in wait inside the enclosure, rushed at the poor girl, seized her in his formidable jaws, scrambled up the banks of the river, holding the shrieking, struggling girl well up in the air by the middle of her body, and plunged heavily into the river outside of the stake. A smothered scream, a ripple upon the water, a few bubbles, and the frightful scene was closed.

As we saw in the last chapter, ships used to have makara prows as a talisman against the terrors of the sea. Even today, Ganga on her makara is often worshipped as protection against catastrophe on a boat journey.[96] Propitiation of the makara forms the basis of the

Makarasnan held yearly at Namkhana (in the 24-Parganas), the steamer berth for Sagar Island. In the festival at Dostpur, also in the 24-Parganas, Ganga's vehicle is portrayed as a shark, an equally terrifying animal. Sebastian Manrique reports incredulously that Sagar Island pilgrims would sometimes perform their puja and then, with a solemn vow, enter the sea with the hope of being consumed by sharks. At times a sated shark would reject the offering: "They then look upon this escape . . . as an event full of ill-luck and misfortune, and hence leave the sea weeping and lamenting loudly, believing that owing to their sins . . . they were not considered worthy to have their sacrifices accepted."[97] Sharks are often known to attack bathers at the mouth of the Hughli River.[98]

The best-known Ganga festival in Bengal is the Mela at Sagar Island. The site is an ancient one mentioned as early as the *Mahabharata*. In the epic, the sage Pulastya promises great spiritual reward for a person who visits the spot "where Ganga mingles with the sea."[99] A Bengali poem, the *Manasamangal,* describes the voyage of the merchant Chand, whose fleet set sail from a port in the Ganges Valley. Passing through Bengal, it anchored at Gangasagar, where the merchant performed worship before departing for Patan in Gujarat. In the medieval period, the island often served as a naval base, at one time for the Hindu ruler Pratapaditya, at another for the pirates ravaging the coast of Bengal. Manrique comments on the Portuguese and Magh pirates of Arakan, whose ships "often call at this island to rest and also . . . to seize and carry off the pilgrims [as slaves]."[100] In the early nineteenth century, several attempts at cultivation met with failure as workmen fell prey to sickness and tigers. In 1833, a severe hurricane swept away all the houses and other facilities, and the island reverted once again to what it has always been: a place of pilgrimage.[101]

That pilgrimage is not an easy one. In the past, the only means of transport was by country boat, and the twelve-hour journey from Calcutta often met with disaster. Even now a year seldom passes without a handful of boats capsizing. At one time, Sagar was also the haunt of tigers. Captain Alexander Hamilton's memoirs from the early eighteenth century relate that the island was infested with them and that a hungry tiger might swim out to a boat at night and make off with a sleeping pilgrim.[102] A Bengali journal of 1853 reports that a company of artillery personnel was deputed to frighten off the man-eaters of the Sundarbans by constantly firing heavy guns.[103] In spite of such government precautions, three persons were devoured during the Mela.

The first worship begins at 3 A.M. with a prayer to Kapila Muni, the sage who cursed the sons of Sagara. It is said that Kapila came to Sagar, where he built his hermitage and spent his days in meditation.[104] The pilgrimage is supposed to yield its full benefits only if the devotee remains three days and nights. On the last and most auspicious day, known as *makara sankranti,* people wake in the darkness and drift slowly down to the beach (Figure 46). The first wisps of sunlight turn the gray sand gold as the puja begins with offerings from a dala—a pot containing flowers, coconut, a scented candle, sweets, and a piece of cloth that represent one's earthly possessions. As the day wears on, the pilgrims board their country boats for the long journey home. The regular population of Sagar is roughly twenty thousand. On my visit in 1974, the numbers had swelled to half a million.

In Bengali festivals and literature, Ganga is found in conjunction with other deities, sometimes the indigenous gods of the delta. The association provides the local figures some entry into the Hindu fold. This assimilating process is a common feature of Hinduism, begun as early as the *Rig Veda.* In the Maldah village of Gohilla, for example, a bathing festival is held for Ganga and the local goddess Chandi. The Ganga shrine is permanent, but no temple or image exists for Chandi. Manasa, the indigenous serpent goddess, is also connected with Ganga. In the poem *Manasamangal,* Ganga is asked to help sink the boats of a merchant who has offended the serpent goddess. When Ganga refuses, Manasa threatens to poison the river so that none would drink its water and the river would lose its sanctity. Ganga is terrified and agrees to help. In the older versions of the poem, Manasa worship is prescribed as taking place on Dasahara, the same day that Ganga is worshipped, and the custom has prevailed to this day.[105]

At the village of Amarkundu, an annual celebration is held for Ganga and the sun god on the last Sunday of Shravana (July-

Figure 46. Ladies in Saris. Religious Bathing at the Ganga Sagar Mela. Courtesy of Michael Putnam.

August). The twin images, housed in a temple, are together known as Gangaditya. The custom goes back at least to the seventeenth century, for Friar Manrique remarks that the Hindus, while divided into different sects, all worship the sun and the river Ganges.[106] Today sick people from Calcutta often go to Tarakeshvar, thirty-five miles from the city, carrying two pots of Ganges water in a sling. They pour the water over a stone slab representing an indigenous sun god assimilated to Shiva. The village is twenty-five miles from the nearest point of the Ganges. Sometimes water is collected from Kali Ghat, which adds another twenty to twenty-five miles. In the hot season, professional carriers of Ganges water sometimes make the trip, dressed as warriors and traveling in a large procession.

Hindu and Muslim practices have often coalesced in Bengal.[107] The sacred river has provided a common theme for both religions. Dharaf Khan's *Ganga-Stotra,* a Sanskrit hymn to the goddess, is still sung today. The big Ganga festival at Berhampur-Murshidabad illustrates the synthesis. Essentially a Muslim event, the Bera celebration draws people of both communities, from near and far. It is traditionally dedicated to Khaja Khizr, patron saint of the waters. On the last Thursday of Bhadra (August-September), a square platform is built by lashing together several banana trunks, the structure measuring thirty feet square. On top the artisans place four 20-foot boats made of bamboo strips covered with black paper. Their prows are shaped like makaras. The float is then decorated with flags, minarets, and a cardboard replica of a palace. In earlier days, members of the nawab's family would tie flower garlands on the makara head of the boat. Then a musical procession would make its way to the nawab's palace, carrying bread, sweets, and a gold candle. The boat and offerings were placed on the float. After that, the gold candle was lit, along with several others, and a gun was fired from the nawab's house to mark the beginning of the festival. The ropes were then cut and the platform drifted slowly on the current.[108]

We can find several Hindu elements in the celebration. For one thing, one notes its strong resemblance to the Sedo festival, in which Hindu women launch small banana-trunk boats containing candles and flowers. For another, the musical accompaniment is contrary to Muslim law, especially at religious festivals. Moreover, the event follows the Hindu calendar and has no connection with the Muslim Hidjri reckoning. We can also recognize the makara feature of the boat and the choice of Ganga as the location. Even today the Bera festival is remarkable and attracts huge crowds on both sides of the Ganges. In the days when the nawabs of Murshidabad ruled the country, the spectacle must have been much greater still.

12
The Image of Ganga in the West

NOT SURPRISINGLY, the fame of Ganga is known wherever Indian culture has spread: in Asia as far afield as Mongolia and Indonesia. But from early times the image of the river also took hold on western imagination. By the fourth century B.C., the western world had come to know of Ganga. From Alexander the Great to Christopher Columbus eighteen hundred years later, the river spoke the greatness and mystery of Asia. It is also mentioned by many classical writers as the farthest limit of the known world; the Christian Fathers regarded it as a river of paradise. In this chapter we will examine Ganga in western literature and the image it has created in people's minds.

Classical Knowledge of India and the Ganges

It is difficult to say when the classical world first became aware of India. In the Near East, recollections of trade with the old Indus civilization faded with the crumbling of empires, while an oblique reference to Babylon in the *Jatakas* provides no lasting clue.[1] Early in the eighth century B.C., we find Greek settlements around the Black Sea: the Ionians, with their passion for exploration and trade, established a colony at Sinope, halfway along its southern shore. But at this time there was no India, properly speaking, and few wonders to quicken travelers' tales.

The first clear awareness broke upon the Greeks when the Persian Empire under Darius conquered the Punjab as far as the Indus. We read in Herodotus that the king, wishing to know where the Indus emptied into the ocean, sent a number of men to travel the river.[2] The party, under Scylax, reached the Arabian Gulf and explored the coast westward to the Red Sea. Invasion followed, and from this time (ca. 510 B.C.) the Indus Valley and the Punjab remained part of the Persian Empire—its twentieth satrapy—for almost two hundred years, while in Asia Minor the Ionian states also passed under Persian rule. As subjects of the same dominion, the ever curious citizens of Samos and Miletus must have learned things about the farthest part of the empire. From the eastern provinces, merchants, soldiers, and civil servants carried with them intimations of another civilization beyond their kingdom.

From Hecataeus to Alexander

Yet nothing tangible remains before Hecataeus (549–486 B.C.), a citizen of Miletus and the first Greek to mention India with any degree of authority. Even before him, Anaximander had sketched a map of the world with its seas and rivers,[3] but this map is now lost, and we will never know how far east it extended—if it included the Indus or any other parts of India. Hecataeus as well has not come down to us directly: we do, however, glimpse his work and the details of his map in the writings of Herodotus, Athenaeus, and later from Stephanus of Byzantium. To judge from the details, his knowledge of India must have been based on direct reports. He notes, for example, "that artichokes grow in the region of the Indus."[4] He mentions Caspatyrus, the town on the river from which Scylax began his voyage. His observations are all the more surprising if we remember that India became a part of the Persian Empire during his lifetime, and it seems likely that Hecataeus had before him reports of Darius' Indian expedition.[5]

As best we can construct it, Hecataeus' map divides the world into two continents, Europe and "Asia," both enclosed by the great river Oceanus. The Nile is fed from the encircling ocean, as is the Indus, which lies just east of the Tigris and Euphrates along the same stretch of land. Thus, as early as the sixth century B.C., Hecataeus pictures the four great rivers of Asia. His map, as the standard work of the fourth and fifth centuries B.C., left a permanent mark on ancient and medieval geography.[6] In time this image of the four great rivers grew into tradition, becoming subject to myth and speculation. Gradually the Indus is more or less forgotten and its place is taken by the Ganges. Herodotus, with his details about the Indian troops in Xerxes' army, provides a fuller account of India. He elaborates on the idea that India lies at the limits of the world. "The Indians," he remarks, "dwell nearest to the east and the rising of the sun. After them, all is desert."[7] Like his predecessor, he describes the Indus and reed boats fashioned by the people dwelling on its banks. He mentions also the enormous amount of gold that Darius received from his Indian satrapy.[8] Of the land beyond the Indus, Herodotus tells us nothing.

The first major work on India comes from the pen of Ctesias, a Greek physician who spent seventeen years at the Persian court. From 416 to 399 B.C., he served two kings, Darius II and Artaxerxes Mnemon. During this time, he met officials and merchants traveling between the capital and its easternmost province. From these reports he fashioned his *Indica,* a mélange of fabulous creatures and straightforward geographical commentary. Though the original is lost, we find copious extracts made by Photius, bishop of Constantinople in A.D. 858. Like Herodotus, Ctesias tells of gold, found on many high-towered mountains.[9] He also describes a river, the Hyparkhos, which may be the first reference to Ganga in western literature. "Through India," he notes, "there flows a certain river . . . called in the Indian tongue Hyparkhos, which means in Greek . . . the bearer of all things good . . . in the upper part of its course . . . it flows among the mountains."[10] Pliny in the role of scholiast observes: "Ctesias says that in India is a river, the Hyperbarus, and that the meaning of its name is the bearer of all good things. It flows from the north into the Eastern Sea."[11] To Alexander, over three centuries before Pliny, the Ganges had become *par excellence* the river of the Eastern Sea.[12] The classical scholar Christian Lassen also equates the Hyparkhos with the Ganges.[13]

From Ctesias to the time of Alexander, there is virtually no mention of India or its rivers. Aristotle, probably writing before Alexander's journey, repeats Herodotus on India and the Indus as the eastern boundary of the known world.[14] To Aristotle, the Indus is still "the greatest of all rivers."[15]

From the Time of Alexander

Evidently India was in people's minds. Alexander, as Strabo puts it, "reached out for India . . . since many men had been describing it to him, though not too clearly."[16] Reports of Ganga must have increased during this time, for according to several biographers the Ganges had become the goal of Alexander's expedition through Asia. Unfortunately, firsthand narratives of the campaign, by men like Aristobolus and Onesicritus, have long since disappeared, and we must rely on later historians, especially Arrian and Curtius. Arrian, one of the most reliable chroniclers, records the speech of Alexander to his weary soldiers: "If any one desires to hear what will be the end of our warfare, let him learn that the distance still remaining before we reach the Ganges and the Eastern Sea is not great."[17] Plutarch repeats the incident, adding to it from his storyteller's art: "Alexander at first in vexation and rage withdrew to his tent, and shutting himself up lay there feeling no gratitude towards those who had thwarted his purpose of crossing the Ganges."[18]

Abandoning his plans to reach the end of the world, Alexander and his men turned south along the Indus, where they encountered several hostile armies in their march to the sea. The soldiers were depressed at the thought of unending battles and Alexander rallied them, pointing out, according to Curtius, that "those of whom they were afraid were weak and unwarlike; that after the conquest of these tribes there was nothing in their way, once they had traversed the distance now between them and the ocean, to prevent their coming to the end of the world, which would also be the end of their labours; that he had given way to their fears of the Ganges and of the numerous tribes beyond that river, and turned his arms to a quarter where the glory would be equal but the hazard less."[19]

Though Alexander never reached his destination, later romances carry him to the sacred river, where improbable things befall him.

Such stories are part of medieval legend; we will examine them further on.

After Alexander, India with its wonders became part of the classical world. The great conqueror died on his journey home and the empire was divided among his generals. The region from Babylon to the Indus fell to Seleucus Nicator, who dreamed the dreams of Alexander but was thwarted by Chandragupta Maurya, king of the first great Indian empire. After several unsuccessful battles, Seleucus established diplomatic relations with Chandragupta, and embassies were exchanged between Pataliputra and Babylon. Seleucus sent a Greek wife and the ambassador Megasthenes, who spent several years at the Mauryan court.

Megasthenes' impressions were recorded in a book that remained for a long time the most influential Greek work on India. As we saw in Chapter 8, Megasthenes notes the voyage from Palibothra to the ocean but did not make the journey himself. He describes the Ganges as reaching the Eastern Sea, which to the Greeks meant the easternmost part of an essentially four-sided world. To Megasthenes, Ganga is the greatest river of the earth, "which neither the Egyptian Nile, nor the Danube . . . can for a moment be compared with."[20] One of the geographical conundrums of the ancient world was the source of the Nile. Accordingly, Megasthenes gathers different opinions on the origins of Ganga: "Some have asserted that this river, like the Nile, rises from unknown sources . . . while others trace its source to the Scythian mountains."[21] From still other accounts, "it bursts from its fountain with a thundering roar, and tumbling down a steep rocky channel, lodges in a lake as soon as it reaches the level plain, whence it issues forth with a gentle current."[22]

Such observations provide the seeds for later writers, influencing their belief in an endless mountain chain dividing Asia and giving rise to its great rivers. In certain places, we recognize the *Mahabharata* and Purana descriptions of the Ganges—falling from Meru with a terrible roar, tumbling over the rocks, and entering a lake (see chapter 2)—while the fountain from which it flowed added to other legends of Ganga, leading medieval writers to regard it as a river of Eden.

The idea of a single mountain chain running the length of Asia is further elaborated by Eratosthenes, keeper of the great library at Alexandria. Writing half a century after Megasthenes (ca. 240 B.C.), he locates the Ganges at the eastern end of the earth. According to Strabo, he placed the limits of the known world in the west at the Pillars of Hercules and in the east at "the capes and most remote peaks of the mountain chain that forms the northern boundary of India."[23]

In the second half of the second century B.C., hostilities between Rome and Persia closed the overland route to India. But the growing passion for Indian goods, as well as Hippalus' discovery of the monsoon for navigation, led to greatly expanded maritime activity.[24] Writing shortly before A.D. 17, Strabo comments: "In early times . . . not so many as twenty vessels would dare to traverse the Arabian Gulf . . . but at present even large fleets are dispatched as far as India."[25] As a result, "these regions have become far better known to us of today than our predecessors."[26] At Myos Hormos, a port on the Red Sea, Strabo is told that upwards of 120 ships make the voyage every year. From the Red Sea ports, cargo was forwarded to Alexandria and transshipped to Rome. Alexandria at this time became the center of east-west trade and the most cosmopolitan city of the empire, filled with merchants, scholars, and travelers from all the countries of the east. Among the people in Alexandria, Dio Chrysostom mentions Bactrians, Scythians, Persians, and Indians.[27] It was here at Alexandria, during this period, that the western world learned what it did about the east and India and its sacred rivers. This maritime trade flourished until A.D. 200 and continued in dwindling importance for another two hundred years, providing a steady supply of fact and fable.

But essentially the picture was complete. Following Megasthenes, later writers placed India at the farthest end of the world and had the Ganges flowing into the Eastern Sea. So Artemidorus attempted to calculate the distance, down to the last mile, from Gades to the mouths of the Ganges. The Peutingerian Table, a road map of the Roman Empire, separates the world into twelve divisions stretching from Britain to the mouths of the Ganges.

Another important conception was the formidable mountain

range running from the Euxine—the Black Sea—continuously through northern India and producing the great rivers of Asia. "The whole of India," in Strabo's words, "is traversed by rivers. . . . They have their sources, one and all, in the Caucasus."[28] (See Map 3.) "It is sufficiently agreed," he continues, "that the Ganges is the largest of known rivers in the three continents."[29] Similarly, Arrian and Curtius, writing in the first century A.D., describe the Ganges, the greatest river of Asia, as flowing from the Caucasus.[30] Arrian injects the idea that the Indus, the Tigris, and the Euphrates also take rise from the same mountain range. In his *Library of History,* Diodorus comments that "the Euphrates and Tigris, the most notable . . . of all the rivers of Asia after the Nile and Ganges, have their sources in the mountains of Armenia."[31] This idea later influenced those medieval writers who situated paradise, with its four rivers, in the Armenian Caucasus, thereby contributing to Ganga's image as a river of Eden.

Along with sober geographical speculation on India came descriptions of exotic creatures that combined human and animal parts or possessed great feet or had ears large enough to sleep in. Such imaginative descriptions go back to Ctesias, and some later writers simply repeat them, adding a skeptical commentary. So Strabo mentions the tales of certain people who "live round the sources of the Ganges; and they sustain themselves by means of vapours from roasted meats and odours from fruits and flowers, since instead of mouths they have only breathing orifices."[32]

Until the end of the classical world—at the time of Ptolemy and Pliny—the image of India and the Ganges remained unchanged. The sacred river captured the fancy of poets and often appears in story. In the *Aeneid,* Virgil compares the Ganges in spate to angry armies marching off to war;[33] in the *Georgics,* he promises to carve upon a temple door, "in gold and solid ivory, the battles of the Ganges' tribes."[34] The tribes of Ganga, the Gangaridae, are also mentioned by Valerius Flaccus in his *Argonautica.*[35]

Among the more beguiling fabulists, Apollonius of Tyana claims to have spent thirteen years in India. During his travels he is entertained by one Iarchus, the "chief of Brahmans," who in a previous incarnation had been a great king named Ganges. The king "had

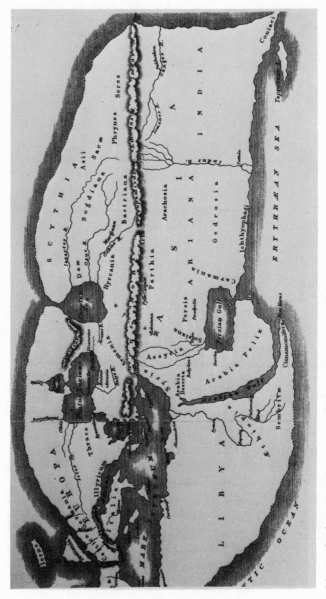

Map 3. Strabo's Map. By courtesy of Edward Stanford, Ltd., London.

rendered his father, the Ganges river, propitious to India, by inducing it to keep within its banks."[36] But Apollonius gives himself away in describing his itinerary by claiming that he traveled down toward the sea, keeping the Ganges on his right and the Hyphasis on his left. Unfortunately the opposite is true. His depictions of strange and exotic animals read like a page from Ctesias. While exploring the Caucasus, he comes upon the chains of Prometheus, who was banished to the mountain for his act of hubris. Another story, spuriously attributed to Plutarch, leaves us the following to ponder:

> The Ganges is a river of India called so for the following reason: The nymph Kalauria bore Indus a son of notable beauty, by name Ganges, who in the ignorance of intoxication had connections with his mother. But when later he learned the truth from his nurse, in passion of remorse he threw himself into the river Chliaros, which was named the Ganges after him.[37]

Clearly, by this time, the Ganges had become the stuff of legend. Dionysius Periegetes (meaning the guide or tourist), an Alexandrian of the second century A.D., anticipates Rama of the *Raghuvamsha* when he describes the wanderings of Bacchus, "who set up pillars by the Ganges and the eastern Ocean."[38] Ovid, after his banishment to the Black Sea, also recalls the journey of Bacchus to Persia and the "broad-flowing Ganges."[39]

The Ganges and the Rivers of Eden

Beginning with Eusebius in the third century A.D., we find growing agreement among Christian writers that the Phison, a river of Eden, was none other than the Ganges. By the ninth or tenth century, the idea had become almost universal, despite what might seem to us the geographical obstacles involved. To understand the reasons for this belief, we must examine several geographical conceptions of the Middle Ages.

The Medieval World View

With the onset of Christianity, the classical vision dissolves. Slowly it is refashioned to the image of faith. Medieval thinkers follow Genesis as their chief guidebook to geography. Systematic observation, so prized by the Greeks, succumbs to the explorers of the spiritual world. Under these circumstances, geographical knowledge of the sea, of Asia, and of Africa grows more and more tenuous, until the line between fact and fable eventually disappears. Political conditions quicken the change, as large parts of the Roman Empire are reclaimed by primitive tribes and revert once again to *terra incognita.*

But the classical works are never completely lost, and by the fourth century people begin to find in them ideas that clarify and support the truths of the Bible. Theories that run counter to Scripture are rejected; others, of a noncontroversial nature, appear in the secular margins of early Christian thought.

The Confusion of India with Africa

One belief that eventually draws Ganga into the realm of paradise is the proximity of Africa and India. Ptolemy is chiefly responsible for the idea that the southern part of Africa extended far to the east. At the same time, eastern Asia is carried southward, so that the two eventually join, making the Indian Ocean an inland sea. The result is to place the ancient kingdom of Ethiopia *en face* with India. (See Map 4.) This geographical fancy is implied as early as Homer.[40] Aeschylus certainly subscribes to it; in *Prometheus Bound* he portrays the wanderings of Io from Europe to Asia.[41] On her journey she touches the farthest land, whose swarthy people (the Indians) dwell by the fountain of the sun, source of the Ethiopian river. Followings its banks she reaches a cataract of the Nile that issues from the Bibline mountains.[42]

Evidently this ancient notion prevailed, for Alexander, on reaching the Indus, thought he had discovered the sources of the Nile. As Arrian relates: "He thought the Nile rises somewhere or other in India."[43] Apollonius of Tyana, embroidering on the theme, offers us the following reminiscence: "There was a time," the Brahman Iarchas informs him, "when the Ethiopians, an Indian race, dwelt in this country, and when Ethiopia as yet was not. . . . At that time of which I speak, the Ethiopians . . . were subject to King Ganges." He continues, obviously warming to the

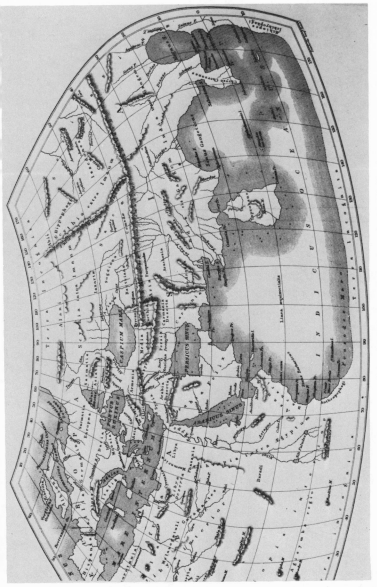

Map 4. Ptolemy's Map. From *History of Ancient Geography*, vol. 2, by E. H. Bunburye.

tale: "Now this Ganges, it seems, was ten cubits high, and in personal beauty excelled any man the world has yet seen, and when his own father (also named Ganges) inundated India, he himself turned the flood into the Red Sea."[44]

The confusion survives the classical world. Procopius, a sixth-century Christian writer whose sympathies lie clearly with the ancients, describes the Nile as flowing from India into Egypt, dividing the land into two equal parts up to the sea.[45] Such anomalies are reflected in medieval maps. On an eighth-century *mappamundi* from the library of Albi in Languedoc, the world is shaped like a horseshoe, with Africa placed along the right spur. Starting from an indentation, presumably the Red Sea, the Ganges runs down through Africa, while the Nile joins the Red Sea and the Mediterranean.[46]

The belief remained alive as late as the fourteenth century, for we find it in the *Travels of Sir John Mandeville*, long accepted as an authentic and valuable itinerary. Like Apollonius of Tyana and other later imposters, it appropriated from every conceivable source. The book further helps us to understand the incredible ignorance of geographical knowledge at this time. The river Nile, explains Sir John,

> cometh running from Paradys terrestre between the deserts of Ind and after it sinks into land and runneth long time many countries under the earth and after it goeth out under an high hill . . . between Ind and Ethiopia . . . and goeth all along from the land of Egypt into the city of Alisandre . . . and there it falleth into the sea.[47]

We may judge the popularity of the book by the fact that it was translated into almost all the major western languages.[48]

The Location of Paradise

To the Greeks, the Blessed Isles lay somewhere west of Italy. Though some later writers also situated paradise in the Atlantic beyond the Pillars of Hercules,[49] most Christians followed the biblical narrative and imagined paradise as eastward in Eden. To orthodox Christians, the location became a geographical fact and the

object of many journeys, fanciful and real. "Paradise is a place ly-
ing in the eastern parts," affirms Isidore of Seville in his *Etymologies,*[50] one of the most pervasive geographical commentaries of the
Middle Ages; likewise Epiphanius[51] and Athanasius, who regarded
it as near India.[52] The *Image du Monde* (about A.D. 1245) explains:
"The first regyon of Asia the greate is paradys terrestre. This is a
place whiche is ful of solace, of playsances and of delices."[53]

In time the Eastern Paradise became a permanent feature on medieval maps. One of the earliest and most influential of these maps
was drawn by Cosmas, an Egyptian monk who had spent several
years as a merchantman. (See Map 5.) During his travels, Cosmas
reached as far as Ceylon and for this reason was called Indicopleustes, the Indian voyager. Afterward he retired to a monastery
and settled down to write his *Christian Topography,* a book that
colored a thousand years of Christian speculation on the shape of
the earth.[54] In spite of his maritime experience, Cosmas relies more
on the chronicles of Alexander the Great and other dusty manuscripts. According to Cosmas, the earth resembles an indented rec-
tangle, surrounded by an ocean, with another landmass encircling
it. East of the outer earth lies paradise.[55]

As we have seen, medieval writers often reinterpreted classical
works in the light of Christian doctrine. One such piece is the
anonymous *Description of the Whole World and Its Races.* The
original fourth-century Greek text describes the Brahmins of India.
In its later Latin version, a Christian writer has added the Garden of
Eden, portraying its good inhabitants with the words previously
used to describe the Brahmins, whose name is now deleted:

> In the regions of the East they tell us dwell the peoples of the
> Camarini, whose land Moses described by the name Eden. From
> here a mighty river is said to flow forth and then to branch off
> into four streams. . . . Now the men who dwell in the aforesaid
> lands are extremely pious and good. No blemish is to be found in
> their bodies or in their minds.[56]

Medieval geographers continued to regard India and the Ganges
as the end of the world. To Martianus Capella in the fifth century,
the Ganges flows into the eastern ocean.[57] "Asia," says Orosius,
"begins in the East where lies the mouth of the River Ganges."[58]

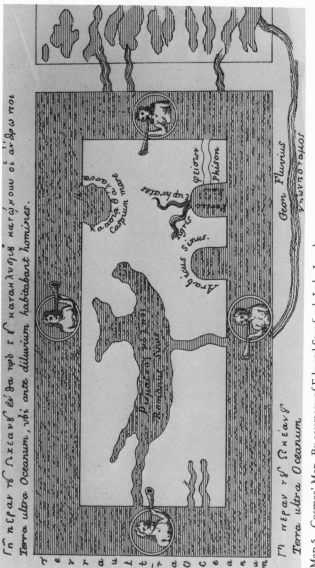

Map 5. Cosmas' Map. By courtesy of Edward Stanford, Ltd., London.

The *Image du Monde* assures us that "the Yndes ben closed with the Grete See that enuyronneth them round about."[59] At times the river is still confused with the Indus, for we read in St. Basil that the Indus, greatest of streams, flows from the winter solstice in the east.[60] But by and large the image of the eastern horizon is the image of Ganga. Dante pictures dawn and the sun rising on the river:

> Night wheels on, while the sands of the Ganges
> tip the scales of time.
>
> *Purgatorio* 2.4–6

> And noontide scorches down on Ganges' flood,
> so rode the sun . . .
>
> *Purgatorio* 27.4–5

Since paradise was a living reality located at the eastern end of the world—along with India and the Ganges—it seemed natural that the three would find their way together. This is exactly what happened. Aside from Cosmas' rough sketch, the earliest graphic representation is a *mappa mundi* drawn by an anonymous geographer of Ravenna (around A.D. 650) showing paradise as an island off the coast of India and facing the Ganges. (See Map 6.) The writer seems to have relied heavily on Greek sources, but here the Sacred Isle is transposed to the eastern sea. We find the same disposition in the Hereford map (ca. 1280): there paradise is a circular island at the mouth of the Ganges. Another group of maps follows the design of the Spanish priest Beatus, whose great work, the *Commentary on the Apocalypse* (ca. 776), contains a map illustrating the universal spread of Christianity. In the Beatus maps, paradise appears not as an island but on the mainland. One such map (ca. 1030), executed in the Aquitaine convent of St. Sever and now in the British Museum, shows the terrestrial paradise between Seres (China, the land of silk) and Bactria. The Garden of Eden, containing Adam and Eve, is ringed by a high mountain chain. Similarly the "London" Beatus or Spanish-Arabic map (ca. 1109) shows Eden in the region of India and the Caucasus. Sir John Mandeville and others also place paradise on a mountain.

The location of paradise in or near India gave rise to several legendary journeys, such as the tale of Eirek the Norwegian, who

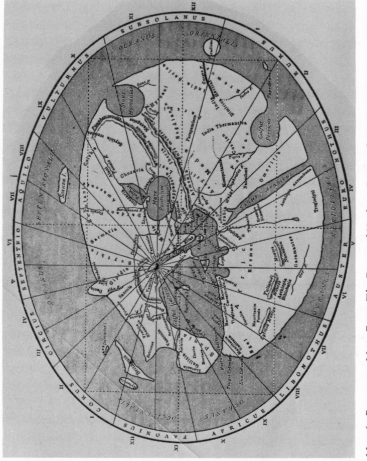

Map 6. Ravennese Map. From *The Dawn of Modern Geography* by C. R. Beazley published by Oxford University Press.

vowed to find the Earthly Garden. After securing directions from the emperor of Byzantium, he set out for *Paradisus extra Gángem*. Encountering deep forests and endless plains, at last he came upon a lovely park encircled by a river, which he recognized from his instructions as paradise and the river Phison. The only access lay across a small stone bridge blocked by an enormous dragon. Whereupon Eirek drew his sword and marched into the dragon's mouth. At once the monster disappeared and Eirek passed over into paradise.[61]

One widely held twelfth-century belief was the existence of Prester John, a powerful Christian king who ruled a great part of Asia, including India. In 1165, the Byzantine Emperor Manuel received a letter reputedly written by Prester John and describing his kingdom. "In one of the heathen provinces," it relates, "there flows a river called the Indus, which, issuing from Paradise, extends its windings . . . through all the country."[62] The letter excited great wonder and prompted the Vatican to dispatch a mission east in the hope of enlisting Prester John's aid against the Saracens. In reality there was no Prester John; the letter may have been written for political reasons by the archbishop of Mainz. But at the time, it was accepted without question and further strengthened the belief of paradise in India. We can judge its popularity by the fact that over a hundred manuscripts of the letter are still preserved. Similarly another twelfth-century text, the *Account of Elysaeus*, partly based on the letter, informs us that the earthly paradise is found in India at the top of a mountain.[63] The *English Faustbuch* (1592) portrays Doctor Faustus looking down on Scythia and India from a peak in the Caucasus. Through the valley flow the four rivers of paradise: the Ganges or Phison, the Nile or Gihon, the Euphrates, and the Tigris.[64]

In a tenth-century representation known as the Anglo-Saxon map, paradise is omitted and its place is taken by Taprobane or Ceylon, an island positioned at various points on the Greek maps and often greatly magnified in size. The fifteenth-century Andrea Bianco world map locates the earthly paradise beside Cape Comorin, with the four rivers flowing through the center of India.[65] John Marignolli, who reached Ceylon in the fourteenth century, describes a glorious mountain (probably Adam's Peak) barely forty miles from paradise, according to the natives. And from the height, the water falling from the fountain of paradise divides into four rivers that flow through the country.[66] "The second river," relates Marignolli, "is called the Phison, and it goes through India, circling all the land of Evilach."[67] Though he does not name the river, Marignolli's description points to the Ganges, for on its banks are

> great and noble cities, rich above all in gold. And on that river excellent craftsmen have their dwellings, occupying wooden houses, especially weavers of silk and gold brocade [Banaras?], in such numbers . . . as in my opinion do not exist in the whole of Italy.[68]

Following custom, Marignolli notes that the river Gyon (Gihon), after passing through Ceylon, encircles the land of Ethiopia and flows into Egypt. Such a belief is based on the ancient theory of subterranean watercourses flowing deep in the earth, under oceans and between continents. This belief, as old as Pindar, was later revived by Christian writers to explain the rivers of paradise flowing into the world from some remote point in the east.

Rivers in the Earth

We find it in Pindar and in a dozen other classical writers, the story of the maid Arethusa who escaped from her suitor Alpheus by being changed into a river.[69] From the Peloponnesus, she passed beneath the Ionian Sea through underground caverns and rose as a fountain on the island of Ortygia, all the while pursued by the river god Alpheus.[70] Pausanias, dallying on the myth, cites an old poem:

> Somewhere in the misty reaches of the sea
> Where Ortygia lies by Sicily
> Alpheus' eager mouth tastes of
> Arethusa's bubbling spring.[71]

The story may derive naturally from the limestone country of Greece, where many rivers lose themselves underground and reappear at some far-off point. But regardless of the origin, it soon became an accepted theory of classical geography, Aristotle's skepticism notwithstanding.[72] All the cavities of the earth, says Plato, "are joined together underground by many connecting channels, some narrower, some wider, through which, from one basin to another, there flows a great volume of water—monstrous unceasing subterranean rivers of water."[73] The following passage might well describe Cosmas' map of paradise and the four rivers issuing from their distant source:

> Some [rivers] flow in on the opposite side from where they came out, and others on the same side, while some make a complete circle, and winding like a snake . . . round the earth, descend as far as possible before they again discharge their waters. . . . Among these many various and mighty streams there are four in particular.[74]

Callimachus describes the ubiquitous Nile rising in Delos as the stream Inopus in that season when the Ethiopian river descends in torrent from its unknown height.[75] The incident is repeated by Pausanias, who records several stories of underground rivers that surface in distant places. The most imaginative—recalling the febrile speculations of Sir John Mandeville—claims that "the Nile itself is really the Euphrates, which disappears into a marsh and rises again beyond the Ethiopians."[76]

The theory of underground watercourses fitted well with a paradise located at the eastern limits of the world. Thomas Aquinas quotes St. Augustine: "It is supposed that since the site of Paradise is far removed from the knowledge of men . . . the rivers whose sources are said to be known have gone underground and after traversing vast distances have issued forth in other places."[77] Isidore of Seville affirms that "all the waters and torrents return by secret channels to the abyss from which they came."[78] After Isidore the theory remained popular throughout the Middle Ages.[79] It explained how the Nile, the Tigris, and the Euphrates could flow from a common source while their headwaters lay so far apart. It also led several Christian writers to place the Garden of Eden in the mountains of Armenia, among the endless Caucasus from which flowed "the great rivers of Asia." Philo, a bridge to the classical tradition, contemplates the location of paradise. He is perhaps the first scriptural writer to suggest that it may be "in some distant place far from our inhabited world, and has a river flowing under the earth, which waters many great veins so that these rising send water to other recipient veins, and so become diffused.''[80]

Cosmas, carrying the theory to its ultimate conclusion, describes how the rivers of paradise ''cleave a passage through the ocean and spring up in this earth.'' We read in his *Christian Topography* (bk.2) that:

> Divine scripture, with a view to show the diameter of Paradise, how great it is, and how far it extended eastward, mentions the four rivers only, and thence we learn that the fountain, which springs up in Eden and waters the garden, distributes the residue of its waters among the four great rivers which cross over into this earth and water a large part of its surface.

Consciously or not, later writers followed the pattern laid down by Cosmas. The thirteenth-century *Image du Monde* observes that ''the second of the four flodes is named Gyon or Nylus, whiche entreth in to therthe by an hool, and renneth vnder the erthe,'' encircling Ethiopia and flowing through Egypt.[81]

The idea of underground watercourses is a universal theme. We have come upon it in the Bengali stories of Ganga filling the sacred temple wells. Hebrew literature also mentions the subterranean waters issuing from the stone beneath the temple and flowing to the ends of the earth.[82]

Ganga as a River of Eden

Josephus was the first to suggest it. He had access to the classical writers and knew of the Ganges at the eastern end of the world. He had spent time in Alexandria shortly after A.D. 69 and may have heard further stories there about India and its sacred river. As a scholar and a Jew, he had probably read Philo, stimulated perhaps by his comment on the eastern site of paradise with its underground river. Josephus speaks of the garden, ''watered by a single river whose stream encircles all the earth and is parted into four branches. Of these the Phison . . . runs toward India and falls into the sea, being called by the Greeks Ganges.''[83] He identifies the other rivers as the Tigris, the Euphrates, and the Nile (the Geon).

The belief in Ganga as a river of Eden was greatly reinforced by the geographical position of India and the Ganges, coupled with the eastern location of paradise and the theory of underground watercourses. For it is often reaffirmed by the Church Fathers: Eusebius early in the fourth century and Augustine in the fifth.[84] St. Ambrose mentions that the Phison, "so called by the Hebrews but named Ganges by the Greeks, flows in the direction of India."[85] Guided by the figurative interpretations of Philo, he explains that the word *Phison* "stands for prudence. Hence it has pure gold, brilliant rubies, and topaz stones. We often refer to wise discoveries as gold; as the Lord says, speaking through the Prophet: 'I gave them gold and silver.' "[86]

Later the gold of Indian rivers, notably the Ganges, became the subject of legend, especially to medieval writers. In Indian tradition as well, Ganga above all others was the river of gold—for example, in the *Mahabharata* story cited in chapter 5. It was this gold of the Indies, the gold of King Solomon, brought from Ophir, that Columbus fourteen hundred years later thought he had found in the New World. Ambrose equates the gems in the river with the sparkling jewel of the soul, concluding that "the Phison is rightfully the first of rivers." St. Jerome also identifies Ganga with the Phison, which brings from its source in paradise emeralds and carbuncles and gleaming pearls, "which our great ladies so ardently desire."[87] John Marignolli, while in Ceylon, is assured by the natives that the river of paradise often carries down "precious stones, such as the carbuncle and sapphire, and also certain fruits with healing virtues." We can measure the popularity of the belief by the fact that it appears in *Mandeville's Travels:*

> The first of these floods [of Eden], which is called Phison or Ganges, springs up in India under the hill Orcobares, and runs eastward through India into the great sea Ocean. In that river are many precious stones . . . and mickle gravel of gold.[88]

This passage may have been lifted from the *Image du Monde*, considering that, in all probability, Sir John was a Frenchman. Caxton's English rendering of the *Image*, his *Mirror of the World*, describes the realm of paradise:

> Ther withinne sourdeth and spryngeth a fontayne or welle whiche is deuyded in to four flodes; of whom that one is called Vngages [Goussin's Old French translation of Phison or Ganges] that renneth

a longe thurgh the Royame of Ynde, and departeth in to many armes or braces. It sourdeth of the monnt that is called Ortobares, and whiche is to ward thorient and falleth in to the see Occian.[89]

Borrowing a page from Apollonius, Mandeville further explains: "It is called Ganges for a king that was in India, the which men called Gangarus; and for it runs through his land it was called Ganges."

Cosmas, in his *Christian Topography,* identifies the Phison with the Ganges or the Indus,[90] while Isidore, the "father of medieval geography," also observes that the "River Ganges, which the holy scripture calls Phison, flows from Paradise to the realms of India."[91]

Other curious incunabula of the Middle Ages locate the Phison in India. As we have seen, the spurious letter of Prester John equates the Phison with the Indus. In 1122, an obscure event took place in Rome that caused a great stir in the papal curia. The anonymous account tells of a Patriarch John of India, who arrived in Rome to receive confirmation in his office after the death of his predecessor. The story would seem doubtful at best, if not for a letter from an abbot of Rheims who was there at the time.[92] While in Rome, the patriarch gave a lecture on his native country in which he mentioned the principal city, Hulna, on the river Phison. He also spoke of the gold and gems in the river and its source in paradise.

By this time, India and the Ganges had long since passed into legend and found their way into other contemporary myths. Probably the most popular is the *Romance of Alexander* (third century A.D.), which recounts the deeds of the great conqueror. A fifth-century interpolation, attributed to Palladius, mentions the Brahmans, who dwell "near the Ganges, the river of India. . . . This river Ganges is in our opinion that which is called in the Scripture the Phison, one of the rivers which are said to go out from Paradise."[93] In the *Iter ad Paradisum,* a later addition written in the twelfth century, Alexander actually reaches the Ganges and, boarding a ship with five hundred picked men, embarks upon the river. After a month's journey, he anchors before a great walled city but is refused entrance. On returning, he is told that this was paradise, where the spirits of the just remain until the last judgment.[94]

The end of the medieval world was quickened by the great age of discovery. One by one, the geographical beliefs of a thousand years began to fade. The new men of science, methodically following the scriptural charts of the Middle Ages, arrived at unexpected destinations. Just as the Ganges had been the final goal of Alexander, one of the first great explorers of antiquity, so it was with Columbus, one of the first great explorers of the modern world.

Columbus had read Ptolemy and Mandeville and the Church Fathers from Ambrose to Isidore. In his journey westward, Columbus was seeking India on the southern coast of Asia and China on its eastern edge. In addition to the other charts and documents, Columbus may have been influenced by Martin Behaim's globe of 1492. Beneath the region of the Ganges, Behaim inscribed the following:

> In the Book of Genesis it is stated that this country through which flows the Ganges is called Havilla. The best gold in the world is said to grow there. In Holy Writ, in the Third Book of Kings . . . it is written that King Solomon sent his ships hither and had brought from Ophir to Jerusalem of this gold and valuable pearls and precious stones. This country of Gulat and Ophir, through which flows the River Ganges or the water of Gion, belonged together.[95]

Ptolemy, fourteen hundred years earlier, had underestimated the distance between western Europe and the east coast of Asia by at least fifty degrees longitude.[96] Thus, Columbus, relying heavily on Ptolemy, continued to believe he had reached Asia. On the third voyage, he coasted along Venezuela and encountered the Orinoco. From the Gulf of Pearls (modern Gulf of Paria), as he described in a letter to the crown, "the water runs constantly with great force towards the east."[97] Columbus was certain he had come upon the earthly paradise:

> For its situation [in the east] agrees with the opinions of those holy and wise theologians, and also the signs are very much in accord with this idea, for I never read or heard of so great a quantity of fresh water flowing into the sea . . . and if it does not come from there, from paradise, it seems to be a still greater marvel, for I do not believe that there is known in the world a river so great and so deep.[98]

On the fourth voyage, Columbus left the southern shore of Cuba and charted his course southwest toward India. The coast of Honduras he regarded as Ciamba (lower Cathay). The plan, as G. E.

Nunn describes it, "was to follow this coast in a southerly and ultimately westerly direction past Java Major . . . the Strait of Malacca, and into the Indian Ocean to the India of the Ganges."[99] Eventually the fleet dropped anchor off the Panama coast and the admiral went ashore, where the natives of Veragua confirmed his belief. We may wonder at the problems of translation; what he heard may well have been what he had hoped to hear. At any rate, he reports in a letter to the king, dated 7 July 1503, that according to the natives "the province of Ciguare lies inland to the west nine days' journey. They say that the sea surrounds Ciguare, and that from there it is ten days' journey to the River Ganges."[100]

Columbus was forced to return for lack of provisions, and so, like Alexander, he never reached the sacred river. To the end, he felt that at Veragua he had found the land of Ophir and brought King Solomon's mines under control of the Spanish crown.[101]

Throughout this book we have examined the many myths and legends connected with Ganga. We will never know which ones found their way to Alexandria and into the minds of those later writers who identify the Ganges as a river of Eden. The popular belief that paradise lay somewhere in the Caucasus corresponds to the image of Ganga flowing from the same mountain chain; as early as the third century B.C., Megasthenes records that the river originated high in the mountains of Asia. Some Christian writers such as Cosmas and Mandeville describe the four rivers issuing from a well or lake; in Indian tradition, as we have seen, Ganga, along with three other mighty streams, originates in Lake Manasarovar. The Apocalypse of Paul, from the Apocryphal New Testament, describes the rivers of Eden flowing from the roots of a tree;[102] the same is said of Ganga in the *Mahabharata* and the *Shiva Purana*. The Apocalypse further mentions a great river that falls from heaven and waters the earth.[103] The image brings to mind Gangavatarana, the well-known descent of the Ganges. The parallels are many.[104]

In the end, all is conjecture. But it is not unlikely that some of these descriptions, together with the geographical speculations of the ancient and medieval world, helped make Ganga what she has always been to those who know and love her: *lokanadi,* the River of the World.

Notes

CHAPTER 1

1. In Egyptian religious art, a lotus flower is used as a symbol for the remote mountains of the upper Nile, which concealed the source of the river.

2. Alberuni, the Muslim historian who visited India in the eleventh century, gives a traveler's report of a river "which is several times crossed on bridges consisting of planks tied with cords to two canes, which stretch from rock to rock, and are fastened to milestones constructed on either side. People carry the burdens on their shoulders over such a bridge, whilst below, at a depth of a hundred yards, the water foams as white as snow, threatening to shatter the rocks." See Alberuni, *Alberuni's India,* trans. E. C. Sachau (Delhi, 1964), vol. 1, p. 201.

3. Kanti Nautiyal, *The Archaeology of the Kumaon* (Varanasi, 1969), p. 153.

4. Swami Maharaj Tapovan, *Ishwara Darshan* (Madras, 1969), p. 139.

5. Birch bark is strong yet malleable and since early times has been used as a form of clothing by ascetics living in the forests.

6. Abul Fazl, *Ain-i-Akbari,* trans. H. Blochmann (Delhi, 1871), vol. 1, p. 58. Even among Muslims the custom goes back at least to Muhammed bin Tughluq (1325-1351), sultan of Delhi. See Aziz Ahmad, *Islamic Culture in the Indian Setting* (Oxford, 1964), p. 177.

7. Jean Baptiste Tavernier, *Travels in India* (London, 1925), vol. 2, pp. 253-254.

8. Hiuen Tsiang, *Travels of Hiuen Tsiang,* trans. Samuel Beal (Calcutta, 1957), vol. 2, p. 226.

9. Abul Fazl, vol. 1, p. 32.

CHAPTER 2

1. *Katha Upanishad* IV.6.

2. *Rig Veda* II.35.9, 10.

3. Sam Higginbottom, *India's Agricultural Problems* (New York, 1954), p. 11.

4. See B. M. Bhatia, *Famines in India* (Bombay, 1967); Hari Srivastava, *The History of Indian Famines* (Agra, 1968).

5. William Crooke, *The Northwest Provinces of India* (London, 1897), p. 46.
6. William Crooke, *The Popular Religion and Folklore of Northern India* (Delhi, 1968), vol. 1, p. 89.
7. *Rāmāyaṇa.* Bāla-kāṇḍa 38.
8. Percy Brown, *Indian Architecture,* vol. 1: *Buddhist and Hindu Period* (Bombay, 1965), p. 78.
9. Ibid.
10. *Rāmāyana.* Bāla-kāṇḍa 43.
11. The style flourished in Orissa from the eighth to the twelfth centuries, though the carvings are late copies of an old design. See note by Percy Brown in A. Annanadale, "A Working Model of the Origin of the Ganges in a Temple in Ganjam," *Memoires of the Asiatic Society of Bengal* 8(1924): 265.
12. *Vishṇu Purāṇa* II.8.
13. *Bhāgavata P.* 8.21.1–3; *Kūrma P.* 1.16.56; *Vāmana P.* 65.32–34.
14. *Mahābhārata.* Ādi-parvan 98.
15. C. Sivaramamurti, "The Story of Gaṅgā and Amṛita at Paṭṭaḍakal," *Oriental Art* 3(1957):20–24.
16. *Mahābhārata.* Śalya-parvan 44.
17. *Mahāsuka Jātaka,* no. 429.
18. Āśramavāsika-parvan, trans. C. V. Narasimhan.

CHAPTER 3

1. Like the Ganges Valley, the Indus region also receives the monsoon, though the amount of precipitation may have been less than half, to judge from modern figures. Allahabad, for example, receives 34 inches between June and September, Lahore nearly 15. Over the entire year, the difference amounts to 39.1 versus 19.6 inches. See O. H. K. Spate, *India and Pakistan* (London, 1957), p. 44. Judging from some of the tropical animals found on the Indus seals—elephant, rhinoceros, tiger—annual rainfall may have been higher in the Indus region four thousand years ago, but no firm evidence supports this suggestion. In Mesopotamia, the Tigris and Euphrates do not traverse a uniform zone. Syria and Assyria still receive winter rains from the Atlantic sufficient for modest growth of cereals without irrigation. In ancient Egypt, the Nile south of Cairo experienced semimonsoon conditions. See V. Gordon Childe, *New Light on the Most Ancient East* (New York, 1952), pp. 31, 102.
2. Dorothy Mackay, "Ancient River Beds and Dead Cities," *Antiquity* 19 (1945):138.
3. Ibid., p. 137.
4. Sir Mortimer Wheeler, *The Indus Civilization,* 3rd ed. (Cambridge, 1968), p. 33.
5. Mackay, p. 142.
6. D. D. Kosambi, *The Culture and Civilization of Ancient India* (London, 1965), p. 62.
7. Wheeler, p. 67.
8. S. R. Rao, "Shipping and Maritime Trade of the Indus People," *Expedition* 8(1965):30–37.
9. G. R. Sharma, *The Excavations at Kauśāmbī* (Allahabad, 1960), p. 6.
10. S. C. Malik, *Indian Civilization: The Formative Period* (Simla, 1968), p. 140.
11. W. T. Sedgwick and H. W. Tyler, *A Short History of Science* (New York, 1939), p. 31.

12. A. H. Sayce, *The Religions of the Ancient Babylonians* (London, 1887), p. 240.
13. Eric Neumann, *The Great Mother* (Princeton, 1955), p. 48.
14. Ernest Mackay, *Early Indus Civilizations* (London, 1948), p. 16; Wheeler, p. 43.

CHAPTER 4

1. Because of the limited archaeological evidence, there is considerable controversy over using the word *Aryan* to describe these early settlers. The term *Vedic* may reasonably include the period ca. 1200–800 B.C., when the four Vedas were composed, while *Brahmanic* covers the period ca. 900–700 B.C., which gave rise to the Brāhmaṇa literature. For our purposes, Aryan will refer to those people associated with both sets of scriptures.
2. For a discussion of the size and characteristics of herding societies, see Gerhard Lenski and Jean Lenski, *Human Societies* (Englewood Cliffs, N.J., 1974), pp. 267–270.
3. Richard Thurnwald, "The Psychology of Acculturation," *American Anthropologist* 34(1932):562.
4. Ralph Beals, "Acculturation," in A. L. Kroeber (ed.), *Anthropology Today* (Chicago, 1953), p. 627.
5. D. D. Kosambi, *The Culture and Civilization of Ancient India* (London, 1965), p. 81.
6. T. Burrow, *The Sanskrit Language* (London, 1959), p. 387.
7. Thurnwald, p. 562.
8. *Rig Veda* III.3310; III.34.11–13.
9. *RV* I.140.12.
10. V. Gordon Childe, *The Aryans* (London, 1926), p. 87.
11. The *Rig Veda* often mentions ships and the sea. While most passages may describe small craft and rivers, some refer unmistakably to the sea.
12. Childe, p. 83. For a general discussion of Aryan society, see his chap. 4, pp. 78–94.
13. N. N. Bhattacharyya, *History of Indian Cosmogonical Ideas* (New Delhi, 1971), p. 13.
14. *RV* I.112.11.
15. Kosambi, p. 80.
16. *RV* VI.21.9; VII.56.25; X.97.1; X.97.17; X.1351. The tree as a primal substance of creation is a common Aryan myth. Viśvakarman, the divine craftsman of the *Rig Veda,* fashions the world from a tree. "What indeed was the wood? What the tree?" questions the scripture, "from which they fashioned the heaven and earth?" (*RV* X.81.4). While probably of European provenance, the idea provides a point of contact with the vegetal substratum.
17. *RV* X.16.3; X.58.4–7, 9–12, abridged.
18. Jean Przyluski, "Totémisme et végétalisme dans l'Inde," *Revue de l'histoire des religions* 96(1927):359.
19. Lucien Levy-Bruhl, *How Natives Think* (New York, 1966), p. 346.
20. X.24.5–6; I.159.14; V.43.13; I.185.1, 5.
21. X.125.7. In several ways, the goddess serves the same end as the Logos in Greek and Christian thought.
22. G. R. Sharma, *The Excavations at Kauśāmbī* (Allahabad, 1960), p. 5.
23. Bridget Allchin and Raymond Allchin, *The Birth of Indian Civilization* (Baltimore, 1968), p. 211.
24. Walter Fairservis, *The Roots of Ancient India* (New York, 1971), p. 352. At Atranjikhera—on the upper Ganges—the lower levels of painted gray ware

are carbon dated 1024 B.C. plus or minus 110 years and appear above an ochre-colored ware. At first the new ceramic comprises less than 10 percent of the total complex, which includes several other traditions as well. The gradual increase of painted gray ware implies a peaceful assimilation of these and other styles to the new inhabitants. See S. C. Malik, *Indian Civilization* (Simla, 1968), p. 126.

25. The introduction of iron in Europe—in Danubian Period VII—produced a similar effect on settlement patterns. Previously, in Period VI, a crop-and-fallow agriculture plus the bronze axe and harvesting tools allowed for villages of thirty-five to forty houses. In Periods VII and VIII, use of the iron plow, along with other agricultural innovations, stimulated the growth of fortified cities covering twelve or more acres. See Betty J. Meggars, "Environmental Limitations on the Development of Culture," *American Anthropologist* 56 (1954):814.

26. H. C. Raychaudhuri, *Political History of Ancient India,* 7th ed. (Calcutta, 1950), p. 33.

27. *Mahābhārata.* Ādi-parvan 128; Udyoga-parvan 89, 94; Sānti-parvan 9. Also Āśramavāsika-parvan 5.

28. *Vājasaneyī Saṃhitā* XXIII.18.

29. Kosambi, p. 90.

30. Charles Singer et al. (eds.), *A History of Technology,* vol. 1: *From Early Times to the Fall of Ancient Empires* (London, 1954), p. 713.

31. Gideon Sjoberg, "The Preindustrial City," *American Journal of Sociology* 55(1955):438.

32. S. C. Singh, *Changes in the Course of Rivers and Their Effects on Urban Settlements in the Middle Ganga Plain* (Varanasi, 1973), pp. 86–87.

33. V.19.8; XX.94.6; X.46.2.

34. Such as iron-smelters, car-builders, horse-keepers. XXX.6–22.

35. *Atharva Veda* III.15.1, 2, 5.

36. *AV* XI.4.13 and X.1.42; *Vājasaneyī Saṃhitā* I.11; *Śatapatha Brāhmaṇa* V.3.3.2–6 and XII.7.1.9. In modern times Allahabad, with about forty inches of rain, forms a dividing line between the rice and wheat-barley areas. Proceeding east, the balance shifts dramatically, with the Patna region producing three times more rice than barley. In the Mālda district of Bengal, barley disappears. See Indras, *Lost Sarasvatī* (Vallabh Vidyanagar, 1967), p. 22; Spate, pp. 178–179.

37. *AV* VIII.7.9; *Taittirīya Saṃhitā* I.4.45; *AV* II.3.6; *Vājasaneyī Saṃhitā* XII.94; *AV* III.31.10.

38. According to scholar and statesman K. M. Panikkar, "the distribution of the indigenous races even today in the uplands of South Bihar and in the eastern areas of Madhya Pradesh, and the persistence of the Bhils in the Aravali and Vindhya ranges show that as a population movement the Aryan invasion ceased to have any momentum after it reached the Gangetic Valley." See K. M. Panikkar, *Geographical Factors in Indian History* (Bombay, 1959), p. 93.

39. It is in the Brāhmaṇa literature of the seventh and eighth centuries B.C. that the mother goddess makes her reappearance as a major figure.

CHAPTER 5

1. E. W. Hopkins, *The Religions of India* (Boston, 1895), p. 31; E. Thomas, in R. D. Oldham, "On the Probable Changes in the Geography of the Punjab and Its Rivers," *Journal of the Asiatic Society of Bengal* 55(1886):341. The

argument is chiefly linguistic: with Avestan *h* becoming *s* in Sanskrit, the two names are cognate.

2.   R. D. Oldham, p. 340ff; O. H. K. Spate, *India and Pakistan* (London, 1957), pp. 486–488; A. B. Keith and A. A. Macdonell, *Vedic Index* (Delhi, 1912), vol. 2, pp. 435ff. See also C. F. Oldham, "The Sarasvati and the Lost River of the Indian Desert," *Journal of the Royal Asiatic Society* 25(1893): 49–76. For a stimulating if erratic discussion, see Indras, *Lost Sarasvatī* (Vallabh Vidyanagar, 1967).

3.   The linguistic evidence provides a case of what historian Nilakantha Sastri calls "that transfer of river names which is of common occurrence from very early times in the *topographia sacra* of India." See his *Cultural Contacts between Aryans and Dravidians* (Bombay, 1967), p. 35; see also Hopkins, p. 31.

4.   See John Marshall, *Mohenjo-Daro and the Indus Valley Civilization* (London, 1931), vol. 1, pp. 5–6, for further references.

5.   VI.61.14.

6.   *Vishṇu Dharma Śāstra* I.8; I.12; I.15.

7.   *RV* VI.61.11; V.43.11.

8.   *Skanda Purāṇa.* Kedār-kāṇḍa III.56–60.

9.   *RV* VI.61.2. Later literature, eager to preserve the memory of the Vedic river, often repeats the earlier descriptions. Compare *Vāmana Purāṇa XI.4.*

10.   *Mārkaṇḍeya Purāṇa* 56.6.

11.   *RV* VII.95.2; *Mbh.* Śalya-parvan 35.

12.   *RV* VI.61.7: *Mbh.* Droṇa-parvan 60; Śalya-parvan 44.

13.   The later *Vāmana Purāṇa* (XI.3) also notes that Sarasvatī "was born of a fig tree."

14.   *Mbh.* Vana-parvan 144. The *Śiva Purāṇa* repeats the theme of Gaṅgā flowing "from the branches of an Udambara [fig] tree." Koṭirudra Saṃhitā XXVII.4.

15.   *Skanda Purāṇa* VII.1.35.25, 26.

16.   "The divine sin-dissolving Bhāgīrathī, flowing on the earth, was, in the beginning, water in the vessel of the Primeval Grandfather [Brahma]." See Śaṅkarāchārya, *Gaṅgāshṭakam,* in A. Avalon and E. Avalon (trans.), *Hymns to the Goddess* (Madras, 1966), p. 41.

17.   *Mbh.* Bhīshma-parvan 6.

18.   *Vāmana Purāṇa* XVI.37; XVI.35–36.

19.   *RV* I.3.10–12. *Śatapatha Brāhmaṇa* V.2.213; V.3.4.25; VII.5.1.31; IX.3.1.17.

20.   A. B. Keith, *The Religion and Philosophy of the Vedas and Upanishads* (Delhi, 1925), pt. 1, p. 173.

21.   *Aitareya Āraṇyaka* III.16.

22.   Skanda Purāṇa Kedār-kāṇḍa III.21–25.51.56.91–95; *Mbh.* Anuśāsana-parvan 26.

23.   Bāṇa, *Harsha-Carita,* trans. E. B. Cowell and F. W. Thomas (London, 1929), p. 158.

24.   *Vishṇu Dharma Śāstra* XIX.6; XIX.10–11.

25.   *RV* III.54.13; *Hiraṇyakeśin Gṛihya Sūtra* I.6.20.1.

26.   *Mbh.* Ādi-parvan 95.

27.   *Mbh.* Śalya-parvan 51.

28.   Sir A. Cunningham, *Archaeological Survey of India: Reports* (Varanasi, 1970), vol. 14, pp. 103–105.

29.   Cunningham, *ASI Reports,* vol. 9, p. 60.

30. *Mbh.* Vana-paran 130.
31. The *Matsya Purāṇa,* one of the oldest Purāṇas (ca. third century A.D.), omits all reference to the invisible Sarasvatī joining Gaṅgā and Yamunā at the saṅgam, though its section on the Greatness of Prayāg (chaps. 103–112) gives a detailed account of the area and its main sites.
32. III.56.3.
33. X.76.90.
34. *Mbh.* Śalya-parvan 37.
35. *Mbh.* Vana-parvan 85.
36. *Mbh.* Vana-parvan 86. See also U. N. Roy, *Studies in Ancient Indian History and Culture* (Allahabad, 1969), vol. 1, pp. 181, 213–214.
37. *Skanda Purāṇa.* Kedār-kāṇḍa 3.111–115.
38. S. Sivaramamurti, *Some Aspects of Indian Culture* (New Delhi, 1969), pp. 23–24, fig. 15.
39. Kaśinath, "Serpent Worship," *Indian Antiquary* 2(1873):124. Vāsuki's temple is built near the pond of the serpent king, mentioned as early as the *Mahābhārata* (Vana-parvan 85) and the *Matsya Purāṇa* (106.46).
40. Thomas Watters, *On Yuan Chwang's Travels in India* (Delhi, 1961), vol. 2, p. 364.
41. Of the four places where the amṛita fell, two are located on the Ganges. I am told that a temple at Nasik is located near a river also called Gaṅgā. The temple is opened every twelve years, during the Kumbha Mela. At that time, it is said, the water of the original Gaṅgā comes to the temple. I have not inquired about Ujjain, but it would not be surprising to find a similar belief there. If so, Gaṅgā water might indeed have been the amṛita to the authors of the legend.
42. Other rivers like the Kṛishṇa and the Narmadā are endowed with rich traditions all their own.
43. *Mbh.* Vana-parvan 85; Anuśāsana-parvan 25.
44. *Mbh.* Vana-parvan 85.

CHAPTER 6

1. Martin Nilsson, *History of Greek Religion* (Oxford, 1925), p. 28; R. E. Witt, *Isis in the Graeco-Roman World* (Ithaca, 1971), p. 142.
2. Witt, p. 142.
3. Gertrude Levy, *The Gate of Horn* (London, 1948), p. 4 passim; Eric Neumann, *The Great Mother* (Princeton, 1955), p. 270.
4. R. Briffault, *The Mothers* (New York, 1931), p. 166.
5. Joseph Campbell, *The Masks of God: Primitive Mythology* (New York, 1959), p. 313.
6. Briffault, p. 246.
7. *Hymn to Artemis* 3.15–25.
8. Nilsson, p. 82.
9. E. O. James, *The Cult of the Mother Goddess* (London, 1959), p. 130.
10. Levy, p. 223.
11. *Mbh.* Svargārohina-parvan 97.
12. Pausanias 2.30.2; Hesiod *Theogony* 411–452; Virgil *Aeneid* 4.
13. Pausanias 2.35.3–4.
14. Walter Otto, "The Meaning of the Eleusinian Mysteries," in Joseph Campbell (ed.), *The Mysteries* (New York, 1955), p. 20.
15. Plutarch, *De fact. in orb. lun.* 28, as noted in Jane Harrison, *Prolegomena to the Study of Greek Religion* (New York, 1959), p. 275.
16. Childe, *The Aryans,* pp. 5, 81, passim.
17. Callimachus *Hymn to Artemis* 3.5–15; Diodorus 5.72.5.

18. Herodotus 1.181.
19. H. Frankfort, *The Birth of Civilization in the Near East* (Garden City, N.Y., 1951), p. 56.
20. C. G. Jung, *The Archetypes and the Collective Unconscious* (Princeton, 1959), p. 81 passim.
21. *Matsya Purāṇa* 121.29–30.
22. *Mbh.* Ādi-parvan 172.
23. IV.2.
24. Gilbert Murray, *Five Stages of Greek Religion*(Garden City, N.Y., 1955), p. 61.
25. For a more detailed examination of the goddess in her Indo-European setting, see Joseph Campbell, *The Masks of God: Occidental Mythology* (New York, 1964), pp. 3–93.

CHAPTER 7

1. Already in the *Taittirīya Brahmāṇa* (II.8.9.6), Brahman is considered the forest and the tree from which the worlds are fashioned.
2. For Saṃsāra in the Upanishads: *Bṛhadāraṇyaka* III.2.13 and VI.2.2; *Śvetaśvatara* V.11–12; *Kaushītaki* I.2; *Chandogya* V.10.7; *Muṇḍaka* I.2.7, 9, 10; *Katha* V.7.
3. Heinrich Zimmer, *Myths and Symbols in Indian Art and Civilization* (New York, 1946), p. 25.
4. Paul Devandan, *The Concept of Maya* (London, 1950), p. 68.
5. *Atharva Veda* XII.1.19.
6. F. D. K. Bosch, *The Golden Germ* (The Hague, 1960), p. 84.
7. Kālidāsa, *Meghadūta* 51.
8. *Śatapatha Brāhmaṇa* I.6.3.23; I.1.1.20.
9. *Mbh.* Śalya-parvan 37.
10. "On the gateways of Sānchī, tree worship occupies as much space as Buddhist subjects. Men and women are depicted as paying homage to the trees." See V. S. Agrawala, *Ancient Indian Folk Cults* (Varanasi, 1970), p. 125.
11. As observed by S. Kramrisch, *Indian Sculpture* (Calcutta, 1933), pp. 16, 29.
12. In promoting his policy of religious integration, Aśoka declares that the deities of former times be mingled with the gods of the higher religion. See *Rupnath Minor Rock Edicts, I* and passim.
13. High in a tree, a gandharva guards the dwelling place of soma. "Wondrous, he protects the generation of the Gods" (*RV* IX.83.4).
14. A. Coomaraswamy, *Yakshas* (Delhi, 1971), pt. 2, p. 14.
15. X.2.32.
16. The village god is generally lodged in a small primitive shrine or by itself at the base of a tree. In many cases, the image is lacking and the tree itself personifies the deity. See N. V. Ramanayya, *An Essay on the Origin of the South Indian Temple* (Madras, 1930), p. 4.
17. Ibid., p. 52.
18. A. Annandale, "A Working Model of the Origin of the Ganges in a Temple in Ganjam," *Memoires of the Asiatic Society of Bengal* 8(1924):255.
19. *Artha Śāstra* IV.3.
20. *Zend-Avesta,* trans. James Darmesteter (New Delhi, 1965), pt. 2, *Ābān Yasht* I.1; I.6; XXI.85; XXI.87; XXVIII.121, passim.

CHAPTER 8

1. J. C. Jain, *Ancient India as Depicted in the Jain Canons* (Bombay, 1947), p. 274.
2. *Mahāparinibbāna Sutta* V.

3.   *Mahājanika Jātaka,* no. 539.

4.   Jain, p. 251.

5.   *Chullavagga* XII.2.1. Later seals from Vaiśālī include the imprint of traders and transport merchants plus a boat with three decks and a large oar, together suggesting the presence of waterborne traffic. See R. C. Majumdar and A. S. Altekar, *The Vākāṭaka-Gupta Age* (Delhi, 1954), p. 355; H. Chakraborti, *Trade and Commerce of Ancient India* (Calcutta, 1966), p. 189.

6.   Arrian *Indica* 4. Similarly, the Son River: *Indica* 1.22b.

7.   *Dīgha Nikāya* VI.28.8.

8.   *Mbh.* Sabha-parvan 27.

9.   Mrs. C. F. Rhys-Davids, "Early Economic Conditions in North India," *Journal of the Royal Asiatic Society,* October 1901, p. 876.

10.   To judge from its metallic sound, it was sturdier than the earlier painted gray ware and was produced in a far greater variety of shades. The ceramic was highly valued, for we find the broken pieces of several pots held together by copper rivets. See N. R. Banerjee, *The Iron Age in India* (Delhi, 1965), p. 201.

11.   *Alinachitta J.,* no. 156; *Cullaka-seṭṭhi J.,* no. 4; *Mahā-ummaga J.,* no. 546; *Samudra-vanija J.,* no. 466.

12.   A. S. Altekar and V. Mishra, *Report on the Kumrahar Excavations, 1951–1955* (Patna, 1959), p. 25.

13.   *Uvāsaga Dasāo* I.105, as noted in A. L. Basham, *The Wonder That Was India* (New York, 1954), p. 216.

14.   *Artha Śāstra* II.28.126; II.16.98.

15.   *Mahāvastu* III.286. See also III.113.

16.   *Manu Dharma Śāstra* VIII.157; VIII.412. *Milinda-pañha* VI.21.

17.   *Periplus* 64.63.60.

18.   *Avadāna-Śataka* I.1; I.3; IV.6; IX.1.

19.   *Āvaśyaka-Bṛihadvṛitti,* as noted in K. P. Jayaswal, "The Muruṇḍa Dynasty and the Date of Pādalipta," in *Mālaviya Commemorative Volume* (Banaras, 1932), p. 185. See also *Vikrama's Adventures,* trans. F. Edgerton (Cambridge, Mass., 1926), p. 251.

20.   P. Pelliot, "Le Fou-Nan," *Bulletin de l'École française d'Extrême Orient* 3(1903):271, and "Quelques textes chinois concernant l'Indochine Hindouisée," in *Études Asiatiques* (Hanoi, 1925), vol. 2, pp. 243–265. The sixth-century *Shui-Ching-Chu* (I.55) relates that the king of Tan Mei (Tāmralipti) had sent an embassy to the Chinese court in the third century A.D. which probably traveled by sea.

21.   Fa-hien, *A Record of Buddhist Kingdoms,* trans. James Legge (New York, 1886), chap. 27.

22.   *Harshacarita* III.95.

23.   *Raghuvaṃśa* XIV.30.

24.   Śūdraka, *Mṛicchakaṭika,* act 2.

25.   *Nārada Smṛiti* III.16.

26.   *Travels,* bk. 2, p. 242; bk. 4, pp. 401–402.

27.   Hwui-lih, *Life of Hiuen-Tsiang,* trans. S. Beal (London, 1911), p. 172.

28.   *Raghuvaṃśa* IV.36.

29.   John F. Fleet, *Corpus Inscriptionum Indicarum,* vol. 3: *Inscriptions of the Early Gupta Kings* (Varanasi, 1970), p. 217.

30.   F. Kielhorn, "Khalimpur Plate of Dharmapāla," *Epigraphia Indica* 4(1896–1897):252.

31.   John Jourdain, *The Journal of John Jourdain* (Cambridge, 1905), p. 162.

32.   Peter Mundy, *Travels in Asia* (Cambridge, 1907–1936), vol. 2, pp. 87–224.

CHAPTER 9

1. Levy, pts. 1 and 2.
2. *ŚB* XIII.8.1.1.
3. *RV* X.18.13.
4. Agrawala, *Ancient Indian Folk Cults*, p. 132.
5. *RV* X.18.4.
6. *ŚB* XIII.8.2.2.; VII.1.1.12. Even today, communities such as the Todas, Kurumbas, and Irulas use stone circles as grave markers. The most primitive graves of South India and the Deccan are "the simple ring of stones, with three stones in the centre, marking the place where the dead body is buried." See Ramanayya, *Essay on the Origin of the South Indian Temple*, p. 76.
7. *ŚB* VII.4.1.7.
8. XIII.8.1.17.
9. A. M. Hocart, *Kings and Councillors*(Chicago, 1936), p. 64.
10. Benjamin Rowland, *The Art and Architecture of India: Buddhist, Hindu, Jain* (London, 1953), p. 23.
11. *ŚB* XIII.8.1.5.
12. Levy, p. 218. Arthur Evans, *The Mycenaean Tree and Pillar Cult* (London, 1901), p. 44.
13. *RV* I.59.1; III.5.10.
14. *AV* X.7.4, 6.
15. *AV* X.7.41. Cf. I.2.1. See also Bosch, *The Golden Germ*, p. 164.
16. *RV* VII.21.5; X.99.3.
17. I.70.2.
18. *ŚB* VII.1.1.2.
19. *AV* VI.81.2.
20. *Bṛhadāraṇyaka Up.* 6.4.2–3.
21. *Mbh.* XIII.141.
22. *Matsya P.* XI.20–21.
23. Ramanayya, p. 2.
24. Ibid., pp. 2–3.
25. Mrs. Sinclair Stevenson, *The Rites of the Twice-Born* (London, 1920), p. 396.
26. Madanjeet Singh, *Himalayan Art* (New York, 1968), p. 102.
27. Such as Tiruvannamallai, See G. Jouveau-Dubreuil, *Iconography of Southern India* (Paris, 1937), p. 12.
28. See Mircea Eliade, *Patterns in Comparative Religion* (Cleveland, 1963), pp. 231–232.
29. Frankfort, *Births of Civilization in the Near East*, p. 56.
30. Stella Kramrisch, *The Hindu Temple* (Calcutta, 1946), vol. 1, p. 161.
31. *Rāmāyaṇa* V.15.43.
32. Fleet, *Corpus Inscriptionem Indicarum*, vol. 3, p. 78; *Samarāṅgana* 55.3.
33. C. D. Diehl, *Instrument and Purpose* (Lund, Sweden, 1956), p. 254.
34. E. B. Havell, *The Himalayas in Indian Art* (London, 1924), p. 26.
35. Walter Leifer, *Himalaya: Mountain of Destiny* (London, 1962), p. 2.
36. Lucien Levy-Bruhl, *How Natives Think* (New York, 1966), p. 330.
37. Diehl, p. 66.
38. *Agni Purāṇa* 102.17.
39. "Altar, 'pillar,' mountain, cave, enclosure and gate," says Kramrisch. "Singly and conjointly they are the themes of sacred architecture in India, as they have been in the Mediterranean and Near Eastern civilizations since the days of Megalithic art." See *The Hindu Temple*, vol. 1, p. 16.
40. "The temple and statutes," says Kramrisch, "are so many stages in the

approach to moksha." See *The Art of India* (London, 1954), p. 10.

41.   Similarly, in an architectural commentary the *Agni Purāṇa* (104.29–30) indicates the evolution from tree to pillar support at the entranceway: "The ornamental branches overhanging the doors should be made to culminate in the images of celestials."

42.   S. Giedion, *The Eternal Present*, vol. 2: *The Beginnings of Architecture* (New York, 1964), p. 97.

43.   See Goblet d'Alviella, *The Migration of Symbols* (New York, 1956), p. 153.

44.   Such as the Ghateśvar temple, Badoli. See Odette Viennot, *Les Divinités fluviales Gaṅgā et Yamunā* (Paris, 1964), p. 40a.

45.   *Odyssey* 7–8.

46.   Neumann, *The Great Mother*, p. 159.

47.   Akshay Kumar Maitra, "The River-Goddess Gaṅgā," *Rūpam* 6 (1921):4.

48.   *RV* II.24.5; I.128.6.

49.   *AV* IX.3.22; *RV* II.3.5.

50.   *Aitareya Up.* I.1.3.

51.   *Sāṅkhyāyana Gṛihya Sūtra* III.3.2.9.

52.   The classifications differ. For a discussion see Bosch, *The Golden Germ*, pp. 88–89; Mircea Eliade, *Yoga: Immortality and Freedom* (New York, 1958), pp. 236–240.

53.   *RV* I.29.3; II.26.11.

54.   For the union of fire and water, see C. G. Jung, *Psychology and Alchemy* (New York, 1953), p. 140, fig. 72; as irreconcilables, see *Iliad* 21.

55.   *Haṭhapradīpikā* III.106. The spinal cord itself is called the Sushumnā, a term equated in the text (III.4) with Śiva's burning ground.

56.   Ibid., III.23.

57.   J. C. Harle, *Temple Gateways in South India* (Oxford, 1963), p. viii.

58.   Diehl, *Instruments and Purpose*, p. 106.

59.   *Agni P.* 21.9–11.

60.   Diehl, p. 106.

61.   James Pritchard (ed.), *Ancient Near Eastern Texts* (Princeton, 1955), pp. 331, 333.

62.   *Mbh.* III.144; also the Tibetan *Kailāsa Purāṇa*. See Swami Pranavananda, *Kailāsa-Mānasarovar* (Calcutta, 1949), p. 8. See also *Mārkaṇḍeya P.* 56.7–9; *Kūrma P.* 1.44.7.

63.   *Mārkaṇḍeya P.* 57.18.

64.   *Vishṇu P.* II.2 and II.8; *Bhāgavata P.* 5.17; *Kūrma P.* 1.44.28–33.

65.   *Matsya P.* 121.38–41; *Brāhmaṇḍa P.* 2.18.39–41.

66.   IV.3.208.

67.   *Rāmāyaṇa* I.35; *Kena Up.* III.25.

68.   *ŚB* VII.4.1.8.

69.   *ŚB* X.5.2.7–8. "The entrance of the garbha-gṛihya," says Kramrisch, "is the sculptural metamorphosis of the natural tīrtha." See *The Hindu Temple*, vol. 2, p. 315. In Egypt, "la naissance ou la renaissance par le lotus . . . est un thème de l'iconographie et de la liturgie de tous les dieux." See A. Moret, "Le lotus et la naissance des dieux," *Journal Asiatique* 9(1917):505.

70.   *Kathāsaritsāgara* XVIII.70.171.

71.   VII.31.

72.   *ŚB* VII.1.1.12.

73.   *Kaṭha Up.* IV.6.

74.   *Bhāgavata P.* IV.24.14.

75.   *Mbh.* XIII.14. According to Cope, "the traditional Christian font-rituals . . . give full expression to the sexual aspect of the regenerative process of

baptism. The font is unmistakably a womb, and in the Holy Saturday ceremonies the Paschal candle signifies the contribution of the masculine spirit. The massive candle is plunged three times into the font, and in some rites, the liquid wax is made to drip into the water." See Gilbert Cope, *Symbolism in the Bible and the Church* (New York, 1959), p. 102.

76. Jouveau-Dubreuil, *Iconography of Southern India,* p. 16.

77. Diehl, *Instrument and Purpose,* p. 241.

78. Ibid.

79. Stevenson, *Rites of the Twice-Born,* p. 375.

80. Tamonash Das Gupta, *Aspects of Bengali Society from Old Bengali Literature* (Calcutta, 1935), pp. 111–112. A story in the *Kathāsaritsāgara* (IX.56) describes the adventures of Nala, famous for his skill in chariot driving and cooking. The hero is bitten by a snake and his body is inhabited by a black figure named Kali, tantamount to dying. Eventually he recovers from the snakebite, frees himself from the demon, and finds employment as a cook. His skill is such that "waters gushed up in pots and pans without being put in." Here Nala's recovery may be seen as a return from the dead, the waters as those of the underworld.

81. Raphael Patai, *Man and Temple* (London, 1947), p. 56. We may also recall the Old Testament story of Moses and the rock. "And Moses lifted up his hand, and with his rod he smote the rock twice: and the water came out abundantly" (Numbers 20:11).

82. Lucian, *De dea Syria* 13.48; Pausanias 1.18.17.

83. Giedion, *Eternal Present,* vol. 2, p. 243, fig. 145.

CHAPTER 10

1. A. Coomaraswamy, *History of Indian and Indonesian Art* (New York, 1927), p. 45.

2. J. Ph. Vogel, "Le Makara dans la sculpture de l'Inde," *Revue des Arts Asiatiques* 6(1929–1930):145.

3. The makara—as cognate of the Nāga and of the dragon Vṛitra in the *Ṛig Veda*—may follow the same evolution as the yakshas: indigenous pre-Vedic elements, at first denounced and rejected, later admitted into the Hindu pantheon as surrogates of the gods.

4. Ernest Mackay, *Further Excavations at Mohenjo-Daro* (Delhi, 1938), vol. 2, pl. 19, no. 4.

5. Ernest Mackay, *Early Indus Civilizations* (London, 1948), p. 133.

6. G. Combaz, *L'Inde et l'Orient classique* (Paris, 1937), vol. 1, p. 152.

7. A. L. Basham, *The Wonder That Was India* (New York, 1954), p. 226.

8. *Avadāna-śataka* IV.6.

9. *Kathāsaritsāgara* XVIII.70.121.

10. *Rājataraṅgini*. Marco Polo (A.D. 1294), in his journey around the coast of India, reports the following tale that must have come from native sources: "In consequence of the gulf being infested with a large kind of fish, which often proves destructive of the [pearl] divers, the merchants take the precaution of being accompanied by a certain class of enchanters belonging to a class of Brahmans, who, by means of their diabolical art, have the power of constraining and stupefying these fish, so as to prevent them from doing mischief" (*Il Milione* 3.20.1).

11. Alberuni, *Alberuni's India,* trans. E. C. Sachau (Delhi, 1964), vol. 1, p. 205.

12. *Arthaśāstra* X.2; *Mbh.* VI.69.

13. *Mārkandeya P.* 68.17–19.

14.   John Rosenfeld, *The Dynastic Arts of the Kushans* (Berkeley, 1967), p. 179, pls. 2 and 2b.

15.   *On the Characteristics of Animals* 11.41.

16.   Manuel de Faria y Sousa, *History of the Discovery and Conquest of India by Portugal,* trans. Capt. John Stevens (London, 1695), vol. 2, p. 404.

17.   *Agni P.* 51.15. See T. Gopinath Rao, *The Elements of Hindu Iconography* (Delhi, 1928), vol. 2, pt. 2, p. 529.

18.   According to the *Vishṇudharmottaram,* a fourth- or fifth-century iconographic text, Varuṇa is flanked on either side by statues of Gaṅgā and Yamunā, with Gaṅgā on a fish or makara.

19.   René Guénon, *Symboles fondamentaux de la Science sacrée* (Paris, 1962), p. 359.

20.   Joseph Henderson, *The Wisdom of the Serpent* (New York, 1963), p. 43.

21.   Mircea Eliade, *Rites and Symbols of Initiation* (New York, 1958), p. 35.

22.   In myth, the dragon of Vaucluse, in France, was said to devour children of the surrounding region. L. Berenger-Feraud, *Superstitions et survivances étudiées au point du vue de leur origines et leurs transformations* (Paris, 1895), vol. 1, p. 211. See also the Chimu pottery design from Peru, depicting a man escaping from the mouth of a sea dragon. H. Leicht, *Indianische Kunst und Kultur* (Zürich, 1944), p. 85.

23.   C. G. Jung, *The Archetypes and the Collective Unconscious* (Princeton, 1959), p. 166.

24.   *White Yajur Veda* V.33; *Taittirīya Saṃhitā* V.5.13.

25.   In the European Rogationtide festivals—such as those in Sicily and England—the dragon represented the source of springs and rivers, and had to be subdued to prevent it from flooding instead of fructifying the land. See Theodore Gaster, *Thespis* (New York, 1950), p. 250.

26.   I have tried to avoid the main lines of Coomaraswamy's well-known study, which deals chiefly with the makara's vegetal affinities. See his *Yakshas* (Delhi, 1971), pt. 2.

27.   Universally, the fundamental element in the dragon's powers is the control of water. Both in its beneficial and destructive aspects, water was regarded as animated by the dragon. See G. Elliot Smith, *The Evolution of the Dragon* (Manchester, 1919), p. 78.

28.   *Mbh.* Ādi-parvan. 218.

29.   Eberhard Fischer and Haku Shah, *Mogra Dev* (Ahmedabad, 1971), p. 37.

30.   Sir Ernest Budge, *The Gods of the Egyptians* (London, 1894), vol. 2, pp. 355–358.

31.   Jung, p. 271.

32.   Berenger-Feraud, vol. 1, p. 208.

33.   As related by Athenagoras, in C. C. Richardson et al. (eds.), *Early Christian Fathers* (New York, 1953), vol. 1, p. 316.

34.   Similarly, the Tibetan goddess Lha-mo is described as "she of the lion face and she of the makara face." Her two acolytes are Makaravaktra and Simhavaktra. Antoinette Gordon, *Tibetan Religious Art* (New York, 1963), pp. 35, 58.

35.   See especially Bosch, *The Golden Germ,* pl. 9b.

36.   W. Norman Brown, *Man in the Universe* (Berkeley, 1966), p. 75.

37.   Viennot, pp. 53, 69, passim.

38.   *AV* X.2.32.

39.   *Bṛihadāraṇyaka Up.* 5.15.1.

40.   *ŚB* IV.1.5.1–12.

41.   *Rāmāyaṇa* II.14–15.

42.   XIII.26.

43. 102.3-8.
44. *Rām.* I.38; *Mbh.* I.131, 168. For Greek and Christian modes, cf. Plato *Timaeus* 41d, e; Jessie L. Weston, *From Ritual to Romance* (Garden City, N.Y., 1957), p. 76.
45. *Agni P.* 41.17-20.
46. G. Conteneau, *Manuel d'archéologie orientale* (Paris, 1927), vol. 2, p. 748, fig. 528.
47. André Parrot, *Sumer: The Dawn of Art* (New York, 1961), p. 272, fig. 339.
48. Neumann, *The Great Mother,* p. 128.
49. *RV* I.105.8; II.29.5; VII.10.2; IX.13.1; IX.20.1; X.56.6; X.57.2; X.130.1-2; X.106.1; *Brihadāranyaka Up.* 3.6; 3.7.1; 3.8.3; *Śvetāśvatara Up.* 6.10.
50. A. Coomaraswamy, *Elements of Buddhist Iconography* (Cambridge, Mass., 1934), p. 89.
51. V. S. Agrawala, *Gupta Art* (Lucknow, 1948), p. 16.
52. J. Allan, *Catalogue of the Coins of the Gupta Dynasties* (London, 1914), p. 14, pl. 2; A. Altekar, *Catalogue of Gupta Coins in the Bayana Hoard* (Bombay, 1954), p. 296.
53. The stone is amazingly durable. Among scores of images seven hundred years old or more, not one shows any effect of time. See H. Zimmer, *The Art of Indian Asia* (New York, 1955), vol. 1, p. 127. The ancient Egyptians called their country the Black Land, a name acknowledging the dark life-giving mud carried down by the Nile. The sacred god of the river was represented in statues carved from dark stone. See Witt, *Isis in the Graeco-Roman World,* p. 14.

CHAPTER 11

1. K. Bagchi, *The Ganges Delta* (Calcutta, 1944), p. 39.
2. W. W. Hunter, *A Statistical Account of Bengal* (London, 1875), vol. 1, p. 24.
3. Bagchi, p. 92.
4. Radhakamal Mukerjee, *The Changing Face of Bengal* (Calcutta, 1938), p. 79.
5. S. C. Majumdar, *Rivers of the Bengal Delta* (Calcutta, 1941), p. 123.
6. Ramaranjan Mukherji and S. C. Maity, *Corpus of Bengal Inscriptions* (Calcutta, 1967), pp. 39-40.
7. In Richard Hakluyt, *The Principal Navigations, Voyages, Traffiques and Discoveries of the English Nation* (New York, 1927-1928), vol. 3, p. 295.
8. Sebastian Manrique, *The Travels of Sebastian Manrique* (London, 1926-1927), vol. 2, p. 135.
9. Jean Tavernier, *Travels In India* (London, 1925), vol. 1, p. 102.
10. Elisee Reclus, *The Earth and Its Inhabitants,* vol. 3: *India and China* (London, 1884), p. 226.
11. Hunter, vol. 2, p. 27.
12. H. T. Colebrook, "On the Course of the Ganges through Bengal," *Asiatick Researches* 8(1803):2.
13. Ibid., p. 21.
14. Ibid., p. 20.
15. Observation by Captain Sherwill. Recorded in L. S. S. O'Malley, *Bengal District Gazetteers: Murshidabad* (Calcutta, 1914), p. 6.
16. Mukerjee, *Changing Face of Bengal,* p. 45.
17. *Mbh.* Droṇa-parvan 119; Karṇa-parvan 22; Sabhā-parvan 29.
18. H. B. Sircar, "The Port of Tāmraliptī in Fiction and History," in Perala Ratnam (ed.), *Studies in Indo-Asian Art and Culture* (Delhi, 1972), vol. 1, p. 223.
19. B. B. Lal, "Excavations at Hastināpura and Other Explorations in the Upper

Gaṅgā and Sutlej Basins," *Ancient India* 10–11(1954–1955):145.

20. T. N. Ramachandran, "Tāmraliptī," *Artibus Asiae* 14(1951):235 and pl. 5.
21. *Mahāvaṃsa* XI.28–31; XIX.4–6.
22. Basham, *The Wonder That Was India*, p. 228.
23. Gungwu Wang, *The Nanhai Trade* (Kuala Lumpur, 1958), p. 15.
24. *Shui-Ching-Chu* 1.55; *Liang Shu*. See Paul Wheatley, *Golden Khersonese* (Kuala Lumpur, 1961), p. 16.
25. Daṇḍin, *Daśakumāracarita*, trans. Arthur Ryder (Chicago, 1927), p. 164.
26. K. S. Ali Khan, *Memoires of Gaur and Pandua* (Calcutta, 1931), p. 42.
27. B. K. Basu, "Trade of Bengal from the Earliest Times down to the Great War," *Journal of Indian History* 6(1928):278.
28. L. S. S. O'Malley, *Bengal, Bihar, and Orissa* (London, 1917), p. 145.
29. In Col. Henry Yule, *Cathay and the Way Thither* (London, 1866), vol. 2, p. 459.
30. Nalini Bhattasali, *Coins and Chronology of the Early Independent Sultans of Bengal* (Cambridge, 1922), p. 170.
31. Ludovico di Varthema, *The Travels of Ludovico di Varthema* (London, 1863), p. 212. The identification of Gaur with Bengala has been a subject of considerable controversy. For an extended discussion, see Varthema, pp. cxiv–cxxi; Duarte Barbosa, *The Book of Duarte Barbosa* (London, 1921), vol. 2, pp. 135–145n.
32. Faria y Sousa, *Discovery and Conquest of India*, vol. 1, pp. 415–417.
33. W. W. Hunter, *The Annals of Rural Bengal* (London, 1897), p. 29. Given the sandy soil of the region, the river continues to shift. H. Creighton, writing in 1807, describes it as nine or ten miles from Gaur; see *The Ruins of Gaur* (London, 1817), p. 7. J. H. Ravenshaw in 1873 estimates it as some six miles from the city; see *Gaur* (London, 1878), p. 1. Both are classical studies of the site and its surroundings.
34. Manrique, *Travels,* vol. 2, p. 126.
35. Ibid., p. 128.
36. In Yule, *Cathay*, p. 457.
37. John Huyghen van Linschoten, *The Voyage of John Huyghen van Linschoten* (London, 1885), vol. 1, p. 94.
38. Manrique, *Travels,* vol. 2, p. 123.
39. Francois Bernier, *Travels in the Mogul Empire* (Delhi, 1891), p. 457.
40. Ibid., p. 442. We gain a similar impression from the French jeweler Tavernier (vol. 2, pp. 140ff) and from Thomas Bowrey (1670), *Geographical Account of the Countries round the Bay of Bengal* (London, 1903), p. 172.
41. Ghulam Husain Salīm, *Riyāzu-s-salatīn*, trans. Maulavi Abdus Salem (Calcutta, 1902), p. 248.
42. O'Malley, *Murshidabad*, p. 187.
43. Mukerjee, *Changing Face of Bengal*, p. 166.
44. In Hakluyt, *Principal Navigations*, vol. 2, p. 230ff.
45. Samuel Purchas (ed.), *Hakluytus Posthumus, or Purchas His Pilgrimes* (Glasgow, 1905–1907), vol. 10, pp. 113–114.
46. J. Horton Ryley, *Ralph Fitch: England's Pioneer to India and Burma* (London, 1899), p. 114.
47. Mukerjee, *Changing Face of Bengal*, p. 190.
48. Majumdar, *Rivers of the Bengal Delta*, p. 75.
49. Bowrey, *Geographical Account*, p. 174.
50. *Dohakośa*, in D. L. Snellgrove, *The Hevajura Tantra* (London, 1959), vol. 1, p. 37.
51. S. Das Gupta, *Obscure Religious Cults* (Calcutta, 1969), p. 97.

52. P. Mahapatra, *Folk Cults of Bengal* (Calcutta, 1972), p. 35.
53. Matilal Das and P. Mahapatra, *Lalan Gitika* (Calcutta, 1958), song 429.
54. Ibid., song 210.
55. Lalan, *Songs of Lalan Shah*, trans. Abu Rashd (Dacca, 1964), p. 49, song 34.
56. Das and Mahapatra, *Lalan Gitika*, p. 104.
57. Deben Bhattacharya, *The Mirror of the Sky: Songs of the Bāuls from Bengal* (London, 1969), p. 106.
58. Mahapatra, *Folk Cults of Bengal*, p. 104.
59. Rāmprasād Sen, *Rāmprasād's Devotional Songs*, trans. Jadunath Sinha (Calcutta, 1966), song 27.
60. Ibid., song 219.
61. Ibid., song 88.
62. Ibid., song 11.
63. Ibid., song 107.
64. R. C. Dutt, *Cultural Heritage of Bengal* (Calcutta, 1962), p. 81.
65. Jayadeva, *Gītā-Govinda*, trans. George Keyt (Bombay, 1940), p. 105.
66. Ibid., p. 9.
67. Subhadra Jha, *The Songs of Vidyāpati* (Banaras, 1954), poem 159.
68. Vidyāpati, *Love Songs of Vidyāpati*, trans. Deben Bhattacharya (New York, 1963), p. 134.
69. *Chandravatī* XII.
70. *Rūpavatī* V.
71. *Andha Bandhū.*
72. *Mahua* V.
73. E. T. Prideaux, "River Songs of Bhagalpur," *Man in India* 25(1945):20–21.
74. Asutosh Bhattacharyya, *Vanglar Loka-Sahitya* (Calcutta, 1971), vol. 5, p. 79.
75. Sondra Sen, "Concepts of Physical and Spiritual Health and Their Relation to Food Habits among Middle-Class Hindu Bengalis," M.A. thesis, University of Pennsylvania, 1969, p. 54.
76. Ibid., p. 56.
77. *Caitanya Caritāmṛita:* Ādi Lilā, Madhya Lilā.
78. Sondra Sen, "Concepts," p. 57.
79. Ibid., p. 42.
80. Asutosh Bhattacharyya, *Vangiya Loka-Samgit Ratnākar* (Calcutta, 1967), vol. 3, p. 1404.
81. *Caitanya Bhāgvat.* Ādi-kāṇḍa. See Phulrenu Datta, *La société bengalie au XVIe siècle* (Paris, 1938), pp. 67–68.
82. Sondra Sen, "Concepts," p. 51.
83. Datta, *La société bengalie*, p. 71.
84. Jayānanda, *Chaitanya Maṅgal*, in Datta, p. 74.
85. Tara Basu, *The Bengal Peasant from Time to Time* (Bombay and Calcutta, 1962), p. 122.
86. Rāmprasād Sen, song 44.
87. E. J. Thompson and A. M. Spencer, *Bengali Religious Lyrics: Śākta* (Calcutta, 1923), p. 75.
88. In Purchas, *Hakluytus Posthumus*, vol. 10, p. 161.
89. Gautier Schouten, *Voiage aux Indes Orientales 1658-1665* (Amsterdam, 1707), vol. 2, p. 161.
90. Sondra Sen, "Concepts," p. 52.
91. Faria y Sousa, *Discovery and Conquest of India*, vol. 2, p. 402.
92. Linschoten, *Voyage*, vol. 1, p. 93.

93. Bowrey, *Geographical Account,* p. 216.
94. G. Coedes, *Les États Hindouisés d'Indochine et d'Indonésie* (Paris, 1964), p. 111.
95. Mahapatra, *Folk Cults of Bengal,* p. 138.
96. P. K. Maity, *Historical Studies in the Cult of the Goddess Manasā* (Calcutta, 1966), p. 205.
97. Manrique, *Travels,* vol. 1, p. 75.
98. B. L. Choudhari, assistant superintendent of the Natural History Department, Indian Museum, Calcutta, in Manrique, vol. 1, p. 75n.
99. *Mbh.* Vana-parvan 85.
100. Manrique, *Travels,* vol. 1, p. 74.
101. W. H. Carey, *The Good Old Days of Honorable John Company* (Calcutta, 1906), vol. 2, p. 125.
102. Captain Alexander Hamilton, *A New Account of the East Indies* (Edinburgh, 1727), vol. 2, p. 4f.
103. *Sambād Pravākar,* 21 January 1853.
104. For references to the medieval temples and tīrthas on the island, see D. C. Sircar, *Studies in the Geography of Ancient and Medieval India* (Delhi, 1960), pp. 181–182.
105. Maity, *Historical Studies,* p. 206.
106. Manrique, *Travels,* vol. 1, p. 67.
107. Ralph Nicholson, "Vaishṇavism and Islām in Rural Bengal," in David Kopf (ed.), *Bengal: Regional Identity* (East Lansing, 1969), p. 34.
108. O'Malley, *Murshidabad,* p. 211.

CHAPTER 12

1. *Bāveru Jātaka,* no. 339.
2. Herod. 4.44.
3. Herod. 5.49. More specifically, see Walter How and Joseph Wells, *Commentary on Herodotus* (New York, 1928), vol. 2, p. 20.
4. Athenaeus *Deipnosophists* 2.70a, b.
5. William A. Heidel, *Frame of the Ancient Greek Maps* (New York, 1937), p. 50. See also J. Oliver Thomson, *History of Ancient Geography* (Cambridge, 1948), p. 80f.
6. Heidel, p. 133; Thomson, *Anc. Geog.,* p. 99.
7. Herod. 3.98.
8. Herod. 3.94–95.
9. John W. McCrindle, *Ancient India as Described by Ktēsias* (London, 1882), frag. 1.12; Felix Jacoby, *Die Fragmente der griechischen Historiker* (Leiden, 1923–1958), pt. 3C, no. 688.
10. McCrindle, *Ktēsias,* frag. 1.19.
11. *Nat. Hist.* 37.39.
12. Arrian *Anabasis* 5.26.
13. C. Lassen, *Indische Alterthumskunde* (Bonn, 1842–1861), vol. 2, pp. 641ff.
14. *Meteor.* 2.5.362b.
15. *Meteor.* 1.13.350a.
16. *Geog.* 15.1.26.
17. *Anabasis* 5.26. Cf. Diodorus 18.93.2.
18. *Alex.* 62. See also J. R. Hamilton, *Plutarch's Alexander: A Commentary* (Oxford, 1969), p. 171.
19. Curtius, *History of Alexander.* 9.4.
20. John W. McCrindle, *Ancient India as Described by Megasthenes and Arrian* (London, 1877), frag. 1.2. See B. C. J. Timmer, *Megasthenes en de Indische Maatschappij* (Amsterdam, 1930), esp. pp. 1–10.

21. McCrindle, *Megasthenes,* frag. 1.22b.
22. Ibid.
23. *Geog.* 2.1.1.
24. Literature on the contact is voluminous. Some of the better-known earlier book-length studies include H. G. Rawlinson, *Intercourse between India and the Western World* (Cambridge, 1917); E. Warmington, *The Commerce between the Roman Empire and India* (Cambridge, 1928); Osmand Priaulx, *The Indian Travels of Apollonius of Tyana and the Indian Embassies to Rome* (London, 1873). More recently, see M. L. West, *Early Greek Philosophy and the Orient* (Oxford, 1971).
25. *Geog.* 17.1.13.
26. *Geog.* 2.5.12.
27. *Discourses* 22.40.
28. *Geog.* 15.1.13.
29. *Geog.* 15.1.35.
30. Curtius, *History of Alexander.* 8.9; Arrian *Anabasis* 5.5.
31. 2.11.1; Also Arrian *Anabasis* 5.5.
32. *Geog.* 15.1.57.
33. *Aeneid* 9.31.
34. *Georgics* 3.27; see also 2.136–138.
35. 6.66.
36. Philostratus *Life of Apollonius* 3.20.
37. As noted in William Crooke, *The Popular Religion and Folklore of Northern India* (Delhi, 1968), vol. 1, p. 36.
38. *Dion. Per.* 1164–1165 passim, in McCrindle 1901.
39. *Tristia* 5.3.23.
40. *Odyssey* 1.22–24.
41. *Prometheus Bound* 790ff.
42. *Suppliants* 284–286.
43. *Anabasis* 6.1.
44. 3.20.
45. *De aedificiis* 6.1.6.
46. Map in C. R. Beazley, *The Dawn of Modern Geography* (New York, 1949), vol. 1, p. 385.
47. *Mandeville's Travels,* ed. J. P. Hamelius (London, 1919–1923), vol. 1. p. 28.
48. Beazley, *Dawn of Modern Geography,* vol. 3, p. 319.
49. See William Babcock, *Legendary Islands of the Atlantic: A Study in Medieval Geography* (New York, 1922).
50. 14.3.2.
51. *Adversus haereses* 2.1.64.
52. *Quaest. ad Antiochum* 47.
53. 1.14.
54. Leo Bagrow, *History of Cartography* (London, 1964), p. 47.
55. Bk. 2.
56. M. L. W. Laistner, "The Decay of Geographic Knowledge and the Decline of Exploration, A.D. 300–500," in Arthur P. Newton (ed.), *Travel and Travellers of the Middle Ages* (London, 1926), p. 27.
57. *Satyricon* 6.695.
58. *Historia adversos paganos* 1.2.
59. 1.11.
60. *Hexaemeron* 3.5.6.
61. Sir Charles Oman, *The Unfortunate Colonel Despard and Other Studies* (London, 1922), p. 221.
62. Sir E. Denison Ross, "Prester John and the Empire of Ethiopia," in Newton,

Travel and Travellers, p. 176.

63. Howard R. Patch, *The Other World* (Cambridge, Mass., 1950), p. 149.

64. *English Faustbuch,* ed. H. Logeman (Ghent and Amsterdam, 1900).

65. See George Kimble, *Geography in the Middle Ages*(London, 1938), p. 185.

66. The cascade, as Yule remarks, may be the Sītalagaṅgā; see Yule, *Cathay,* vol. 2, p. 360. Besides the longest river—the Mahāvaligaṅgā—several other Singhalese rivers have Gaṅgā as part of their name. See J. C. De, "Gaṅgā in Ceylon and India," *Indian Historical Quarterly* 7(1931):359–362.

67. John Marignolli, "Recollections of Travel in the East," in Yule, *Cathay,* vol. 2, p. 349.

68. Marignolli in Yule, *Cathay,* vol. 2, p. 350.

69. Pindar *Nemean Odes* 1.144.

70. *Aeneid* 2.695; Ovid *Met.* 5.

71. Pausanias 5.7.3.

72. *Meteor.* 1.13.350b–351a.

73. *Phaedo* 111d.

74. Ibid., 112e–113a.

75. *To Delos* 4.206; *To Artemis* 2.170.

76. Pausanias 2.5.2. See also Terrot Glover, *Springs of Hellas* (New York, 1946), p. 5; James Reuel Smith, *Springs and Wells in Greek and Roman Literature: Their Legends and Locations* (New York, 1922), pp. 669–672.

77. *Summa* 1.102.2, citing Augustine *De gen. ad litt.* 8.7.

78. *Etymol.* 13.20.

79. See John Kirtland Wright, *The Geographic Lore of the Crusades* (New York, 1925), pp. 27, 185, passim.

80. *Quaest. in Gen.* 1.12.

81. 1.10; Caxton, p. 69.

82. Ezek. 47:1. For detailed references, see Raphael Patai, *Man and Temple* (London, 1947), pp. 86, 101.

83. *Antiq.* 1.38.

84. *De gen. ad litt.* 8.7.

85. *Paradisus* 3.14.

86. 3.15.

87. *Letter to Rusticus,* no. 75, ca. A.D. 411.

88. Egerton text, pp. 215–216.

89. 1.10; Caxton, pp. 68–69.

90. Bks. 2, 9.

91. *Etymol.* 13.21.8.

92. Wright, *Geographic Lore of the Crusades,* p. 279.

93. *Palladius* 3.7, in McCrindle 1901.

94. Paul Meyer, *Alexandre le Grand dans la litterature français du moyen âge* (Paris, 1886), vol. 2, pp. 47–48. See also George Cary, *The Medieval Alexander* (Cambridge, 1956), pp. 19–21. Alexander's journey to paradise must have originated before A.D. 500, since it appears in the Babylonian Talmud. See D. J. A. Ross, *Alexander Historiatus* (London, 1963), p. 35.

95. E. G. Ravenstein, *Martin Behaim: His Life and His Globe* (London, 1908), p. 94.

96. John Keane, *The Evolution of Geography* (London, 1899), p. 33.

97. Christopher Columbus, *Select Documents Illustrating the Four Voyages of Columbus,* trans. and ed. Cecil Jane (London, 1932), vol. 2, p. 34.

98. *Select Documents,* vol. 2, p. 38.

99. G. E. Nunn, *The Geographical Conceptions of Columbus* (New York, 1924), p. 73.

100.   *Select Documents,* vol. 2, p. 82.
101.   *Select Documents,* vol. 2, p. lxxxvi.
102.   Apoc. of Paul 45.
103.   Ibid., 21, 31.
104.   See, for example, F. Lenormant, "Ararat and Eden," *Contemporary Review,*
       September 1881, pp. 453–478. For an early nineteenth-century Christian in-
       terpretation of the similarities, see George S. Faber, *Pagan Idolatry* (London,
       1816), vol. 1, pp. 314–356.

Bibliography

SANSKRIT AND PALI WORKS

Agni Purāṇa.
Aitareya Āraṇyaka.
Aitareya Brāhmaṇa.
Amarakośa.
Arthaśāstra.
Āryaśūra. *Jātakamālā.*
Aśvaghosha. *Buddhacarita.*
Atharva Veda.
Avadānaśataka.
Bāṇa. *Harshacarita.*
Baudhyāyana Dharmaśāstra.
Bhāgavata Purāṇa.
Brahmāṇḍa Purāṇa.
Cullavagga.
Daṇḍin. *Daśakumāracarita.*
Dīgha Nikāya.
Gṛihya Sūtras.
Harivaṃśa.
Jātakas.
Jayadeva. *Gītā-Govinda.*
Kalhaṇa. *Rājataraṅgiṇī.*
Kālidāsa. *Kumāra-Sambhava.*
_____. *Mālavikāgnimitra.*
_____. *Meghadūta.*
_____. *Raghuvaṃsa.*
_____. *Śakuntala.*
Kāmandaki. *Kāmandakīya Nītisāra.*
Kaushītaki Brāhmaṇa.

Mahābhārata.
Mahāparinibbāna Sutta.
Mahāvagga.
Mahāvaṃsa.
Mahāvastu.
Manu Dharmaśāstra.
Mārkaṇḍeya Purāṇa.
Matsya Purāṇa.
Milinda-pañha.
Nārada Smṛiti.
Pāṇini. *Ashṭādhyāyī.*
Rig Veda Saṃhitā.
Śatapatha Brāhmaṇa.
Śiva Purāṇa.
Skanda Purāṇa.
Somadeva. *Kathāsaritsāgara.*
Śūdraka. *Mṛicchakaṭika.*
Svātmārāma. *Haṭhapradīpikā.*
Taittirīya Saṃhitā.
Upanishads.
Vājasaneyī Saṃhitā.
Vālmīki. *Rāmāyaṇa.*
Vāmana Purāṇa.
Vasishṭha Dharmaśāstra.
Vikramacarita.
Viśākhadatta. *Mudrārākshasa.*
Vishṇu Dharmaśāstra.
Vishṇudarmottaram.
Vishṇu Purāṇa.

GREEK AND LATIN WORKS

Aelian. *On the Characteristics of Animals* (Loeb ed.).
Aeschylus. *Prometheus Bound.*
_____. *The Suppliants.*
Ambrosius. *Paradisus.*
Apocryphal New Testament.
Aquinas, Thomas. *Summa theologiae.*
Aristotle. *Meteorologica* (Loeb ed.).
Arrian. *Anabasis of Alexander.*
_____. *Indica.*
Athanasius. *Quaestiones ad Antiochum.*
Athenaeus. *Deipnosophists* (Loeb ed.).
Augustine. *De genesi ad litteram.*
Basil. *Hexaemeron.*
Brehaut, Ernest. *An Encyclopedist of the Dark Ages: Isidore of Seville.* New York, 1912.
Callimachus. *Hymns and Epigrams* (Loeb ed).
Cosmas Indicopleustes. *Topographia Christiana.* Translated by J. W. McCrindle. London, 1897.
Curtius. *History of Alexander.*
Dio Chrysostom. *Discourses* (Loeb ed.).
Diodorus Siculus. *Library of History* (Loeb ed.).
Epiphanius. *Adversus haereses.*

Eusebius. *Ecclesiastical History* (Loeb ed.).
Herodotus. *Persian Wars.*
Hesiod. *Theogony.*
Homer. *Odyssey.*
Isidore of Seville. *Etymologies.*
Jerome. *Selected Letters* (Loeb ed.).
Josephus. *Antiquities* (Loeb ed.).
Lucian. *De dea Syria.* (Loeb ed.).
Martianus Capella. *Satyricon.*
McCrindle, John W. *Ancient India as Described in Classical Literature.* Westminster, 1901.
———. *Ancient India as Described by Ktesias the Knidian.* London, 1822.
———. *Ancient India as Described by Megasthenes and Arrian.* London, 1877.
———. *Ancient India as Described by Ptolemy.* Calcutta, 1927.
Orosius. *Historia adversos paganos.*
Ovid. *Metamorphoses.*
———. *Tristia* (Loeb ed.).
Pausanias. *Guide to Greece.*
The Periplus of the Erythraean Sea. Translated by Wilfred Schoff. New York, 1912.
Philo. *Quaestiones in Genesis* (Loeb ed.).
Philostratus. *Life of Appollonius of Tyana* (Loeb ed.).
Pindar. *Nemean Odes* (Loeb ed.).
Plato. *Phaedo.*
Pliny. *Natural History* (Loeb ed.).
Plutarch. *Life of Alexander* (Loeb ed.).
Procopius. *On Buildings* (Loeb ed.).
Strabo. *Geography* (Loeb ed.).
Valerius Flaccus. *Argonautica* (Loeb ed.).
Virgil. *Aeneid.*
———. *Georgics* (Loeb ed.).

OTHER WORKS

Books
Acharya, P. K. *Hindu Architecture in India and Abroad.* Bombay, 1946.
Agrawala, V. S. *Ancient Indian Folk Cults.* Varanasi, 1970.
———. *Gupta Art.* Lucknow, 1948.
———. *India as Known to Panini.* Varanasi. 1963.
Ali Khan, K. S. Abid. *Memoires of Gaur and Pandua.* Calcutta, 1931.
Allan, J. *Catalogue of the Coins of the Gupta Dynasties.* London, 1914.
Allchin, Bridget. *The Stone Tipped Arrow.* New York, 1966.
Allchin, Bridget and Raymond Allchin. *The Birth of Indian Civilization.* Baltimore, 1968.
Allen, Richard H. *Star Names: Their Lore and Meaning.* New York, 1899.
Altekar, Anant. *Catalogue of Gupta Coins in the Bayana Hoard.* Bombay, 1954.
Altekar, Anant and V. Mishra. *Report on the Kumrahar Excavations, 1951-1955.* Patna, 1959.
Andrae, W. *Das Gotteshaus und die Urformen des Bauens im Alten Orient.* Berlin, 1930.
Avalon, Arthur and Ellen Avalon (trans.). *Hymns to the Goddess.* Madras, 1966.
Awasthi, A. B. L. *Studies in Skanda Purāṇa.* Pt. 1. Lucknow, 1965.
Babcock, William. *Legendary Islands of the Atlantic: A Study in Medieval Geography.* New York, 1922.
Bagchi, Kanagopal. *The Ganges Delta.* Calcutta, 1944.

Bagrow, Leo. *History of Cartography*. London, 1964.

Balasubrahmanyam, M. D. (ed.). *K. Chattopadhyay Felicitation Volume*. Allahabad, 1972.

Banerjee, N. R. *The Iron Age in India*. Delhi, 1965.

Barbosa, Duarte. *The Book of Duarte Barbosa*. 2 vols. Translated by M. L. Dames. London, 1921.

Basham, A. L. (ed.). *Paper on Kanishka*. Leiden, 1968.

_____. *The Wonder That Was India*. New York, 1954.

Basu, Tara Krishna. *The Bengal Peasant from Time to Time*. Bombay and Calcutta, 1962.

Beazley, C. R. *The Dawn of Modern Geography*. 3 vols. New York, 1949.

Berenger, Feraud. L. *Superstitions et survivances étudiées au point du vue de leurs origine et leurs transformations*. 5 vols. Paris, 1895.

Bernier, Francois. *Travels in the Mogul Empire*. Translated by A. Constable. Delhi, 1891.

Bhandarkar, D. R. *Ancient Indian Numismatics*. Calcutta, 1921.

Bhargava, Manoharlal. *The Geography of Rgvedic India*. Lucknow, 1964.

Bhargava, Purushottam Lal. *India in the Vedic Age*. Lucknow, 1971.

Bhattacharji, Sukumari. *The Indian Theogony*. Cambridge, 1970.

Bhattacharya, Deben (ed. and trans.). *The Mirror of the Sky: Songs of the Bāuls from Bengal*. London, 1969.

Bhattacharyya, Asutosh. *Vangiya Lok Sangeet*. Vols. 1–4. Calcutta, 1964–68.

_____. *Vanglā Mangal Kabyer Itihas*. Calcutta, 1969.

_____. *Vanglar Loka-Sahitya*. Vol. 5. Calcutta, 1971.

Bhattacharyya, Narendra Nath. *History of Indian Cosmogonical Ideas*. Delhi, 1971.

_____. *Indian Mother Goddess*. Calcutta, 1971.

Bhattasali, Nalini. *Coins and Chronology of the Early Independent Sultans of Bengal*. Cambridge, 1922.

_____. *Iconography of Buddhist and Brahmanical Sculptures in the Dacca Museum*. Dacca, 1929.

Bloch, R. et al. *Le symbolisme cosmique des monuments religieux*. Rome, 1957.

Bosch, F. D. K. *The Golden Germ*. The Hague, 1960.

Bose, Atindranath. *Social and Rural Economy of Northern India*. 2 vols. Calcutta, 1961.

Bose, Subodh Chandra. *Land and People of the Himalaya*. Calcutta, 1968.

Bowrey, Thomas. *Geographical Account of Countries round the Bay of Bengal*. London, 1903.

Briffault, R. *The Mothers*. New York, 1931.

Brown, Percy. *Indian Architecture*. Vol. 1: *Buddhist and Hindu Period*. Bombay, 1965.

Brown, W. Norman. *Man in the Universe*. Berkeley, 1966.

Budge, Sir Ernest. *The Gods of the Egyptians*. London, 1894.

Burgess, James. *The Buddhist Stūpas of Amarāvatī and Jaggayyapeta*. Varanasi, 1970.

Campbell, Joseph. *The Masks of God: Occidental Mythology*. New York, 1964.

_____. *The Masks of God: Primitive Mythology*. New York, 1959.

_____ (ed.). *The Mysteries*. New York, 1955.

Carey, W. H. *The Good Old Days of Honorable John Company*. 2 vols. Calcutta, 1906.

Cary, George. *The Medieval Alexander*. Cambridge, 1956.

Caxton, William. *Caxton's Mirrour of the World*. London, 1913.

Chakraborti, Haripada. *Trade and Commerce of Ancient India*. Calcutta, 1966.

Chand, Amar. *Hastinapura*. Banaras, 1952.

Chatterji, S. K. *Indo-Aryan and Hindi*. Calcutta, 1969.
Chattopadhyay, Bhaskar. *The Age of the Kushanas*. Calcutta, 1967.
Chattopadhyaya, Sudhakar. *Early History of North India*. Calcutta, 1958.
_____. *The Sakas in India*. Śantiniketan, 1955.
Childe, V. Gordon. *The Aryans*. London, 1926.
Coedès, George. *The Making of Southeast Asia*. Berkeley, 1966.
_____. *Les États Hindouisés d'Indochine et d'Indonésie*. Paris, 1964.
Columbus, Christopher. *Select Documents Illustrating the Four Voyages of Columbus*. Translated and edited by Cecil Jane. 2 vols. London, 1929–1932.
_____. *Select Letters of Christopher Columbus*. 2 vols. Translated and edited by R. H. Major. London, 1847.
Combaz, Gisbert. *L'Inde et l'Orient classique*. 2 vols. Paris, 1937.
Conteneau, G. *Manuel d'archéologie orientale*. 4 vols. Paris, 1927.
Coomaraswamy, A. *Elements of Buddhist Iconography*. Cambridge, Mass., 1934.
_____. *History of Indian and Indonesian Art*. New York, 1927.
_____. *Time and Eternity*. Ascona, Switzerland, 1947.
_____. *The Transformation of Nature in Art*. New York, 1934.
_____. *Yakshas*. Delhi, 1971.
Cope, Gilbert. *Symbolism in the Bible and the Church*. New York, 1959.
Creighton, H. *The Ruins of Gaur*. London, 1817.
Cunningham, Sir Alexander. *Archaeological Survey of India: Reports*. 24 vols. Varanasi, 1966–1972.
_____. *The Stupa of Bharhut*. Varanasi, 1962.
Dani, A. H. *Prehistory and Protohistory of Eastern India*. Calcutta, 1960.
Dante, *Purgatorio*.
Das, Matilal and P. Mahapatra. *Lalan Gitika*. Calcutta, 1958.
Dasgupta, P. C. *The Early Terracottas from Tamralipta*. Calcutta, n.d.
_____. *The Excavations at Pandu Rajar Dhibi*. Calcutta, 1964.
Das Gupta, Shashibhusan. *Obscure Religious Cults*. Calcutta, 1969.
Das Gupta, Tamonash. *Aspects of Bengali Society from Old Bengali Literature*. Calcutta, 1935.
Datta, Phulrenu. *La société bengalie au XVIᵉ siècle*. Paris, 1938.
Dey, Nundolal. *The Geographical Dictionary of Ancient and Medieval India*. Delhi, 1927.
Diehl, C. D. *Instrument and Purpose*. Lund, Sweden, 1956.
Dowson, John. *A Classical Dictionary of Hindu Mythology and Religion, Geography, History, and Literature*. London, 1961.
Dube, D. *Purānōō mē gaṅgā*. Prayag, n.d.
Dutt, R. C. *The Cultural Heritage of Bengal*. Calcutta, 1962.
The Egyptian Book of the Dead. Translated by E. A. Wallis Budge. New York, 1895.
Eliade, Mircea. *Patterns in Comparative Religion*. Cleveland, 1963.
_____. *Rites and Symbols of Initiation*. New York, 1958.
_____. *Yoga: Immortality and Freedom*. New York, 1958.
English Faustbuch. Edited by H. Logeman. Ghent and Amsterdam, 1900.
Études asiatiques. 2 vols. Hanoi, 1925.
Evans, A. J. *The Mycenean Tree and Pillar Cult*. London, 1901.
Faber, George S. *Pagan Idolatry*. 3 vols. London, 1816.
Fa-hien. *A Record of Buddhist Kingdoms*. Translated by James Legge. New York, 1886.
Fairservis, Walter. *The Roots of Ancient India*. New York, 1971.
Filliozat, Jean. *Les relations extérieures de l'Inde*. Pt. 1. Pondichéry, 1956.
Fischer, Eberhard and Haku Shah. *Mogra Dev*. Ahmedabad, 1971.

Fleet, John F. *Corpus Inscriptionum Indicarum.* Vol. 3: *Inscriptions of the Early Gupta Kings.* Varanasi, 1970.
Frankfort, Henri. *The Birth of Civilization in the Near East.* Garden City, N.Y., 1951.
Gajjar, Irene. *Ancient Indian Art and the West.* Bombay, 1971.
Gaster, Theodore. *Thespis.* New York, 1950.
Ghulam Husain Salīm. *Riyazu-s-salātin.* Translated by Maulavi Abdus Salem. Calcutta, 1902.
Giedion, S. *The External Present.* Vol. 2: *The Beginnings of Architecture.* New York, 1964.
Glover, Terrot. *The Springs of Hellas.* New York, 1946.
Goblet d'Alviella. *The Migration of Symbols.* New York, 1956.
Goetz, H. and A. Jaenicke. *Mamallapuram.* Wiesbaden, 1966.
Gordon, A. *Tibetan Religious Art.* New York, 1963.
Gordon, D. H. *The Pre-historic Background of Indian Culture.* Bombay, 1960.
Grist, D. *Rice.* London, 1960.
Guénon, René. *La grande triade.* Paris, 1957.
————. *Symboles fondamentaux de la Science sacrée.* Paris, 1962.
Hakluyt, Richard. *The Principal Navigations, Voyages, Traffiques and Discoveries of the English Nation.* 10 vols. New York, 1927–1928.
Hamilton, Capt. Alexander. *A New Account of the East Indies.* 2 vols. Edinburgh, 1727.
Hamilton, J. R. *Plutarch's Alexander: A Commentary.* Oxford, 1969.
Harle, J. C. *Temple Gateways in South India.* Oxford, 1963.
Harrison, Jane. *Prolegomena to the Study of Greek Religion.* New York, 1959.
Havell, E. B. *The Himalayas in Indian Art.* London, 1924.
Heidel, William. *Frame of the Ancient Greek Maps.* New York, 1937.
Henderson, Joseph et al. *The Wisdom of the Serpent.* New York, 1963.
Herskovits, M. J. *Acculturation: The Study of Culture Contacts.* New York, 1938.
Hiuen Tsiang. *Travels of Hiuen Tsiang.* 4 vols. Translated by Samuel Beal. Calcutta, 1957.
Hocart, A. M. *Kings and Councillors.* Chicago, 1936.
Hopkins, E. Washburn. *Epic Mythology,* Strassburg, 1915.
————. *The Religions of India.* Boston, 1895.
Hunter, W. W. *The Annals of Rural Bengal.* London, 1897.
————. *A Statistical Account of Bengal.* 5 vols. London, 1875.
Hwui-lih. *Life of Hiuen-Tsiang.* Translated by Samuel Beal. London, 1911.
Ibn Baṭṭūṭa. *The Travels of Ibn Battuta.* 3 vols. Translated by H. A. R. Gibb. Cambridge, 1958–1971.
Indras. *Lost Sarasvati.* Vallabh Vidyanagar, 1967.
Jain, Jagdish. *Life in Ancient India.* Bombay, 1947.
James, E. O. *The Cult of the Mother Goddess: An Archaeological and Documentary Study.* London, 1959.
Jha, Subhadra. *The Songs of Vidyāpati.* Banaras, 1954.
Johnston, J. *Inland Navigation of the Gangetic Rivers.* Calcutta, 1933.
Jourdain, John. *The Journal of John Jourdain, 1608–1617.* Cambridge, 1905.
Jouveau-Dubreuil, G. *Iconography of Southern India.* Paris, 1937.
Jung, C. G. *The Archetypes and the Collective Unconscious.* Princeton, 1959.
————. *Psychology and Alchemy.* New York, 1953.
————. *Symbols of Transformation.* New York, 1956.
Kane, P. V. *History of the Dharmaśāstra.* 4 vols. Poona, 1930–1953.
Kavirāj, Krishnadāsa. *Chaitanya-charit-amṛita.* Translated by Sir Jadunath Sarkar. Calcutta, 1932.

Keane, John. *The Evolution of Geography*. London, 1899.
Keith, A. B. *The Religion and Philosophy of the Vedas and Upanishads*. 2 vols. Cambridge, Mass., 1925.
Keith, A. B. and A. A. Macdonell. *Vedic Index*. 2 vols. Delhi, 1912.
Kimble, George. *Geography in the Middle Ages*. London, 1938.
Kopf, David (ed.). *Bengal: Regional Identity*. East Lansing, 1969.
Kosambi, D. D. *The Culture and Civilization of Ancient India*. London, 1965.
Kramrisch, Stella. *The Hindu Temple*. 2 vols. Calcutta, 1946.
_____. *Indian Sculpture*. Calcutta, 1933.
Kroeber, A. L. (ed.). *Anthropology Today*. Chicago, 1953.
Lalan. *Songs of Lalan Shah*. Translated by Abu Rashd. Dacca, 1964.
Lassen, Christian. *Indische Alterthumskunde*. 4 vols. Bonn, 1842–1861.
Law, B. C. *Historical Geography of Ancient India*. Paris, 1954.
_____. *India as Described in Early Texts of Buddhism and Jainism*. London, 1941.
_____. *Indological Studies*. Pt. 3. Allahabad, 1954.
_____. *The Magadhas in Ancient India*. London, 1946.
Leicht, H. *Indianische Kunst und Kultur*. Zürich, 1944.
Leifer, Walter. *Himalaya: Mountain of Destiny*. London, 1962.
Lenski, Gerhard and Jean Lenski. *Human Societies*. New York, 1974.
Levy, Gertrude R. *The Gate of Horn*. London, 1948.
Levy-Bruhl, L. *How Natives Think*. New York, 1966.
Linschoten, John Huyghen van. *The Voyage of John Huyghen van Linschoten*. 2 vols. London, 1885.
Lyon, David and George Foot Moore (eds.). *Studies in the History of Religion*. New York, 1912.
Mackay, Ernest. *Further Excavations at Mohenjo-Daro*. 2 vols. Delhi, 1938.
Mahapatra, P. *Folk Cults of Bengal*. Calcutta, 1972.
Mahārāshta Purāna. Translated by Edward Dimock and P. C. Gupta. Honolulu, 1965.
Maity, P. K. *Historical Studies in the Cult of the Goddess Manasa*. Calcutta, 1966.
Maity, S. K. *Economic Life in Northern India in the Gupta Period*. Delhi, 1970.
Majumdar, R. C. *History of Ancient Bengal*. Calcutta, 1971.
_____ (ed.). *The History and Culture of the Indian People*. Vol. 1: *The Vedic Age*. London, 1951.
_____. *History of Medieval Bengal*. Calcutta, 1973.
Majumdar, R. C. and A. S. Altekar. *The Vākāṭaka-Gupta Age*. Delhi, 1954.
Majumdar, S. C. *Rivers of the Bengal Delta*. Calcutta, 1941.
Mālaviya Commemorative Volume. Banaras, 1932.
Malik, S. C. *Indian Civilization: The Formative Period*. Simla, 1968.
Mandeville, Sir John. *Mandeville's Travels*. Edited by J. P. Hamelius. 2 vols. London, 1919–1923.
_____. *Mandeville's Travels*. Edited by Malcolm Letts. 2 vols. London, 1953.
Manrique, Sebastian. *The Travels of Sebastian Manrique*. 2 vols. London, 1926–1927.
Marshall, John. *Mohenjo-Daro and the Indus Valley Civilization*. 3 vols. London, 1931.
Marshall, John and Alfred Foucher. *The Monuments of Sanchi*. 3 vols. London, 1940.
Meyer, Paul. *Alexandre le Grand dans la litterature français du moyen âge*. 2 vols. Paris, 1886.
Mishra, Vishva Nath Prasad. *Padmākar*. Varanasi, 1963.
Mookerji, Radha Kumud. *Indian Shipping: A History of the Sea-Bourne Trade and Maritime Activities of the Indians from the Earliest Times*. Calcutta, 1957.

Mukerjee, Radhakamal. *The Changing Face of Bengal.* Calcutta, 1938.
_____. *The Cosmic Art of India.* Bombay, 1965.
Mukherjee, R. and S. C. Maity. *Corpus of Bengal Inscriptions.* Calcutta, 1967.
Mundy, Peter. *Travels in Asia.* 5 vols. Cambridge, 1907–1936.
Murray, Gilbert. *Five Stages of Greek Religion.* Garden City, N.Y., 1955.
Narain, A. K. *The Indo-Greeks.* London, 1957.
Neumann, Eric. *The Great Mother.* Princeton, 1955.
Newton, Arthur P. (ed.). *Travel and Travellers of the Middle Ages.* London, 1926.
Nilakanta Sastri, K. A. *Cultural Contacts between Aryans and Dravidians.* Bombay, 1967.
_____ (ed.). *The Mauryas and Satavahanas.* Calcutta, 1957.
Nilsson, Martin. *History of Greek Religion.* Oxford, 1925.
Nunn, G. E. *The Geographical Conceptions of Columbus.* New York, 1924.
Oldenberg, Hermann. *Buddha: His Life, His Doctrine, His Order.* London, 1882.
O'Malley, Lewis S. *Bengal, Bihar, and Orissa.* London, 1917.
_____. *Bengal District Gazetteers: Murshidabad.* Calcutta, 1914.
Oman, Sir Charles. *The Unfortunate Colonel Despard and Other Studies.* London, 1922.
Pandey, M. S. *Historical Geography and Topography of Bihar.* Delhi, 1963.
Pandeya, Sudhakar. *Gaṅgālaharī.* Varanasi, 1963.
Parrot, André. *Sumer.* New York, 1961.
Patai, Raphael. *Man and Temple.* London, 1947.
Patch, Howard R. *The Other World.* Cambridge, Mass., 1950.
Petech, L. *Northern India According to the Shui-Ching-Chu.* Rome, 1950.
Phanindranatha Bose. *Principles of Indian Śilpaśāstra.* Lahore, 1926.
Piggott, Stuart. *Prehistoric India.* Baltimore, 1950.
Polo, Marco. *Il Milione.* New York, n.d.
Prakash, Buddha. *Rigveda and the Indus Valley Civilization.* Hoshiapur, 1966.
Priaulx, Osmand. *The Indian Travels of Apollonius of Tyana and the Indian Embassies to Rome.* London, 1873.
Prior, O. H. *L'image du monde de Maître Goussouin.* Lausanne, 1913.
Pritchard, James (ed.). *Ancient Near Eastern Texts.* Princeton, 1955.
Purchas, Samuel (ed.). *Hakluytus Posthumus, or Purchas His Pilgrimes.* 20 vols. Glasgow, 1905–1907.
Puri, B. N. *India under the Kushanas.* Bombay, 1965.
Ramanayya, N. V. *An Essay on the Origin of the South Indian Temple.* Madras, 1930.
Ramprasad Sen. *Ramprasad's Devotional Songs: The Cult of Śakti.* Translated by Jadunath Sinha. Calcutta, 1966.
Rao, T. A. Gopinath. *The Elements of Hindu Iconography.* 4 vols. Delhi, 1928.
Rao, U Shanker. *Inland Water Navigation from Calcutta to Allahabad.* Madras, 1951.
Rapson, E. J. *Cambridge History of India.* Vol 1: *Ancient India.* New York, 1922.
Ratnam, Perala (ed.). *Studies in Indo-Asian Art and Culture.* Vol. 1. Delhi, 1972.
Ravenshaw, J. H. *Gaur.* London, 1878.
Ravenstein, E. G. *Martin Behaim: His Life and His Globe.* London, 1908.
Rawlinson, H. G. *Intercourse between India and the Western World.* Cambridge, 1917.
Raychaudhuri, H. C. *Political History of Ancient India.* 7th ed. Calcutta, 1950.
Rea, A. *Pallava Architecture.* Varanasi, 1970.
Reclus, Elisee. *The Earth and Its Inhabitants.* Vol 3: *India and China.* London, 1884.
Rhys-Davids, T. W. *Buddhist India.* Calcutta, 1957.

Richardson, C. C. et al. (eds.). *Early Christian Fathers. Vol 1.* New York, 1953.

Rosenfeld, John. *The Dynastic Arts of the Kushans.* Berkeley, 1967.

Ross, D. J. A. *Alexander Historiatus.* London, 1963.

Ryley, J. Horton. *Ralph Fitch: England's Pioneer to India and Burma.* London, 1899.

Saletore, Rajaram. *Life in the Gupta Age.* Bombay, 1943.

Samaddar, J. N. *The Economic Condition of Ancient India.* Calcutta, 1922.

Sarkar, Bejoy Kumar. *Inland Transport and Communication in Medieval India.* Calcutta, 1925.

Sarkar, Jadunath. *The History of Bengal: Muslim Period, 1200-1757.* Patna, 1973.

Sastri, K. N. *New Light on the Indus Civilization.* Delhi, 1957.

Sayce, A. H. *The Religions of the Ancient Babylonians.* London, 1887.

Schouten, Gautier. *Voiage aux Indes Orientales 1658-1665.* 2 vols. Amsterdam, 1707.

Sedgwick, W. T. and H. W. Tyler. *A Short History of Science.* New York, 1939.

Sen, Benoychandra. *Some Historical Aspects of the Inscriptions of Bengal.* Calcutta, 1942.

Sen, D. C. *Eastern Ballads.* 4 vols. Calcutta, 1923.

––––––. *Glimpses of Bengal Life.* Calcutta, 1925.

Sen, Sondra Kotzin. "Concepts of Physical and Spiritual Health and Their Relation to Food Habits among Middle-Class Hindu Bengalis." M.A. thesis. University of Pennsylvania, 1969.

Sharma, G. R. *The Excavations at Kauśāmbī.* Allahabad, 1960.

Shukla, D. N. *Hindu Science of Architecture.* Vol. 1: *Vastu Śāstra.* Chandigarh, 1961.

Singer, Charles et al. (eds.). *A History of Technology.* Vol 1: *From Early Times to the Fall of Anicent Empires.* London, 1954.

Singh, Madan Mohan. *Life in North-Eastern India in Pre-Mauryan Times.* Delhi, 1967.

Singh, Satisch C. *Changes in the Course of Rivers and Their Effects on Urban Settlements in the Middle Ganga Plain.* Varanasi, 1973.

Sircar, D. C. (ed.). *The Bhakti Cult and Ancient Indian Geography.* Calcutta, 1970.

––––––. *Inscriptions of Aśoka.* New Delhi, 1967.

––––––. *Studies in the Geography of Ancient and Medieval India.* Delhi, 1960.

Sivaramamurti, C. *Some Aspects of Indian Culture.* New Delhi, 1969.

Sjoberg, Gideon. *The Preindustrial City.* New York, 1960.

Smith, James Reuel. *Springs and Wells in Greek and Roman Literature: Their Legends and Locations.* New York, 1922.

Smith, Vincent. *The Jain Stupa and Other Antiquities of Mathura.* Allahabad, 1901.

Snellgrove, D. L. *The Hevajra Tantra.* 2 vols. London, 1959.

Sousa, Manuel de Faria y. *History of the Discovery and Conquest of India by Portugal.* 3 vols. Translated by Capt. John Stevens. London, 1695.

Spate, O. H. K. *India and Pakistan.* London, 1957.

Stevenson, Mrs. Sinclair. *The Rites of the Twice-Born.* London, 1920.

Stietencron, H. von. *Gangā und Yamunā: zur symbolischen Bedeutung der Flussgottinen an indischen Tempeln.* Wiesbaden, 1972.

Subbarao, B. *The Personality of India.* Baroda, 1958.

Tavernier, Jean Baptiste. *Travels in India.* 2 vols. London, 1925.

Thomson, J. Oliver. *History of Ancient Geography.* Cambridge, 1948.

Thompson, E. J. and A. M. Spencer. *Bengali Religious Lyrics: Śākta.* Calcutta, 1923.

Timmer, B. C. J. *Megasthenes en de Indische Maatschappij.* Amsterdam, 1930.
Toynbee, Arnold J. *A Study of History.* Vol. 7A: *Universal States.* New York, 1963.
Tripathi, R. S. *History of Kanauj.* Delhi, 1964.
Varthema, Ludovico di. *The Travels of Ludovico di Varthema.* London, 1863.
Vats, M. S. *Excavations at Harappa.* 2 vols. New Delhi, 1940.
Viennot, Odette. *Les Divinités fluviales Gaṅgā et Yamunā.* Paris, 1964.
Vogel, J. Ph. *Indian Serpent-Lore or the Nagas in Hindu Legend and Art.* London, 1926.
Wang, Gungwu. *The Nanhai Trade.* Kuala Lumpur, 1958.
Warmington, E. *The Commerce between the Roman Empire and India.* Cambridge, 1928.
Watters, Thomas. *On Yuan Chwang's Travels in India.* Delhi, 1961.
Wheatley, Paul. *Golden Khersonese.* Kuala Lumpur, 1961.
Wheeler, Sir Mortimer. *The Indus Civilization.* 3rd ed. Cambridge, 1968.
Witt, R. E. *Isis in the Graeco-Roman World.* Ithaca, 1971.
Wright, John Kirtland. *The Geographical Lore of the Crusades.* New York, 1925.
Yule, Col. Henry. *Cathay and the Way Thither.* 4 vols. London, 1866.
Zend-Avesta. 3 vols. Translated by J. Darmesteter. Delhi, 1965.
Zimmer, Heinrich. *The Art of Indian Asia.* 2 vols. New York, 1955.

Articles
Allchin, Bridget. "Morhana Pahar, a Rediscovery." *Man* 58(1958):153–155.
Annandale, A. "A Working Model of the Origin of the Ganges in a Temple in Ganjam." *Memoires of the Asiatic Society of Bengal* 8(1924):249–256.
Basu, Basanta Kumar. "Trade of Bengal from the Earliest Times down to the Great War." *Journal of Indian History* 6(1928):275–289.
Bhattacharyya, Asutosh. "Medieval Narrative Bengali Poetry on Historical Themes." *Indian Historical Quarterly* 20(1944):21–35.
Chakravarti, Prithivis C. "Naval Warfare in Ancient India." *Indian Historical Quarterly* 6(1930):645–664.
Chapekar, N. G. "Traces of Totemism in the Ṛig Veda." *Sociological Bulletin* 1(1952):95–98.
Colebrook, H. T. "On the Course of the Ganges through Bengal." *Asiatick Researches* 8(1803):1–32.
Cowell, E. B. "Three Episodes from the Old Bengali Poem 'Chandi.'" *Journal of the Asiatic Society of Bengal* 71(1902):1–46.
Darian, Steven. "The Economic History of the Ganges to the End of Gupta Times." *Journal of the Economic and Social History of the Orient* 13(1970):62–87.
———. "Gaṅgā and Artemis: Cultural Differentiations of a Theme." *Journal of the Ganganatha Jha Kendriya Sanskrit Vidyapeetha* 29(1973):229–240.
———. "The Ganges in Indian Art." *East and West* 23(1973):307–325.
———. "The Significance of Hardvar." *Bhavan's Journal,* 26 May 1974, pp. 14–18.
De, J. C. "Ganga in Ceylon and India." *Indian Historical Quarterly* 7(1931):359–362.
Dey, Nundolal. "The Early Course of the Ganges." *Indian Antiquary* 50(1921):8–14.
"The Ganges Delta." *Calcutta Review* 32(1859):1–25.
Ghosh, A. "Rājgir 1950." *Ancient India* 7(1951):66–79.
Goloubew, Victor. "La Descente de la Gange sur Terre." *Ars Asiatica* 3(1921):23–25.
Gopal, Lalanji. "Art of Shipbuilding and Navigation in Ancient India." *Journal of Indian History* 40(1962):313–328.

Hornell, James. "The Boats of the Ganges." *Memoires of the Asiatic Society of Bengal* 8(1924):173-198.
_____. "The Fishing Methods of the Ganges." *Memoires of the Asiatic Society of Bengal* 8(1924):199-237.
_____. "The Origins and Ethnological Significance of Indian Boat Designs." *Memoires of the Asiatic Society of Bengal* 7(1923):139-256.
Jain, Niraj. "Jaina Purātattva mē Yamunā-Gaṅgā." *Anekānta Vīrseva Mandir* 16(1963):40-41.
Jayaswal, K. P. "Bhīṭā Excavations, on the Hindu War, on the Kushans, and on Vākāṭaka Seals and Inscriptions." *Journal of the Bihar and Orissa Research Society* 19(1933):291-300.
Kasinath. "Serpent Worship." *Indian Antiquary* 2(1873):124.
Kielhorn, F. "Khalimpur Plate of Dharmapāla." *Epigraphia Indica* 4(1896-1897): 243-254.
Lal, B. B. "Birbhanpur, a Microlithic Site in the Damodar Valley." *Ancient India* 14(1958):4-48.
_____. "Excavations at Hastināpura and Other Explorations in the Upper Gaṅgā and Sutlej Basins." *Ancient India* 10-11(1954-1955):1-151.
_____. "Protohistoric Investigations." *Ancient India* 9(1953):80-102.
Lenormant, F. "Ararat and Eden." *Contemporary Review,* September 1881, pp. 453-478.
Levi, Sylvain. "Notes on the Indo-Scythians." *Indian Antiquary* 32(1903):381-389.
Mackay, Dorothy. "Ancient River Beds and Dead Cities." *Antiquity* 19(1945): 135-144.
Maitra, Akshay Kumar. "The River-Goddess Gaṅgā." *Rūpam* 6(1921):2-10.
Meggers, Betty J. "Environmental Limitations on the Development of Culture." *American Anthropologist* 56(1954):801-824.
Moret, A. "Le lotus et la naissance des dieux." *Journal Asiatique* 9(1917):499-513.
Mus, Paul. "Cultes Indiens et indigènes au Champā." *Bulletin de l'École française d'Extrême Orient* 33(1933):367-410.
Oldham, C. F. "The Sarasvati and the Lost River of the Indian Desert." *Journal of the Royal Asiatic Society* 25(1893):49-76.
Oldham, R. D. "On Probable Changes in the Geography of the Punjab and Its Rivers." *Journal of the Asiatic Society of Bengal* 55(1886):322-343.
Pelliot, P. "Le Fou-Nan." *Bulletin de l'École française d'Extrême Orient* 3(1903): 248-303.
Piggott, Stuart. "Prehistoric Copper Hoards in the Ganges Basin." *Antiquity* 18 (1944):173-182.
Prideaux, E. T. "River Songs of Bhagalpur." *Man in India* 25(1945):17-23.
Przyluski, J. "Totémisme et végétalisme dans l'Inde." *Revue de l'histoire des religions* 96(1927):347-364.
Ramachandran, T. N. "Tāmraliptī." *Artibus Asiae* 14(1951):226-239.
Rao, S. R. "Shipping and Maritime Trade of the Indus People." *Expedition* 8 (1965):30-37.
Rhys-Davids, Mrs. C. F. "Early Economic Conditions in North India." *Journal of the Royal Asiatic Society,* October 1901, pp. 859-889.
Richards, F. J. "Geographic Factors in Indian Archaeology." *Indian Antiquary* 62(1933):231-243.
Sandhyākara Nandi. "Ramacarita." Edited by M. M. Hariprasād Śāstri. *Memoires of the Asiatic Society of Bengal* 3(1910-1914):1-55.
Sarasvati, S. K. "Temple Architecture in the Gupta Age." *Journal of the Indian Society of Oriental Art* 8(1940):146-158.

Singh, S. D. "Iron in Ancient India." *Journal of the Economic and Social History of the Orient* 5(1962):212–216.

Sivaramamurti, C. "The Story of Gaṅgā and Amṛita at Paṭṭadakal." *Oriental Art* 3(1957):20–24.

Sjoberg, Gideon. "The Preindustrial City." *American Journal of Sociology* 55 (1955):438–455.

Thurnwald, Richard. "The Psychology of Acculturation." *American Anthropologist* 34(1932):557–569.

Touche, T. H. (ed.). "The Journals of Major James Renell." *Memoires of the Asiatic Society of Bengal* 3(1910):1–148.

Viennot, Odette. "Le Makara dans la décoration des monuments de l'Inde ancienne: positions et fonctions." *Ars Asiatica* 5(1958):183–206 and 272–292.

Vogel, J. Ph. "Le Makara dans la sculpture de l'Inde." *Revue des Arts Asiatiques* 6(1929–1930):133–147.

Index

A note on pronunciation: spelling in the index follows the standard transliteration of Sanskrit. The only symbols that might pose a problem for the non-Sanskritist are ṣ and ś, both of which are pronounced like the *sh* in *sheep*.

ꑣ Production Notes

The text of this book has been designed by Roger J. Eggers and typeset on the Unified Composing System by the Design & production staff of The University Press of Hawaii.

The text typeface is Garamond. The display face is Korinna.

Offset presswork and binding is the work of Vail-Ballou Press. Text paper is Glatfelter P & S Offset, basis 55.